THE ART OF COOKING WITH SPIRITS

The Art of
Cooking with Spirits

ELISE LANDAUER MEYER

Edited and Illustrated by Deirdre Stanforth

BONANZA BOOKS • NEW YORK

Preface

When Elise Meyer sent me a collection of her recipes I felt like a producer discovering a new star. Her originality, imagination, and creative ability with food leapt out of the pages, her passion for cooking glowing almost as visibly as the flambés she loves to serve. The double entendre in the title of this book is no accident . . . it expresses the author's enthusiasm. There never was a more spirited cook than Elise Meyer; she thinks of cooking as an art, rather than drudgery.

Always searching for new and better ways to make things taste good, she has already influenced me away from the slavish follow-the-rules school to the stimulating and rewarding try-it-and-see point of view.

Among other inspired innovations, she has invented mouth-watering new recipes for marinating roasts with Wines and Liqueurs that have everyone who hears about them clamoring to get their hands on the recipes.

It is rather amazing that she is of the first generation in the South that can cook at all. I share this background with her. Our mothers and grandmothers were totally innocent of the most basic kitchen techniques, though they had an uncanny knack for turning field hands into fabulous cooks.

Finally, it is not only a privilege for all of us to be able to share her recipes, but it has been a great pleasure for me to work with her.

DEIRDRE STANFORTH

Contents

Preface	v
Introduction	1
Hors d'Oeuvres, Appetizers, and Aspics	7
Soups	37
Eggs and Cheese	53
Seafood	63
Poultry	95
Meats	131
Vegetables	169
Cooked Fruits	187
Sauces, Salad Dressings, and Stuffings	201
Cakes, Tortes, and Cookies	223
Frostings and Dessert Sauces	251
Desserts	263
List of Spirits Used in This Book	311
Index	313

Recipes for items printed in small capital letters may be found by consulting the index.

THE ART OF COOKING WITH SPIRITS

Introduction

Few of us can afford to eat at the world's finest restaurants every night, but there's no need to settle for second best at home. This cookbook was written for everyone who wants to serve food that is exciting, different, and delicious, and it never could have been written if my temporary jobs as a Kelly Girl had not afforded me the necessary time to do it. It is chiefly a company cookbook, to be used when you want to make a memorable impression, but you can make any meal a festive occasion by adding a dish or two cooked with Spirits.

I have often been asked why I cook with Spirits, but I hasten to add that the question has never been put to me by anyone who has eaten in my home. I want the food I serve my family and friends to be just as good in taste, appearance and nutrition as I can make it, and the use of Spirits in the preparation of food helps me to achieve this goal.

I have found that Wine used in broiling, poaching, boiling, or baking fish or poultry, or in roasting meats blends so perfectly that it cannot be distinguished at the table (in fact the alcohol is cooked away), but it tenderizes, prevents dryness, increases juiciness, and enhances flavor immeasurably.

Sometimes the Spirits serve a dual purpose. The PATE BRANDY STUFFING* and other stuffings included in this book not only taste marvelous, but they also baste the poultry from the *inside* so that the Brandy and Wine ingredients improve the quality of the meat while it is cooking.

Wine can turn an ordinary stew (or for that matter even the lowly hamburger or meat ball) into a treat worthy of any gourmet's palate.

Liqueurs and Wines give sauces of all kinds, ice creams,

* Recipes for items printed in small capital letters may be found by consulting the Index.

mousses, gelatine, and custard desserts a tantalizing flavor. Cakes treated with Spirits after baking not only taste superb, but also retain their freshness far longer. If kept in a covered container, they will be moist and delicious for several weeks rather than the usual few days. Furthermore, when a cake that has been so treated starts to dry out, a few drops of the Spirit brushed on the bottom of the cake will restore it completely. In the case of a layer cake, the slices should be brushed with the Spirit as they are cut if the cake seems to be drying out.

Another gratifying reward from cooking with Spirits is the drama a flambé creates for guests. Aside from the striking addition to taste, the theatrical effect of a BAKED ALASKA or even just a flaming sauce for an ice cream sundae served in a mass of blue flames is impossible to beat. In New Orleans it's an old and delightful custom for the guests to pay tribute to the "chef" when the lights are turned low and the flames leap from the chafing dish or as the flambé is brought to the table. Also, a flambé can be a great morale builder even when there is no company to applaud. On those days when everything seems to go wrong, I prepare for our dinner PORK CHOPS FLAMBE or a RUM OMELET FLAMBE, and during the few moments that the lovely flames dance and flicker as we sit in our darkened dining room, my good spirits are restored. Incidentally both of these dishes are easy to prepare and not very expensive.

They, of course, can be classified as haute cuisine, but like most other dishes that are so classified, they are no more difficult to prepare than ordinary food and need not be very costly. For example, the SHERRY APPLE CAKE is made up of such inexpensive ingredients as apples, raisins, flour, and a few drops of Sherry, but the dessert you produce from them will be outstanding. Inexpensive Wines used for the meat and poultry marinades give excellent results.

Furthermore, it doesn't take any longer to cook with Spirits, as illustrated by the sample menu below. And although I am not suggesting that every meal be composed *entirely* of Spirit-flavored dishes, here is an example of how it can be done:

AVOCADO PEAR AND RUM COCKTAIL

2 minutes to mix the sauce in the afternoon and about 5 minutes at dinnertime to cube the avocado and pour the sauce over it.

SKILLET-BROILED FISH FILLETS

About 20 minutes in all for preparation and cooking, during which time the avocado is prepared, tomatoes grilled, and the butter beans cooked.

TOMATOES GRILLED WITH WHITE WINE AND CHEESE

5 minutes' preparation an hour before dinner—broiled at the same time as the fish.

BUTTER BEANS WITH HOT SAUTERNE MAYONNAISE

15–18 minutes to cook butter beans (frozen) and mix and heat the sauce.

CHOCOLATE BRANDY BISCUIT WITH BAKED PECAN OR ALMOND TOPPING

Both the BISCUIT and the TOPPING can be made in advance and stored for weeks—the Biscuit in the freezer and the topping in the refrigerator. The preparation of the Biscuit takes not more than 15 minutes and the topping 3 minutes to mix and 25 minutes to bake.

After you have used the recipes in this book and discovered the wonderful results to be obtained through the use of Spirits in the preparation of food, you will undoubtedly want to do a little experimenting of your own. It was fun for me to discover that a little French Vermouth is as good for a stuffed baked potato as it is for a Martini, and I am confident that you will get just as much pleasure from your own "revolutionary" discoveries. Don't be frightened by the possibility of failing in your experiments. It's my guess that you'll be amazed by the ratio of your successes to your failures. The notion that recipes must be followed just as they are written was probably created by women who believed that if they could convince everyone of how difficult it was to cook, their own reputations, and consequently their own importance, would be greatly inflated.

Of course I love to keep on experimenting. The recipe for the FRUIT CAKE OF THE TWELVE SPIRITS took twelve seasons to mature. The original recipe came from the cook who worked for my family during my childhood in a happy and beautiful small town named Magnolia, Mississippi. Lu Magee, who actually is responsible for my interest in cooking, was an inspired cook and her fruit cake was good to start with; however, in my early teens when I first started experimenting I began to change measurements and to add and subtract ingredients. It took ten years to achieve the results I wanted, because fruit cakes were baked only once or twice a year, even in the country. When I discovered the excitement of cooking with Spirits I went to work on the recipe all over again, and spent two more years perfecting it.

This is typical of how the recipes in this book came about. Many of them originated in Magnolia, where everyone generously shared recipes; some were derived from well-known French or New Orleans recipes, and others are entirely my own. My latest project was doing something new with the crème brûlée which President Jefferson is supposed to have introduced in this country, and from my knowledge of Mr. Jefferson's tastes I am willing to guess that he might have been pleased by the addition of Benedictine to this recipe he brought from France.

You don't have to be born with a silver spoon in your mouth to serve fabulous food, nor be a graduate of the Cordon Bleu to prepare it!

Hors d'Oeuvres, Appetizers, and Aspics

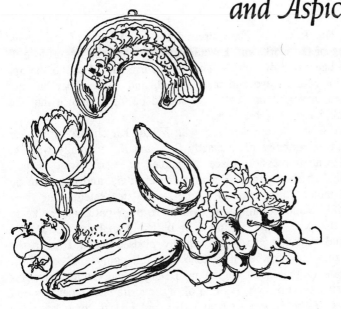

In *The Republic,* Plato stressed the importance of the beginning of the work, and I would equally stress the importance of the beginning of a meal. The first course should excite the appetite with its eye and taste appeal, and if the diner has not eaten in your home before, it should be an assurance that the cook knows her business.

A fruit cocktail flavored with Wine, Kirsch, Cointreau, or White Framboise does exactly this, and if you really want to make an impression, place the chilled sweetened fruit in individual sherbet glasses. Decorate the cocktails and put them on the table. Then, as soon as the guests are seated, pour thoroughly chilled Champagne over the fruit. I particularly like to do this when I have a maid or butler in to help, but I have found that my guests are equally pleased when I pour the Champagne as when it is done with full pomp and ceremony.

For another good beginning, I suggest the CHEESE BISCUITS WITH DEVILED HAM. It's one of my favorite hors d'oeuvres and most of the people to whom they are served come back for more and more and more. Some years ago I decided that I needed for a special dinner an hors d'oeuvre that would be a cross between a highly seasoned cheese straw and a small biscuit with a spicy filling. I started out with a pie dough, which I flavored with Worcestershire and Tabasco sauces. I rolled out the dough, sprinkled it with cheese, rolled it up, wrapped it in wax paper, and placed it in the refrigerator overnight. The next day I rolled out the dough and cut it into small rounds. I tried out various kinds of fillings, but with its first trial I knew that the deviled ham was just what I was seeking. It was not until after I started to concentrate on Spirit cooking that I made a change in this recipe. At that time, I added the dry White Wine and Amontillado Sherry to achieve just the right results.

You will find as you read this chapter that Rum is specified in a number of appetizer, hors d'oeuvres, and aspic recipes. A friend of mine, after eating the LIME-AVOCADO-ASPARAGUS ASPIC, told his wife, who passed it along to me, that ever since he had been in the military service in Trinidad he had adored drinking Rum, but until he tasted the aspic he never knew that Rum "ate" so deliciously.

HORS D'OEUVRES

Hearts of Artichokes Filled with Tomato Juice-Moselle Aspic

12 small boiled hearts of artichokes
TOMATO JUICE-MOSELLE ASPIC (*prepare aspic, using ¼ of each ingredient specified in recipe*)

Remove all leaves, the chokes, and the stems of the small boiled artichokes. Prepare aspic and place in refrigerator. When it is half congealed fill the artichoke hearts with it. Store in refrigerator until aspic is firm.

Hearts of Artichokes Filled with Tomato Juice-Moselle Aspic and Crabmeat

12 small boiled hearts of artichokes
TOMATO JUICE-MOSELLE ASPIC (*prepare aspic, using ¼ quantity of each ingredient specified in recipe*)
¼ cup cooked crabmeat

Remove all leaves, the chokes, and the stems of small boiled artichokes. Prepare aspic and chill until it reaches the consistency of egg white. Stir in crabmeat, and fill artichoke hearts with gelatine. Store in refrigerator until aspic is firm.

Camembert Butter

4 ounces ripe Camembert
  cheese
Dry White Wine
2 tablespoons softened
  butter
⅛ teaspoon cayenne
  pepper

15 1½-inch-diameter toast
   rounds or ¼ inch thick
   slices cucumber or 1-inch
   pieces scraped celery
2 tablespoons toasted almond
   slivers

Remove rind from Camembert cheese. Place cheese in container with tight cover. Cover the cheese with dry White Wine. Put container cover in place. Store in refrigerator overnight. Drain cheese. Combine with butter and pepper. Chill in refrigerator for several hours. Spread on toast rounds or cucumber slices or stuff into hollows of the small pieces of celery. Sprinkle cheese with toasted almond slivers.

Stuffed Celery ※1

20 1¼-inch pieces washed and scraped celery or celery curls
⅔ cup Roquefort cheese
Brandy or Sherry

Prepare celery pieces or curls. Pat dry after celery has been washed. Combine cheese with just enough Brandy or Sherry to soften and beat until mixture is smooth. Fill celery hollows with cheese mixture.

Stuffed Celery ※2

20 1¼-inch pieces washed and scraped celery or celery curls
⅔ cup bleu cheese or any prepared cheese spread
Brandy or Sherry

Prepare celery pieces or curls. After celery is washed, pat dry. Combine cheese with just enough Brandy or Sherry to soften and beat until mixture is smooth. Fill celery hollows with cheese mixture.

Stuffed Celery ※3

20 1¼-inch pieces washed
and scraped celery or
celery curls

⅔ cup cooked crabmeat,
shredded cooked shrimp,
or crawfish or fish flakes
SAUTERNE MAYONNAISE
Worcestershire sauce

Prepare celery pieces or curls. After celery is washed, pat dry. Combine seafood with just enough Sauterne Mayonnaise to moisten it. Add Worcestershire sauce to taste. Fill celery hollows with seafood.

Stuffed Celery ※4

20 1¼-inch pieces washed and scraped celery or celery curls
⅔ cup grated carrot
SAUTERNE MAYONNAISE

Prepare celery pieces or curls. After celery is washed, pat dry. Combine grated carrot with just enough Sauterne Mayonnaise to moisten. Fill celery hollows with carrot and mayonnaise mixture.

Cheese Biscuits with Deviled Ham

1 tablespoon Worcestershire sauce with 6 drops Tabasco sauce and enough dry White Wine to make ⅙ cup liquid
1¼ cups sifted all-purpose flour
½ teaspoon salt
¼ teaspoon baking powder
½ teaspoon sugar
⅜ cup shortening
½ cup grated American cheese
Paprika
2 tablespoons very cold Amontillado Sherry
5 tablespoons deviled ham

Chill Worcestershire sauce mixture thoroughly. Sift flour, measure, and add salt, baking powder, and sugar. Cut shortening into flour mixture with pastry blender or two knives until it is the consistency of coarse corn meal. Stir in Worcestershire sauce mixture with a fork until the dough clings in a ball. Roll dough on floured board or cloth to ¼-inch thickness. Cover with grated cheese and sprinkle liberally with paprika. Roll up like jelly roll; press edges together. Wrap in wax paper and place in refrigerator for at least 12 hours. Roll on floured board or cloth to ⅛-inch thickness. Cut into small rounds and brush one half of the rounds lightly with cold Sherry. On each of the rounds that has been brushed with Sherry, place approximately ½ teaspoon deviled ham. Cover these rounds on which filling has been placed with rounds of cheese biscuit dough. Press edges of rounds together to seal the two rounds so that filling cannot leak out. Bake in 425°F. oven 9–12 minutes.
Makes 32 1⅜-inch biscuits.

Cheese Fondue with Shrimp or Crawfish

1¾ cups grated Swiss
   cheese
¼ cup grated sharp
   Cheddar cheese
1½ tablespoons flour
2 tablespoons water
1 cup dry Chablis Wine
1 teaspoon Worcestershire
   sauce

2 tablespoons minced
   parsley
Salt to taste
⅛ teaspoon cayenne
   pepper
40 medium-size cooked
   shelled deveined lake
   shrimp or crawfish
Small chunks French bread

Place cheese in inset pan of chafing dish. Set pan in water jacket containing boiling water. Stir cheese until melted. Dissolve flour in 2 tablespoons water and beat with fork until smooth. Add to cheese and blend thoroughly. Stir in ¼ cup of Wine and stir until smooth. Add remainder of Wine, ¼ cup at a time, stirring after each addition, until mixture is smooth. With the last quarter cup of Wine add Worcestershire sauce, parsley, salt to taste, and cayenne. Stir until bubbly. Add shrimp or crawfish. Keep warm over hot water. Serve with chunks of French bread.

Serves 8.

Cocktail Patties ※1

18 small cocktail patty shells
1 cup cooked crabmeat,
   chopped cooked shrimp,
   lobster, chicken, or turkey
¼ cup finely chopped green
   pepper

¼ cup thinly sliced cooked
   mushrooms
½ cup Sherry-flavored
   CREAM SAUCE

Heat patties in 400° F. oven. Combine seafood or poultry with remaining ingredients and heat. Fill hot patty shells with mixture.

Cocktail Patties ⚹2

36 small oysters with liquid
¾ cup BROWN SAUCE made
   with oyster water and
   flavored with Amontillado
   Sherry

18 small cocktail patty shells
¼ cup thinly sliced cooked
   or canned mushrooms

Drain oysters and reserve liquid. Prepare Brown Sauce, using the oyster water, and, if additional liquid is needed, bouillon. Flavor with Amontillado Sherry. Heat patty shells in 400° F. oven. Heat Brown Sauce and add oysters and mushrooms. Cook only until oysters puff and edges curl. Fill hot patties with oyster mixture.

Crabmeat or Tuna Balls

1 tablespoon butter or
   oleomargarine
1 tablespoon sifted flour
½ cup White Wine or Sherry
2 tablespoons breakfast
   cream
1 teaspoon Worcestershire
   sauce
¼ cup grated Cheddar
   cheese

1 teaspoon dehydrated
   parsley flakes
¼ teaspoon salt
⅛ teaspoon black pepper
1⅓ rounding cups cooked
   crabmeat or washed and
   drained tuna

Melt butter or oleomargarine, remove from stove, and stir in flour. Return to low heat and cook, stirring constantly, until smooth and thick. Again remove from heat and stir in liquids. Return to low heat and continue stirring until sauce thickens. Add cheese, parsley, salt, and pepper, and stir until cheese is melted and sauce is very thick. Cool. Mix sauce with crabmeat or tuna and let stand in covered dish in refrigerator for at least several hours. Remove from refrigerator and roll into balls about 1 inch in diameter.

TO BAKE:

> *Tuna or crabmeat balls*
> *1 cup melted butter or oleomargarine*
> *1½ cups fine Rice Krispies or Corn Flake crumbs*

Cover cooky tray with aluminum foil. Roll balls first in melted butter or oleomargarine and then in fine crumbs. Place on cooky tray and bake in 350° F. oven for 30 minutes.

OR IF YOU PREFER TO FRY:

> *Tuna or crabmeat balls*   *1 slightly beaten egg yolk*
> *1½ cups fine bread or cracker*   *Deep hot fat*
>   *crumbs*

Roll balls in the bread or cracker crumbs, then dip in yolk and again in the crumbs. Fry in deep hot fat (2–3 inches deep) at 380° F. until golden brown on all sides. Drain on absorbent paper towels.

> *27 baked or fried 1-inch balls.*

Cucumbers Stuffed with Roquefort or Bleu Cheese

> *2 medium-size cucumbers*   *⅓ cup Roquefort cheese*
> *2 cups water*   *combined with ⅓ cup*
> *1 teaspoon salt*   *cream cheese or*
> *Sherry, dry White Wine, or*   *⅔ cup bleu cheese*
>   *Cognac*   *Salt*

Cut unpeeled cucumbers into ¾-inch-thick slices. Scoop out center of each slice about halfway through. Combine water with salt. Soak cucumbers in salt water in refrigerator, keeping container well covered. Drain and pat dry with paper towels. Combine just enough Spirit with the Roquefort and cream cheese mixture or the bleu cheese to soften the cheese. Season to taste with salt. Fill hollows in cucumber slices with the cheese-Wine or cheese-Brandy mixture. Chill and serve.

Serves 6.

Eggs and Caviar in Aspic

1 tablespoon gelatine
½ cup cold water
1 cup boiling bouillon
2 tablespoons lemon juice
2 tablespoons Sherry

⅛ teaspoon salt
3 tablespoons caviar
4 hard-cooked eggs
12 rounds boiled chilled
    celery root

Dissolve gelatine in cold water. Stir in boiling bouillon, lemon juice, Sherry, and salt. Place in refrigerator until mixture reaches consistency of egg white. Pour thin layer of gelatine into shallow, well-oiled pan. Arrange caviar, riced yolks, and grated whites of hard-cooked eggs on gelatine layer. Cover with another layer of gelatine. Return to refrigerator and allow to congeal. When firm, cut rounds of gelatine with a 1½-inch biscuit cutter. Serve rounds on slices of boiled chilled celery root.

Pickled Herring

6 herring with milt
1 lemon sliced
2 medium-size onions
    sliced
Pepper

Double-strength vinegar
Dry White Wine or
    Champagne
3 carrots

Clean, cut open, and then soak herring overnight. Bone and cut herring into small pieces. Add lemon and onion, milt, part of which has been mashed, pepper to taste, and equal parts of vinegar and Wine to cover herring. Let stand several days. Roll pieces around small strips of onion with which herring was pickled. Peel carrots and cut into paper-thin slices (lengthwise) with vegetable parer. Tie each of the herring rolls with a slice of the carrot. Pack rolls in jars and cover with liquid in which herring was pickled. Seal jars and store in refrigerator until ready to use.

Serves 12.

Lime-Avocado-Asparagus Dip

1 medium-size avocado
2 tablespoons chopped onion
1 small can cut green
  asparagus
Juice of 2 limes
2 tablespoons White Rum

1½ teaspoons
  Worcestershire sauce
4 drops Tabasco sauce
Salt to taste
2–3 drops green food
  coloring
Paprika, if desired

Chill all ingredients thoroughly before peeling and cutting avocado. Combine onion, asparagus, and juice of limes in blender and blend until smooth (about 30 seconds). Add avocado, Rum, Worcestershire sauce, and Tabasco. Again run blender until mixture is smooth (about 30 seconds). Season to taste with salt and add coloring. Run blender only long enough to thoroughly mix in color. Chill. If desired, dust with paprika before serving.

Makes 1½ cups (approximate, depending on size of avocado) of dip.

Radishes with Chive Cheese or Bleu Cheese

*15 well-shaped radishes with
  peel*
2 cups water
1 teaspoon salt

*⅓ cup chive cheese or bleu
  cheese*
Dry White Wine
Salt
Cayenne pepper

Cut radishes into rounds about ⅜ inch thick. Combine water and salt. Soak radishes in salt water in a covered container in refrigerator for about 4 hours. Drain and dry thoroughly by patting with paper towels. Combine chive cheese or bleu cheese with just enough dry White Wine to soften cheese. Season to taste with salt and pepper. Spread 1 side of each radish slice with cheese mixture. Chill before serving.
Serves 6.

Steak Bits

*4 pounds round steak, 1 inch
  thick*
Red Burgundy Wine
*2 teaspoons instant meat
  tenderizer*

Salad oil
Juice of ½ lemon
2 teaspoons minced parsley
Pepper to taste

Place steak in long shallow pan and cover with Wine. Let stand in refrigerator for at least 12 hours. When ready to cook, remove meat from Wine and reserve ½ cup Burgundy. Sprinkle tenderizer evenly over entire surface of steak and pierce meat deeply with fork at ¾-inch intervals. Brush meat with oil. Preheat broiler for 10 minutes (it should be around 500°

F.). Broil steak 4 inches below broiler unit 4 minutes on each side. Remove meat from broiler. Put Wine, lemon juice, and parsley into broiler pan. Stir until completely blended with pan juices. Season to taste with pepper. Cut steak into small pieces and impale each piece on a toothpick. Pour Wine-pan juice mixture into dip cup and arrange steak pieces around dip cup. Serve at once.

Makes 48 1-inch cubes.

Plum Tomatoes Filled with Olive Aspic

1½ teaspoons gelatine
¼ cup water
½ cup boiling bouillon
1 tablespoon lemon juice
1 tablespoon Sherry
⅛ teaspoon salt
⅛ teaspoon cayenne pepper
15 plum tomatoes
30 small pimiento-stuffed or anchovy-stuffed olives

Sprinkle gelatine on cold water. Dissolve with boiling bouillon. Add lemon juice, Sherry, salt, and cayenne. Place in refrigerator. Wash plum tomatoes and halve them. Remove pulp and turn upside down. Allow to drain for 20 minutes and then place in refrigerator. When gelatine reaches consistency of egg whites, half fill tomato halves with it. Insert stuffed olive in center of gelatine in each tomato. Return to refrigerator and allow to congeal.

Stuffed Plum or Cherry Tomatoes

12 plum or 24 cherry tomatoes
Salt
¼ cup finely chopped boiled shrimp
¼ cup cooked crabmeat
SAUTERNE MAYONNAISE
1½ teaspoons dehydrated parsley flakes
⅛ teaspoon cumin
⅛ teaspoon turmeric
Salt and pepper
Paprika

Cut off stem end and remove pulp from centers of tomatoes. Lightly sprinkle insides with salt. Turn upside down and drain for 20 minutes. Combine shrimp and crabmeat with just enough Sauterne Mayonnaise to hold seafood together. Add parsley, cumin, and turmeric, and season to taste with salt and pepper. Fill tomato shells with seafood mixture. Chill thoroughly, and just before serving, sprinkle with paprika.

NOTE: If desired, substitute ½ cup chopped boiled or baked turkey or chicken for seafood.

FRUIT APPETIZERS

Apple and Grape Cocktail

2 cups apple balls
Juice of 2 lemons
2 cups ice water
2 cups peeled white seedless
  or seeded grapes
2 tablespoons maraschino
  cherry juice

¼ cup Cointreau
½ cup orange juice
⅓ cup sugar or artificial
  liquid sweetener to taste,
  if desired

Peel apples and with ball cutter or teaspoon scoop into small balls. Combine lemon juice and water and plunge apple balls into lemon water. Drain apple balls and pat dry. Combine with grapes. Mix maraschino juice, Cointreau, and orange juice. Pour over fruit. Chill in refrigerator. If desired, sprinkle fruit with sugar or artificial liquid sweetener.

Serves 8.

Avocado Pear and Rum Cocktail

2 ripe mellow avocado pears
½ cup Rum
3 teaspoons brown sugar
Juice of 1 lemon

Chill avocados thoroughly. Several hours before serving, combine on high speed of blender or mix with rotary egg beater the Rum and brown sugar. Chill. Forty-five minutes before serving place Rum mixture in freezer section of refrigerator. Just before serving time, peel avocados and cut into small cubes. Divide cubes between *4 cocktail glasses* and sprinkle fruit with lemon juice. Pour icy cold Rum sauce over avocados and serve at once.

Grapefruit Halves with Peach or Apricot Preserves

3 grapefruit
½ cup peach or apricot preserves
2 tablespoons Cointreau or Peach Brandy or Apricot Brandy

Cut grapefruit in halves. Remove seeds and loosen sections. Combine Cointreau or Peach Brandy with peach preserves or combine apricot preserves with Apricot Brandy or Cointreau. Spread preserves over grapefruit pulp.

Chill thoroughly and serve, *or*

Broil 4 inches under broiler unit until grapefruit begins to brown, *or*

Place in 375° F. oven and bake until fruit is thoroughly heated.

Serves 6.

Grapefruit and Orange Cocktail

2 cups chilled grapefruit
  sections from which
  membranes and seeds have
  been removed
2 cups chilled orange sections
  from which membranes and
  seeds have been removed
⅓ cup sugar or artificial
  liquid sweetener to taste

Cold Sauterne
8 maraschino cherries that
  have been soaked in equal
  parts of their own juice and
  Maraschino Liqueur for at
  least 4 hours
Mint sprigs if desired

Combine fruit. Sprinkle with sugar or sweetener. Divide among 8 6-ounce sherbet glasses. Cover with cold Sauterne and top each cocktail with a cherry. If desired, garnish with mint and serve at once.

Honeydew Melon and Rum Cocktail

3 cups chilled honeydew melon cubes
½ cup Rum
⅓ cup brown sugar
Juice of 1 lime

Place melon cubes in container with cover. Blend Rum, brown sugar, and lime juice in blender or with rotary egg beater. Pour over melon cubes and cover container. Place in refrigerator for at least several hours, gently stirring cubes from time to time.
Serves 6.

Melon and Cointreau or Triple Sec Cocktail

4 cups chilled watermelon, cantaloupe, and/or honeydew melon
  cubes or balls
½ cup Cointreau or Triple Sec
Sugar or artificial liquid sweetener to taste
Sprigs of mint, if desired

Place melon and/or cantaloupe balls or cubes in container.
Pour Cointreau or Triple Sec over balls or cubes and sweeten
to taste with sugar or artificial liquid sweetener. Store in refrigerator. When ready to serve, divide into *8 6-ounce sherbet
glasses* (both melon and liquid) and if desired, decorate with
sprigs of mint.

Melon and Wine Cocktail

4 cups cold cantaloupe, watermelon, and/or honeydew melon
  cubes or balls
Sugar or artificial liquid sweetener to taste
Thoroughly chilled Sauterne or Champagne
Sprigs of mint, if desired

Cut cantaloupe, watermelon, and/or honeydew melon into
balls or cubes and sweeten to taste with sugar or artificial liquid
sweetener. Divide into cocktail glasses and cover with Sauterne
or Champagne. If desired, decorate with mint. Serve at once.
Serves 8.

Pear or Peach and Wine Cocktail

4 cups chilled peeled and cubed mellow pears or peaches
Juice of 1 lemon
⅓ cup sugar or artificial liquid sweetener to taste
Tenth of (12½ ounces) thoroughly chilled Champagne or Sauterne
8 maraschino cherries soaked overnight in equal parts of their
own juice and Maraschino Liqueur

Sprinkle fruit with lemon juice and with sugar or artificial liquid sweetener to taste. Divide among *8 6-ounce sherbet glasses.* Cover with cold Wine. (If desired, glasses of fruit may be placed on table and wine poured at table.) Garnish with cherries.

Raspberries and White Framboise Liqueur

4 cups chilled whole or
halved raspberries
Sugar or artificial liquid
sweetener to taste

Chilled White Framboise
Liqueur
Sprigs of mint, if desired

Divide raspberries into *8 6-ounce sherbet glasses* just before serving. Sprinkle berries with sugar or liquid sweetener to taste. Then sprinkle berries lightly with White Framboise Liqueur and if desired, garnish with mint.

NOTE: If desired, 2 cups of raspberries may be combined with 2 cups of pineapple cubes or pear cubes.

Strawberries and Grapefruit Cocktail

2 cups chilled whole or
  halved strawberries
2 cups chilled grapefruit
  sections from which
  membranes and seeds have
  been removed

Sugar or artificial liquid
  sweetener to taste
Cold Kirsch, Cointreau, or
  Champagne
Sprigs of mint, if desired

Combine berries and grapefruit. Sweeten to taste with sugar or artificial liquid sweetener. Just before serving, divide into 8 6-ounce sherbet cups and sprinkle with Kirsch or Cointreau, or pour Champagne over the fruit. If desired, garnish with sprigs of mint.

Strawberries and Orange Cocktail

2 cups chilled whole or
  halved strawberries
2 cups chilled orange
  sections from which
  membranes and seeds have
  been removed

Sugar or artificial liquid
  sweetener to taste
Cold Kirsch, Cointreau, or
  Champagne
Sprigs of mint, if desired

Combine berries and orange sections. Sweeten to taste with sugar or artificial sweetener. Just before serving, divide into 8 6-ounce sherbet glasses and sprinkle with Kirsch or Cointreau, or pour the Champagne over the fruit. If desired, garnish with mint.

Strawberries and Pineapple Cocktail

2 cups chilled whole or
halved strawberries
2 cups chilled fresh cooked or
canned pineapple cut in
small chunks

Sugar or artificial liquid
sweetener to taste
Cold Kirsch, Cointreau, or
Champagne
Sprigs of mint, if desired

Combine berries and pineapple. Sweeten to taste with sugar or artificial liquid sweetener. Just before serving, divide into 8 *6-ounce sherbet glasses* and sprinkle with Kirsch or Cointreau, or pour the Champagne over the fruit. If desired, garnish with sprigs of mint and serve at once.

SEAFOOD APPETIZERS

Crabmeat Lorenzo (Cold)

3 cups cooked lump crabmeat
3 tablespoons light dry White
Wine
Salt and pepper to taste
Lettuce, watercress, or endive
1 cup SAUTERNE MAYONNAISE
⅓ cup tomato catsup
1½ teaspoons
Worcestershire sauce

½ cup commercial sour
cream
1¼ tablespoons chopped
chives
Paprika
2 hard-cooked eggs sliced
6 small very thin slices
baked ham

Several hours before serving time sprinkle crabmeat with Wine. Store in refrigerator. Just before serving time remove crabmeat from refrigerator and season to taste with salt and pepper. Arrange on lettuce, watercress, or endive. Combine Sauterne Mayonnaise, catsup, Worcestershire sauce, and fold in

sour cream. Pour over crabmeat. Sprinkle with chives and paprika. Garnish with hard-cooked eggs and ham.
Serves 6.

Seafood Cocktail

48 cold raw oysters or clams
  or 2 cups cold cooked
  shrimp, crabmeat, or diced
  lobster
12 tablespoons chilled
  tomato catsup
6 drops Tabasco sauce
2 teaspoons
  Worcestershire sauce

Juice of 1 lemon
1 tablespoon finely chopped
  celery
½ teaspoon grated
  horse-radish
1 tablespoon chilled Bourbon
  Whisky

Divide chilled seafood among *6 cocktail glasses.* Combine other ingredients and pour approximately 2½ tablespoons of the sauce over the seafood in each glass.

ASPICS

Asparagus in Bouillon Aspic

3⅜ cups of bouillon
2 tablespoons Sherry or dry
  White Wine
Salt and pepper to taste
2 tablespoons unflavored
  gelatine

1½ cups canned or cooked
  asparagus
Lettuce, endive, or romaine
Mayonnaise or SAUTERNE
  MAYONNAISE
Paprika

Combine bouillon and Wine. Season to taste with salt and pepper. Sprinkle gelatine over ½ cup of bouillon mixture. Let stand for 5 minutes. Bring remainder of mixture to a boil. Stir boiling liquid into gelatine and continue stirring until dissolved. Place in refrigerator until gelatine reaches consistency of egg white. Cover bottom of well-oiled rectangular mold with a 1-inch layer of the partly congealed bouillon mixture. Arrange asparagus in rows on top of aspic and then cover with remainder of gelatine. Return to refrigerator for at least 2 hours. When ready to serve, unmold gelatine and cut into serving size rectangles. Arrange the salad greens on individual salad plates and place a rectangle of the aspic on each plate. Top each serving with mayonnaise or Sauterne Mayonnaise and sprinkle with paprika.

Serves 6.

Aspic Ring with Eggs au Pâté

4 hard-cooked eggs	*½ cup cold water*
3 tablespoons pâté de foie gras or liver sausage	*1 cup beef bouillon*
1 teaspoon Worcestershire sauce	*1¾ cups chicken bouillon*
SAUTERNE MAYONNAISE	*¼ cup dry White Wine*
Salt and pepper to taste	*Salt and pepper to taste*
2 tablespoons gelatine	*2 tablespoons sliced pimiento-stuffed olives*

Cut the hard-cooked eggs in halves lengthwise. Remove yolks, mash them, and add the pâté de foie gras or liver sausage, Worcestershire sauce, and just enough Sauterne Mayonnaise to hold the mixture together. Season to taste with salt and pepper. Stuff mixture into hard-cooked egg white halves. Soak gelatine in cold water. Combine beef and chicken bouillons and bring to a boil. Pour over gelatine and stir until dissolved. Add White Wine and season to taste with salt and pepper. Place in refrigerator until aspic begins to set. Pour a ¾-inch layer of the thickened gelatine into the bottom of a well-oiled ring mold. Place eggs with white sides down and arrange the sliced olives around them. Cover with remaining gelatine. Place in refrigerator until firm. Unmold and serve at once.

Serves 8.

Avocado and Grapefruit in Lime Gelatine

6 ounces lime gelatine
3¾ cups boiling water
¼ cup Rum
1 large or 2 small avocados
Juice of 1 lemon or 1 lime

1 cup grapefruit sections
from which seeds and
membranes have been
removed

Dissolve gelatine in boiling water. Stir in Rum. Cool and place in refrigerator until aspic is consistency of egg white. Peel avocado and cut into thin slices. Sprinkle slices with lemon or lime juice. Cover bottom of well-oiled mold with layer of gelatine mixture. Arrange avocado slices and grapefruit sections on gelatine layer. Cover fruit with aspic layer. Alternate layers of fruit and aspic until mold is filled, ending with gelatine layer. Place in refrigerator to congeal.

Serves 8.

Carrot and Pineapple Aspic

2 tablespoons unflavored
gelatine
1 cup cold water
¼ cup Sauterne
¾ cup boiling water
1 cup pineapple juice

½ cup lemon juice
½ teaspoon salt
1 tablespoon sugar
1¼ cups canned diced
drained pineapple
1¼ cups grated raw carrot

Soak gelatine in cold water. Add Sauterne to boiling water and bring mixture to a boil. Dissolve gelatine in boiling liquid. Add pineapple juice, lemon juice, salt, and sugar. Place in refrigerator until aspic begins to set. Fold in pineapple and carrots. Spoon into well-oiled mold and place mold in refrigerator. Let stand until aspic is congealed.

Serves 8.

NOTE: ¼ cup of Cointreau may be substituted for the ¼ cup Sauterne in the above recipe.

Crabmeat Timbales

1½ cups cooked crabmeat
Dry White Wine
2 tablespoons gelatine
1 cup milk
2¼ cups mayonnaise
1 teaspoon onion juice
⅛ teaspoon Tabasco sauce
1½ teaspoons Worcestershire sauce
Salt and pepper to taste
¼ cup chopped ripe olives
⅓ cup chopped celery
3 tablespoons chopped green pepper

3 tablespoons chopped pimiento
3 medium-size cucumbers cut in paper thin slices
4 small firm tomatoes cut in eighths
1 cup commercial sour cream
1 tablespoon chopped chives
2 tablespoons caviar, if desired

Cover crabmeat with dry White Wine. Store in refrigerator for 2 hours. Sprinkle gelatine over milk. Dissolve over boiling water. Add mayonnaise, onion juice, Tabasco sauce, Worcestershire sauce, and salt and pepper to taste. Place in refrigerator until slightly chilled. Drain crabmeat and combine with olives, celery, green pepper, and pimiento. Fold mixture into chilled gelatine and spoon into *8 individual oiled molds.* Let stand in refrigerator until firm. Unmold shortly before serving time. Place each timbale on individual serving plate. Surround with cucumber slices and garnish with tomato sections. Top timbales with sour cream and sprinkle with chopped chives. If desired, place a dab of caviar in center of sour cream on each timbale.

NOTE: If desired, aspic may be congealed in one large oiled mold.

Fruit-flavored Gelatine with Grapefruit and Orange

3 ounces fruit-flavored
  gelatine
1½ cups boiling water
½ cup sweet Sauterne

½ cup grapefruit sections
  free from seeds and
  membranes
½ cup orange sections free
  from seeds and membranes
SAUTERNE MAYONNAISE

Dissolve gelatine in boiling water. Stir in Sauterne. Place in refrigerator until it reaches consistency of egg white. Pour 1-inch layer of gelatine into bottom of well-oiled mold. Arrange fruit sections on gelatine and cover with another layer of gelatine. Alternate layers of fruit and gelatine until mold is filled, topping with gelatine layer. Serve with Sauterne Mayonnaise.
  Serves 4.

Lime-Avocado-Asparagus Aspic

4½ cups LIME-AVOCADO-
  ASPARAGUS DIP
3 tablespoons unflavored
  gelatine
⅜ cup water

⅜ cup *White Rum*
Salt to taste
CREAM OF SHRIMP-SHERRY
  SAUCE

Prepare Lime-Avocado-Asparagus Dip. Sprinkle gelatine over mixture of water and Rum and let stand for 5 minutes.

Dissolve gelatine over boiling water and then stir it into lime-avocado-asparagus mixture. Season to taste with salt. Spoon into greased mold and place in refrigerator to congeal. Unmold and serve with Cream of Shrimp-Sherry Sauce.
Serves 12.

Pear and Pineapple in Lime Gelatine

Follow recipe for AVOCADO AND GRAPEFRUIT IN LIME GELATINE, substituting 6 small canned pear halves for the avocado and 1 cup of canned pineapple chunks for the grapefruit. Add 12 maraschino cherries, which have been soaked overnight in equal parts of their own juice and Maraschino Liqueur, to the pear and pineapple.
Serves 8.

Relish Aspic

6 ounces prepared lemon gelatine	*½ cup chopped drained sweet cucumber pickle*
3 cups boiling water	*2 cups chopped celery*
1 cup White Wine	*⅔ cup chopped drained pimiento*
1 teaspoon salt	*2¼ cups pecans broken into small pieces*
2 tablespoons wine vinegar	

Dissolve gelatine in boiling water. Add Wine. Stir in salt and vinegar. Place in refrigerator and let stand until aspic begins to set. Fold in remaining ingredients. Spoon into well-oiled mold. Place in refrigerator to congeal.
Serves 8.

Seafood Sauce Gelée

1 tablespoon Sauterne
½ cup mayonnaise
¾ cup cooked crabmeat
¾ cup cooked shelled
  deveined shrimp cut in
  ¾-inch segments
Salt and pepper to taste

6 ounces lemon-flavored
  gelatine
3¾ cups boiling water
¼ cup Sauterne
1 cup thinly sliced
  cucumbers

Add 1 tablespoon Sauterne to mayonnaise. Stir in crabmeat and shrimp. Season to taste with salt and pepper. Dissolve gelatine in boiling water. Add ¼ cup Sauterne. Chill seafood and gelatine in refrigerator and when gelatine reaches consistency of egg white, pour a layer into the bottom of a well-oiled mold. Cover with a layer of the seafood mixture. Alternate layers until mold is filled, ending with gelatine layer. Place in refrigerator to congeal. Unmold and serve on bed of thinly sliced cucumbers.
Serves 8.

Shrimp in Clear Aspic

2¼ cups boiled shelled
  deveined shrimp
½ cup Wine-flavored
  FRENCH DRESSING
1½ teaspoons Creole or hot
  prepared mustard
2 tablespoons gelatine
½ cup cold water
2¾ cups chicken bouillon
¼ cup dry White Wine or
  Champagne

½ cup commercial sour
  cream
¾ cup mayonnaise
1 large cucumber cut into
  paper thin slices with a
  vegetable parer and soaked
  in salt water in refrigerator
  for several hours
⅛ teaspoon cayenne pepper,
  if desired

Marinate shrimp in Wine-flavored French Dressing to which mustard has been added. Store in covered container overnight in refrigerator. Drain shrimp. Sprinkle gelatine on water and dissolve with boiling bouillon. Add White Wine or Champagne and place in refrigerator. When aspic begins to set, pour ¾-inch layer into each of *8 oiled individual molds.* Arrange 6–8 shrimp—depending on size and very large shrimp may be cut into 2 segments—on top of the ¾-inch layer in each mold and then cover shrimp with remaining aspic. Return to refrigerator to congeal. Chill sour cream and mayonnaise. Shortly before serving time, drain cucumber slices and pat dry with paper towels. Fold cream and cucumber slices into mayonnaise and if desired add cayenne pepper. Unmold aspics and serve with cucumber sauce.

Shrimp, Lobster, Crawfish, Chicken, or Turkey Aspic

2 cups cooked shrimp,
  lobster, crawfish, chicken,
  or turkey cut in 1-inch
  chunks
Sauterne
2 tablespoons wine vinegar
¼ teaspoon basil
⅛ teaspoon cumin
2 teaspoons dehydrated
  parsley flakes
Mayonnaise
2 tablespoons gelatine

½ cup cold water
½ cup chopped celery
½ cup chopped ripe olives
¾ cup cooked shrimp,
  lobster, crawfish, chicken,
  or turkey, cut in ¾-inch
  pieces[1]
Red caviar
Cucumber slices
Wedges of tomato or plum
  tomatoes

Soak shrimp, lobster, crawfish, chicken, or turkey in just enough Sauterne to cover. Add vinegar, basil, cumin, and parsley. Store in refrigerator in covered container overnight. Drain, reserving ¼ cup of marinade. Put seafood or poultry through

[1] Use the shrimp pieces with the shrimp gelatine, lobster pieces with lobster gelatine, crawfish pieces with crawfish gelatine, chicken pieces with chicken gelatine and turkey pieces with turkey gelatine.

fine blade of meat grinder. Strain the reserved marinade through fine cheese cloth and combine it with ground seafood or poultry. Stir in enough mayonnaise to make 3 cups of mixture. Soak gelatine in cold water. Dissolve over boiling water. Fold gelatine into mayonnaise mixture and then fold in celery, olives, and seafood or poultry. Spoon into well-oiled mold and place in refrigerator to congeal. Just before serving, turn aspic out on cold platter. Sprinkle top with red caviar and garnish with cucumber slices and wedges of tomato or plum tomatoes.
Serves 8.

Thousand Island Aspic

1½ cups mayonnaise
1 cup chili sauce
¼ cup plus 2 tablespoons tomato catsup
1 tablespoon Worcestershire sauce
2 tablespoons unflavored gelatine
½ cup cold water
½ cup light dry Wine

2 large green peppers chopped
4 drained pimientos chopped
4 hard-cooked eggs chopped
6 hearts of artichokes cooked or canned, or 1 cup canned green asparagus, or 1 cup cooked chopped shrimp or lobster or 1 cup cooked crabmeat

Combine mayonnaise, chili sauce, catsup, and Worcestershire sauce. Sprinkle gelatine on a mixture of the cold water and Wine. Let stand for 5 minutes. Melt over boiling water. Fold gelatine into mayonnaise mixture. Place in refrigerator for 10 minutes. Fold in green pepper, pimientos, and hard-cooked eggs. Return to refrigerator, and when gelatine begins to set, pour a 1-inch layer of aspic into oiled mold. Arrange artichoke hearts or asparagus on aspic and cover with remaining gelatine. If using the seafood, after the 1-inch layer has been poured into the mold, fold the seafood into the remainder of the

Thousand Island aspic and spoon into the mold. Place in refrigerator to congeal.
Serves 8.

Tomato Juice-Moselle Aspic

3¼ cups tomato juice
¼ cup Moselle Wine
1 teaspoon basil
¼ teaspoon thyme
1 teaspoon minced
  dehydrated onion
1 teaspoon minced
  dehydrated celery

1 teaspoon minced
  dehydrated parsley
Salt and pepper to taste
2 tablespoons unflavored
  gelatine
2 hard-cooked eggs sliced
½ cup SAUTERNE
  MAYONNAISE

Combine tomato juice, Moselle, basil, thyme, onion, celery, and parsley. Season to taste with salt and pepper. Let stand in covered container in refrigerator overnight. Strain ½ cup of mixture and let stand until room temperature. Sprinkle gelatine over this ½ cup of Wine-flavored tomato juice and soak for 5 minutes. Bring remainder of mixture to a boil. Strain and stir boiling liquid into gelatine until the gelatine is dissolved. Pour into oiled mold. Place in refrigerator to congeal. Unmold and garnish with sliced hard-cooked eggs. Serve with Sauterne Mayonnaise.
Serves 8.

NOTE: 1 cup of any one or any combination of the following may be added to aspic. Prepare TOMATO JUICE-MOSELLE ASPIC and when it reaches consistency of egg white fold in:

chopped celery
sliced cucumbers
cooked or canned asparagus
cooked lobster meat
cooked shelled deveined
  shrimp

cooked crabmeat
cooked crawfish
chopped boiled chicken or
  turkey
chopped roast pork

Pour aspic in oiled mold and congeal in refrigerator.

Soups

One of my first memories is associated with soup. Because my father had often gone hungry when he was young, he was determined that no one was going to want for food if there was anything he could do about it. Our Magnolia home was Mecca for every hobo who traveled Highway 51 or came South via Illinois Central freight cars (we also got all of the return traffic). When the first great flu epidemic struck this country most of the people in our town were stricken and few of them had anyone to do their cooking. Daddy and Mother both had flu, but we had help and we had food, so they went into "conference" with Lu Magee, our cook, and Levi Brown, the porter from our store. As a result, the Meyer family started its own soup kitchen. I can still close my eyes and see Lu cooking tremendous pots of soup on a large wood stove, and then I can see Lu and Levi putting the hot kettles of soup in the back of our mule-driven wagon to make their trip from house to house to take care of any and everyone who was sick and in need of food. I wish that I might have known enough about cooking at that time to suggest to Lu that she add Wine to the soup. I think that it might have added extra strength to the nourishment for our bedridden fellow townspeople and perhaps even hastened some recoveries, as I'm a great believer in the medicinal uses (in moderation, of course) of alcohol.

In this connection, I remember reading in a very old cookbook owned by a Magnolia friend about the different Spirits that could be used in the treatment of practically every ailment then known to mankind. I made a copy of this list, but unfortunately, in the many years that have passed since I left Magnolia, the list has been lost. A few years ago I thought it would be amusing to include it in a cookbook I was compiling for my own use. I went through all the old cookbooks I could find in the New Orleans Public Library and the Tulane University Library with no success, I am sorry to say, but I did find in the translation of an old French cookbook a recipe for CHAMPAGNE ONION SOUP. I was not quite satisfied with the recipe so I went to work on it and made a few changes which resulted in the recipe in this book.

Another soup recipe of which I am very fond, because I sometimes have to get my meals together very quickly (and I have no desire to sacrifice taste to haste) is QUICK CRAB GUMBO. Gumbo is usually cooked for several hours, but with approximately 10 minutes' preparation and 30 minutes' cooking, you have an excellent gumbo when this recipe is used.

Borsch

4 large cooked beets
1 quart clear meat stock
Juice of 1 lemon
1 teaspoon sugar

¼ cup Sherry
Salt and pepper to taste
¼ cup commercial sour
    cream

Grate beets and combine half of grated beets with stock, lemon juice, and sugar. Bring to a boil and allow to cook for 3 minutes. Add Sherry, reduce heat, and cook for 2 minutes. Stir in remaining beets. Check seasoning and, if needed, add salt and pepper to taste. Pour into *6 heated soup bowls* and top each serving with sour cream.

Bouillabaisse

1 red snapper (about 3½ pounds)
6 cups water
½ cup dry White Wine
1 teaspoon salt
⅛ teaspoon white pepper
2 medium-size onions
2 small bay leaves (1 leaf crumbled)
10 sprigs parsley
1 red fish (about 3¼ pounds)
Salt and white pepper

¼ teaspoon thyme
1 small clove garlic minced
¼ teaspoon allspice
¼ cup olive oil
1⅔ cups canned tomatoes
1 small lemon sliced thin
2½ cups fish stock prepared from fish head
1 cup dry White Wine
Salt and pepper to taste
⅛ teaspoon saffron

Cut off head of red snapper. Boil in water to which has been added Wine, salt, pepper, 1 sliced onion, 1 bay leaf and, 5 sprigs of parsley. Cook until liquid is reduced to 2½ cups. Strain and set aside. Cut red snapper into 6 thin slices; cut red fish into 6 thin slices. Sprinkle fish slices on both sides with salt and pepper. Mince remaining parsley and combine with thyme, garlic, 1 crumbled bay leaf, and allspice. Sprinkle each slice of fish on each side with this herb and spice mixture. Pour oil in a pan that is large enough to hold the fish without the slices overlapping. Heat oil and add remaining onion, chopped fine. Lower heat and place fish slices side by side. Cover pan. Cook 5 minutes. Turn fish and cook 5 minutes more.

Remove fish from pan and arrange in deep ovenproof dish or tureen. Keep warm in oven. Pour tomatoes into pan. Bring to a boil. Add lemon slices, fish stock, 1 cup Wine, and season to taste with salt and pepper. Add saffron. Again bring to a boil. Pour over fish and serve at once.

Serves 6.

Bouillon (Chicken, Veal, Beef)

1 hen
10 cups water
2 cups White Wine
2 tablespoons salt

¼ teaspoon black pepper
2 pounds rump of beef
2 pounds veal round
Fat

Place hen in large soup pan and add water and Wine. Bring to a boil. Add salt and pepper. Brown beef and veal in fat. Cut into pieces and add meat and juices that it has drawn to chicken. Bring to a boil. Lower heat. Simmer in covered pan 3½ hours. Place in refrigerator overnight. Skim off fat. Strain. Heat before serving.
Makes 2¾ quarts.

Champagne-Onion Soup

6 medium onions sliced thin
¼ cup butter
5 cups bouillon
1 very small bay leaf
¼ teaspoon nutmeg or mace
Salt and pepper to taste
2 cups dry Champagne
2 egg yolks slightly beaten

⅓ cup Port Wine
2 teaspoons Cognac
Salt and pepper, if desired
½ cup grated Swiss cheese
2 tablespoons grated Gruyère cheese
24 small pieces toasted French bread

Sauté onions in butter until they are a rich brown, stirring from time to time to keep the onions from burning. Add bouillon, bay leaf, nutmeg or mace, and season to taste with salt and pepper. Bring to a boil. Lower heat and allow to simmer in covered pan for 25 minutes over very low heat. Add Champagne. Bring to a boil; lower heat and cook 2 minutes. To the slightly beaten yolks add the Port and Cognac. Stir a small amount of hot soup into eggs and then stir egg mixture into remainder of soup, blending thoroughly. Check seasoning and if needed, add more salt and/or pepper. Pour soup into large heatproof soup bowl or into individual heatproof bowls. Mix Swiss and Gruyère cheeses. Sprinkle the cheese mixture over one side of the pieces of toasted French bread. Float toast on top of soup. If desired, set bowl(s) about 4 inches under broiler unit just long enough to melt cheese slightly (3–4 minutes).

Serves 6.

Consommé, Jellied

> 2 tablespoons gelatine
> ¼ cup cold chicken or beef stock
> 3 cups clear boiling chicken or beef stock
> ¼ cup dry Sherry
> Salt and pepper to taste
> Thin slices of lemon

Sprinkle gelatine on cold, clear chicken or beef stock. Dissolve in boiling stock. Stir in Sherry and season to taste with salt and pepper. Pour into bouillon cups. Place in refrigerator to congeal. Serve with lemon slices.

Serves 6.

NOTE: Consommé may be congealed in one large container and spooned into cups before serving.

Cream of Chicken Soup

> 2 tablespoons butter or oleomargarine
> 2 tablespoons flour
> 3½ cups hot chicken stock
> ½ cup dry White Wine
> 1 bay leaf
> ¼ cup finely ground chicken
>
> ½ cup half-and-half (half milk and half cream)
> ⅛ teaspoon mace
> 1 egg yolk well beaten
> Salt and pepper to taste
> 3 tablespoons crumbled crisp fried bacon, if desired

Melt butter or oleomargarine. Stir in flour. Stir until smooth. Gradually add chicken stock, constantly stirring. When stock is completely blended, add Wine, bay leaf, ground chicken, half-and-half, and mace. Pour into top of double boiler and cook over boiling water until thickened. Add a small amount of hot soup to well-beaten yolk, stirring until completely blended. Then add yolk mixture to remainder of soup and stir vigorously. Season to taste with salt and pepper and remove bay leaf. Pour into heated soup bowls and, if desired, sprinkle with bacon. Serve at once.

Serves 5.

Cream of Vegetable Soup

¼ cup sifted flour
¼ cup butter or
* oleomargarine*
3½ cups hot vegetable,
* meat, or poultry stock*
1¾ cups milk

¼ cup Sherry or White Wine
1 cup vegetable pulp[1]
Salt to taste
⅛ teaspoon pepper
⅛ teaspoon nutmeg or mace,
* if desired*

Measure flour and sift. Melt butter or oleomargarine. Add flour and stir until smooth over low heat. Do not brown. Remove from heat. Stir in stock. Return to heat and cook over low heat, stirring constantly, until thick. Again remove from heat and stir in rest of ingredients. Pour into top of double boiler and cook over boiling water, stirring until thickened.

Serves 6.

[1] The pulp of any one of the following vegetables may be used: cooked asparagus, avocado, dried cooked beans, cooked carrots, cooked cauliflower, cooked celery, cooked corn, cooked mushrooms, cooked peas, boiled potatoes, cooked spinach. The vegetables should be put through a sieve or liquidized in a blender.

Creole Crawfish Bisque

3½ tablespoons salt
3 whole red peppers or ⅜
   teaspoon cayenne pepper
1 bay leaf
½ teaspoon nutmeg
6 cloves
½ teaspoon allspice
8 cups water
6 3-inch pieces celery
10 sprigs parsley
5 pounds cleaned crawfish[2]
2½ cups White Wine
2 cups stale bread cubes
⅔ cup White Wine
3 tablespoons butter, bacon
   grease, or oleomargarine
½ cup minced onion
1 minced clove garlic
2 tablespoons minced shallot
2 tablespoons minced parsley
1 egg well beaten
Salt and pepper to taste

Flour
Deep fat (3–4 inches)
2 tablespoons flour
2 tablespoons butter or
   oleomargarine
⅓ cup minced onion
1¼ cups canned or stewed
   tomatoes
1½ quarts liquid in which
   crawfish were boiled
1 tablespoon minced parsley
⅛ teaspoon thyme
1 bay leaf
Salt and pepper to taste
1 tablespoon Worcestershire
   sauce
½ cup dry White Wine or ⅓
   cup dry Sherry
Small pitcher of warm
   Amontillado Sherry, if
   desired

Add salt, pepper, bay leaf, and spices to 8 cups water. Bring to a boil. Add celery and parsley and pour over crawfish. Again bring to a boil. Boil 10 minutes. Add White Wine. Lower heat and allow to simmer for 5 minutes or until crawfish meat in tails is tender. Drain crawfish, reserving 1½ quarts of liquid in which they were boiled. Strain the reserved liquid. Clean 40 heads to allow 5 for each serving. Shell tails and chop meat very fine.

[2] To clean crawfish, place them in salt water. Rinse several times with clear water until the crawfish are completely free of dirt.

Soak bread in ⅔ cup White Wine. Squeeze most of Wine from bread, reserving the Wine. Melt 3 tablespoons butter, bacon grease, or oleomargarine. Add ½ cup minced onion and cook until it is clear. Stir in bread, garlic, shallot, parsley, and crawfish tails. Cook over medium heat, stirring constantly, for 5 minutes. Add Wine in which bread was soaked and stir the mixture with a fork, mashing so the mixture is smooth and there are no lumps of bread in it. Continue cooking for 3 minutes. Remove from heat and when cool, stir in well-beaten egg. Season to taste with salt and pepper. Stuff heads with mixture. Roll in flour and fry in deep hot fat (360° F.) until golden brown on all sides.

Brown 2 tablespoons flour in 2 tablespoons butter or oleomargarine. Add ⅓ cup minced onion, tomatoes, 1½ quarts of liquid in which crawfish were boiled, parsley, thyme, bay leaf, and salt and pepper to taste. Bring to a boil, lower heat, and allow to simmer 10 minutes. Strain. Add Worcestershire sauce and the stuffed crawfish heads. Simmer over very low heat 15 minutes. Add ½ cup White Wine or ⅓ cup Sherry. Cook 2 minutes. Serve very hot. If desired, a small pitcher of warm Amontillado Sherry may be served with bisque.

Serves 8.

NOTE: Bisque may be put into deep-freeze cartons and kept in deep freeze indefinitely.

Dried Bean Soup (Lima or Red Bean)

*1 cup dried limas or red
beans*
*4½ cups water
(approximate)*
½ pound pickled pork
1 sliced carrot
2 tablespoons chopped celery
*2 tablespoons chopped
parsley*
½ cup thinly sliced onion
*1 teaspoon Worcestershire
sauce*

1½ cups dry White Wine
Salt and pepper to taste
2 bay leaves
¼ teaspoon thyme
1 teaspoon basil
¼ teaspoon marjoram
*2 cups half-and-half (half
milk and half cream)*
¼ cup White Wine
*3 tablespoons grated
Parmesan cheese*

Soak dried beans overnight. Drain. Bring water to boil with pickled pork. Add carrot, celery, parsley, onion, Worcestershire sauce, 1½ cups White Wine, and beans. Cook for 1 hour over low heat. Season to taste with salt and pepper. Cook 30 minutes and add bay leaves, thyme, basil, and marjoram. Cook until beans are tender—about 30–60 minutes more. Remove from heat. Take bay leaves from mixture and then press mixture through a sieve or liquidize in blender. Measure, and, if necessary, additional water to make 4 cups may be added. Stir in half-and-half and wine. Bring to a boil, stirring constantly. Pour into warm soup bowls and sprinkle with cheese.
Serves 8.

Dried Bean Soup (Made in Blender)

4 cups cooked dried beans
1 quart meat or poultry stock
Salt and pepper to taste
¼ cup Sherry or dry White Wine
2 tablespoons grated Parmesan or Gruyère cheese

Cook beans according to recipe for DRIED RED BEANS. Liquidize 1 cup of beans with ¼ cup stock and continue liquidizing operation in blender until all beans are puréed. Place puréed mixture in heavy saucepan and add remainder of stock. Stir well until stock and purée are completely blended. Season to taste with salt and pepper. Add Wine and bring to a boil. Lower heat and cook until thickened. Pour into heated soup bowls and sprinkle with grated cheese.

Serves 8.

Oyster, Crab, and Shrimp Gumbo

3 tablespoons butter, oleomargarine, or bacon grease	4¾ cups water
½ cup finely chopped scallions	1 cup White or Rosé Wine
3 tablespoons flour	2 pounds raw shelled deveined shrimp
1 pint oyster liquid	2 cups crabmeat
2 tablespoons chopped parsley	⅛ teaspoon cayenne pepper
¼ teaspoon thyme	Salt and black pepper to taste
1 bay leaf	24 raw oysters
½ cup celery chopped in small pieces	2⅓ teaspoons gumbo filé (powdered sassafras leaves)

Melt butter, oleomargarine, or bacon grease in deep heavy skillet. When hot, brown scallions in it. Stir in flour and stir until smooth and a rich brown. Add oyster liquid slowly, stirring until smooth and blended and then add parsley, thyme, bay leaf, celery, water, Wine, shrimp, crabmeat, and cayenne pepper. Cover pan and cook over low heat 30 minutes. Season to taste with salt and black pepper. Again cover and continue cooking over low heat for 1¼ hours. Add oysters and cook only until oysters puff and edges curl (3–5 minutes). Remove from stove. Add filé powder and serve at once.

Serves 6.

NOTE: Never reheat gumbo after filé powder is added.

Quick Crab Gumbo

¼ cup butter
½ cup chopped onion
⅓ cup chopped green
 peppers
½ cup lean raw ham cut
 in chunks
1 cup sliced raw okra
1 pint tomato juice
1 cup raw shelled deveined
 shrimp
1 pound crabmeat
1 quart boiling water or
 chicken stock

1 bay leaf
½ teaspoon basil
¼ teaspoon thyme
¼ cup minced parsley
Salt and cayenne pepper to
 taste
½ cup dry White or Rosé
 Wine
⅓ teaspoon gumbo filé
 (powdered sassafras
 leaves), if desired
Steamed rice

Melt and heat butter. Add onion, pepper, ham and okra, and brown. Add tomato juice, shrimp, crabmeat, boiling water or stock, bay leaf, basil, thyme, parsley, and season to taste with salt and cayenne. Bring to a boil; lower heat and let simmer in covered pan for 20 minutes. Add Wine and cook 3 minutes. Remove from heat and stir in filé powder, if desired. Serve with rice.

Serves 6.

NOTE: Never reheat gumbo after filé powder is added.

Madrilène

2½ cups consommé,
 bouillon, or chicken broth
⅓ cup Sherry

1½ cups tomato juice
Salt and pepper to taste
Lemon slices

Combine consommé, bouillon, or chicken broth with Sherry and tomato juice. Season to taste with salt and pepper. Bring

to a boil. Reduce heat and cook over very low heat for 5 minutes. Serve at once, garnished with lemon slices.
Serves 6.

Potato Soup with Swiss or Gruyère Cheese

6 small potatoes
½ cup minced onion
2 tablespoons minced
  parsley
1 tablespoon minced celery
1 quart boiling meat or
  poultry stock
2 tablespoons butter or
  oleomargarine
2 tablespoons flour

¼ cup hot stock
¼ cup dry White Wine or 3
  tablespoons French
  Vermouth
⅛ teaspoon nutmeg or mace
¼ cup scalded whipping
  cream
Salt and pepper to taste
4½ teaspoons grated Swiss
  or Gruyère cheese

Peel potatoes and cut into small cubes. Simmer potatoes, onion, parsley, and celery in 1 quart of stock until potatoes can be easily pierced with a fork. Remove ½ cup of potatoes and mash through a sieve. Gently blend the mashed potatoes with the liquid in which they were cooked, being careful not to break the remaining cubes of potatoes. Melt butter or oleomargarine. Remove from heat and stir in flour. Return to medium heat and continue stirring until thick, but do not brown. Add ¼ cup hot stock and blend thoroughly. Return to low heat and add the Wine or Vermouth, stirring constantly. Then slowly add the potatoes and the liquid in which they were cooked, nutmeg or mace, scalded cream, and season to taste with salt and pepper. Put ¾ teaspoon of grated cheese in each of *6 heated soup bowls.* Pour soup over cheese and serve at once.

Soup Diablo

3 cups beef bouillon
¾ cup SAUCE DIABLO

Combine bouillon and Sauce Diablo. Bring to a boil. Reduce heat and cook over very low heat for 15 minutes. *Serves 4.*

Poultry or Meat Stock

4 pounds beef, fat chicken,
*   or broiler turkey*
10 cups cold water
2 cups White Wine
4 3-inch pieces celery
6 sprigs parsley

2 sliced medium onions
2 small bay leaves
2 tablespoons salt
⅛ teaspoon pepper
Small soup bone, if beef
*   stock is being made*

Place meat or poultry in cold water and Wine. Allow to come to a boil. Add remaining ingredients and bring to a boil once more. Lower heat. Cover pan. Allow to simmer over very low heat for 3 hours. *Makes 2⅔ quarts stock.*

TO CLEAR STOCK:

Poultry or meat stock
1 slightly beaten egg white
1 tablespoon cold water
Shell of egg

Remove grease from top of stock with spoon. Combine egg white, which has been slightly beaten, with cold water. Add mixture and shell of egg to stock. Heat, stirring constantly, until stock boils. Continue boiling for 2 minutes. Allow to stand in warm place for 15 minutes. Strain.

Turtle Soup

18 small chunks turtle meat
Salt and pepper
⅓ cup butter, oleomargarine,
*   or bacon grease*
½ cup chopped onion
1 quart water
1 pint dry White Wine
¼ cup minced parsley
1 tablespoon minced celery
2 tablespoons butter or
*   oleomargarine*
2 tablespoons sifted flour
1 large or 2 small bay leaves
6 whole cloves

⅔ cup canned or stewed
*   tomatoes*
1 tablespoon Worcestershire
*   sauce*
1 sliced lemon
Salt and pepper to taste
½ cup Amontillado
*   Sherry*
2 coarsely chopped hard-
*   cooked eggs*
Small pitcher warm
*   Amontillado Sherry, if*
*   desired*

Wash chunks of turtle meat and pat dry. Sprinkle with salt and pepper. Fry in ⅓ cup butter, oleomargarine or bacon grease (360° F.) until brown on all sides. Place turtle chunks in deep heavy saucepan. Fry chopped onion in same fat in which turtle was cooked until onion is clear. Bring water and Wine to a boil. Add onion. Pour over turtle meat and add parsley and celery. Again bring to a boil. Reduce heat, cover, and cook over low heat for 30 minutes. Melt 2 tablespoons butter or oleomargarine. Remove from heat and stir in flour. Return to heat and cook, stirring constantly, over medium heat until smooth and a rich brown. Stir in 1 cup of the hot turtle broth and cook over low heat, continuing to stir, until blended and thickened. Combine this brown sauce with turtle and broth and stir until the sauce and broth are blended. Add bay leaf, cloves, tomatoes, Worcestershire sauce, lemon, and season to taste with salt and pepper. Simmer in covered pot over very low heat until turtle meat is tender enough to fall away from the bones (1–1½ hours). Remove as many of the bones as possible. Before serving, bring to a boil and add ½ cup Amontillado Sherry. Lower heat and cook 2 minutes. Pour into hot soup bowls or a tureen and sprinkle with the chopped hard-cooked eggs. If desired, serve with a small pitcher of warm Amontillado Sherry.

Serves 6.

Vichyssoise (Chilled)

3 leeks or ½ cup chopped onions
3 tablespoons butter or oleomargarine
3 cups hot chicken or meat broth
4½ cups potatoes sliced very thin[3]
2 tablespoons minced parsley
1 tablespoon minced celery
¼ cup dry White Wine or French Vermouth
¾ cup milk
1¼ cups breakfast cream
Salt and pepper to taste
¼ teaspoon nutmeg or mace
½ cup scalded whipping cream

Lightly brown leeks or onions in butter or oleomargarine. Add broth, potatoes, parsley, and celery. Bring to a boil. Lower heat, cover pan, and allow to simmer over low heat for 30 minutes, stirring from time to time. Press through sieve and add Wine or Vermouth, milk, breakfast cream, salt and pepper to taste, and nutmeg or mace. Bring to a boil, reduce heat and cook 5 minutes, stirring constantly. Strain and add scalded whipping cream. Cool. Place in refrigerator and serve when completely chilled.

Serves 9.

[3] It is recommended that potatoes be sliced with a vegetable parer.

Eggs and Cheese

Eggs and cheese are the lifesavers for most housewives. Since they are usually less expensive than meats, fish, or poultry, we can fall back on them when we find that we have exceeded our food allowance and our budget is taking a beating. As the very apex of kitchen art can be achieved with an egg or a piece of cheese, no apologies are necessary for their use.

For something just a little different, try CHEESE GARLIC BREAD with a bowl of hot soup and a simple dessert for a quick supper. The cheese garlic bread, made with small crusty French loaves, has some of the best features of a toasted cheese sandwich and of garlic bread, but having inherited the good traits from each of its "parents," it is like neither of them.

For a woman in a hurry, with or without a budget problem, I suggest the SPANISH OMELET, SAVORY EGGS, EGGS AU GRATIN, CURRIED HARD-COOKED EGGS, or SPANISH EGGS. Nutritious and delicious, but quick and cheap!

On the more elaborate side but still "quickies" are the CREAMED CHICKEN WITH MUSHROOM OMELET, the SHRIMP AND MUSHROOM OMELET, and the CRABMEAT OMELET. These are excellent dishes for a lunch when two or three old friends get together.

Curried Hard-cooked Eggs

8 hard-cooked eggs
⅛ teaspoon cayenne pepper
2 cups hot Sherry-flavored WHITE SAUCE
Curry powder to taste (1–2 teaspoons)
1 tablespoon minced parsley
Paprika

Cut eggs into eighths. Stir pepper into White Sauce and season to taste with curry. Add eggs and heat thoroughly. Sprinkle with parsley and paprika.
Serves 4.

Curried Hard-cooked Eggs and Shrimp

Follow recipe for CURRIED HARD-COOKED EGGS above, substituting 4 hard-cooked eggs and 1 cup shelled cooked deveined medium-size shrimp for the 8 hard-cooked eggs.
Serves 4.

Eggs au Gratin

8 hard-cooked eggs
½ cup grated American cheese
¼ cup grated Swiss cheese
¼ teaspoon turmeric
2 cups hot Sherry-flavored WHITE SAUCE
¼ cup bread crumbs

Cut eggs in halves. Combine American and Swiss cheese. Remove yolks of eggs and combine yolks with ¼ cup of the grated cheese. Refill whites with yolk and cheese mixture. Place egg halves in greased baking dish. Add turmeric to White Sauce. Sprinkle halves of eggs with ¼ cup grated cheese, cover with white sauce, and top with bread crumbs. Sprinkle crumbs with remaining cheese. Bake in 350° F. oven until cheese is melted and golden brown.
Serves 4.

Eggs à la Turke

18 spring chicken livers
Salt and pepper
¼ cup butter or
  oleomargarine
1 cup fresh sautéed or canned
  mushrooms
¼ cup Madeira or Sherry

2 cups hot BROWN SAUCE
1½ tablespoons finely
  chopped chives or shallot
  tops
12 eggs
Salt and pepper

Cut livers in halves and sprinkle with salt and pepper. Sauté in hot butter or oleomargarine (360°F.). When cooked through, remove livers from skillet and stir in mushrooms, Wine, Brown Sauce, and chives or shallot tops. Cook over very low heat for 5 minutes. Heat 6 individual baking dishes. Grease with butter or oleomargarine. Place 2 eggs in each baking dish and sprinkle with salt and pepper. Cook 4 inches below broiler unit until whites are set. In the meantime, combine broiled livers and sauce and heat thoroughly. As soon as the eggs are removed from the broiler, pour the sauce over the eggs, dividing the mushrooms and livers equally among the six baking dishes.
Serves 6.

Creamed Chicken with Mushroom Omelet

6 eggs
2 tablespoons cream
Salt and pepper
2 tablespoons butter
1 cup chopped cooked
  chicken

1 cup chopped cooked
  mushrooms
½ cup Wine-flavored CREAM
  SAUCE
Salt and pepper

Beat eggs until fluffy. Add cream and season to taste with salt and pepper, continuing to beat while these ingredients are added. Melt butter in skillet over medium heat and, when it bubbles, add eggs. Lower heat and cook slowly over low heat. Combine chicken, mushrooms, and Cream Sauce, and season to taste with salt and pepper. Heat thoroughly. When under-surface of omelet is set, lift edge of omelet with spatula and tilt pan slightly and gently to allow the uncooked egg to run under-neath. Complete cooking over low heat. When omelet is set, transfer to platter. Cover half of omelet with hot creamed chicken and mushrooms. Fold omelet over creamed mixture and serve at once.

Serves 4.

Crabmeat Omelet

½ cup cooked (if available, lump) crabmeat	*Dry White Wine*
	6 eggs
¼ cup cooked or canned sliced mushrooms	*2 tablespoons cream*
	Salt and pepper
1 tablespoon minced parsley	*2 tablespoons butter*

Combine crabmeat, mushrooms, and parsley, and cover with dry White Wine. Bring to a boil. Lower heat and allow to sim-mer for 5 minutes. Beat eggs until fluffy. Add cream and sea-son to taste with salt and pepper, continuing to beat while these ingredients are added. Melt butter in skillet over medium heat and, when it bubbles, add eggs. Lower heat and cook slowly over low heat until the undersurface of the omelet is set. Lift edge of omelet with spatula and tilt pan slightly and gently allow the uncooked egg to run underneath. Complete cooking over low heat and when omelet is set, place on platter. Quickly drain hot crabmeat mixture and cover half of omelet with it. Fold other half of omelet over crabmeat. Serve at once.

Serves 3.

Shrimp and Mushroom Omelet

Follow recipe for CRABMEAT OMELET, substituting ½ cup cooked shrimp, cut in ¾ inch segments, for ½ cup cooked crabmeat.
Serves 3.

Spanish Omelet

6 eggs	*¾ cup hot* SAUCE DIABLO
2 tablespoons cream	*½ cup hot large cooked*
Salt and pepper	*green peas*
2 tablespoons butter	*Sprigs of parsley*

Beat eggs until fluffy. Add cream and season to taste with salt and pepper, continuing to beat while these ingredients are added. Melt butter in skillet over medium heat and, when it bubbles, add eggs. Lower heat and cook slowly over low heat until the undersurface of the omelet is set. Lift edge of omelet with spatula and tilt pan slightly and gently to allow the uncooked egg to run underneath. Complete cooking over low heat until omelet is set. Fold and place on platter. Pour hot Sauce Diablo over top and garnish with the hot peas and parsley.
Serves 3.

Strawberry Omelet

6 eggs separated	*½ cup water*
⅓ teaspoon cream of tartar	*1 pint washed hulled halved*
Salt and pepper	*strawberries*
2 tablespoons butter	*2 tablespoons Kirsch or*
½ cup sugar	*Cointreau*

Beat egg whites just until foamy. Add cream of tartar and beat until stiff. Beat yolks until lemon colored and light. Season to taste with salt and pepper. Fold yolks into stiffly beaten egg whites. Melt butter in a skillet. When it bubbles, pour in eggs. Turn heat as low as possible. Cook 10 minutes. Place skillet in 350° F. oven and cook eggs 12 minutes or until no indentation remains when omelet is lightly touched with finger. In the meantime, after omelet is placed in oven, mix sugar and water. Bring to a boil. Add berries, lower heat, and cook for 5 minutes. Remove from heat and sprinkle berries with Kirsch or Cointreau. When omelet is done, place on platter. Pour half of strawberries and sauce over omelet and then fold it. Pour remainder of strawberries and sauce over eggs and serve at once.

Serves 4.

Savory Eggs

1 cup Sherry-flavored CREAM SAUCE
1 tablespoon minced pimiento
1 tablespoon minced green pepper
8 hot hard-cooked eggs

3 tablespoons hot breakfast cream
⅛ teaspoon black pepper
Anchovy paste
4 slices toast
Paprika

Heat Cream Sauce and add pimiento and green pepper. Cook over very low heat 5 minutes. Cut hot eggs in two lengthwise. Remove yolks and mash. Add cream and pepper and season to taste with anchovy paste. Refill whites of eggs with mixture. Place 4 stuffed egg halves on each slice of toast. Pour sauce over eggs and sprinkle with paprika.

Serves 4.

Spanish Eggs

Hot SAUCE DIABLO   Salt and pepper
8 eggs   4 strips crisp fried bacon

Pour Sauce Diablo to a depth of ½ inch in a greased shallow baking dish. Break eggs on top of sauce. Sprinkle eggs with salt and pepper. Place 4 inches under broiler unit and cook until whites of eggs are set. Garnish with strips of bacon. *Serves 4.*

Hamburger Soufflé

⅔ pound ground beef
2 tablespoons Burgundy or Claret
3 tablespoons butter or oleomargarine
3 tablespoons flour
⅞ cup milk
2 tablespoons Sherry
2 tablespoons grated Swiss cheese
1½ tablespoons Worcestershire sauce

2 teaspoons dehydrated parsley flakes
⅛ teaspoon pepper
Salt to taste
3 tablespoons butter or oleomargarine
2 teaspoons minced onion
Salt to taste
5 eggs separated
¼ teaspoon salt
¼ teaspoon cream of tartar

Combine ground beef and Burgundy or Claret 2 hours before ready to prepare soufflé and store in refrigerator. Melt 3 tablespoons butter or oleomargarine. Remove from stove and stir in flour. Return to medium heat and continue stirring until thickened. Remove roux from heat and stir in milk and Sherry until blended. Then add grated cheese, Worcestershire sauce, parsley, pepper, and salt to taste. Cook over medium heat, stirring constantly, until cheese is melted and sauce is smooth. Melt 3 tablespoons butter or oleomargarine over medium heat in skillet. Add ground beef and onion. Cook until meat grains stand apart. Combine meat mixture and cheese sauce. Let sauce cool until lukewarm. Season to taste with salt. Beat yolks of eggs until lemon colored and light. Stir cheese sauce into yolks. Add ¼ teaspoon salt to egg whites. Beat until foamy. Add cream of tartar and beat until stiff but not dry. Add 2 heaping kitchen tablespoons of whites to yolk mixture and fold in gently. Pour sauce slowly over remaining whites, folding as sauce is poured. Spoon into buttered soufflé dish and bake in 350° F. oven for 25 minutes. Move pan gently in oven and when soufflé barely shakes, it is done. Serve at once. *Serves 6.*

Cheese Garlic Bread

3 small loaves French bread
¼ pound butter
½ teaspoon garlic purée
½ cup grated American cheese

½ cup grated Swiss cheese
5 tablespoons dry White Wine
Paprika

Slice the bread, being careful not to cut through bottom ¾ inch of loaves and cutting slices so they are about 1½ inches thick. Cream butter. Add garlic purée, cheese, and Wine. Mix until completely blended and easy to spread. Spread each side of each slice with cheese mixture, avoiding, if possible, breaking the loaves. Sprinkle slices on both sides and sprinkle the tops of the loaves—all very lightly—with paprika. Wrap each loaf in aluminum foil. Place in 400° F. oven for 10 minutes. Serve at once. *Serves 6.*

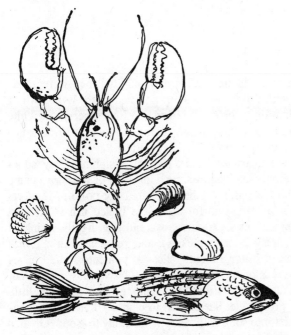

Seafood

White Wine and fish have a natural affinity: they were made for each other! Fillets broiled or poached with Wine, whole fish baked in Wine, shellfish cooked in either Sherry or White Wine, or almost any kind of fish or shellfish with a Wine sauce will please even the most jaded appetite.

Probably the nicest and most sincere compliment my cooking ever received was from a shy young lady of four who came to dinner with her mother. I had prepared my COLD FISH PLATTER, which is a truly colorful dish—the boiled fish is covered with a golden SAUTERNE MAYONNAISE and then lightly sprinkled with green (finely minced pickles) and red (paprika); it has a red pimiento strip for a mouth, slices of pimiento-stuffed olives for eyes, and it is completely surrounded by various green, red, and white salads. As I brought the platter in I saw my little friend's eyes grow wide. She started to clap her hands and spontaneously burst into song with "Happy Birthday to You." Greater praise than this no cook could receive.

Incidentally, the COLD FISH PLATTER can be prepared the night before it is to be served and surrounded with cold salads at the last minute. In working out recipes I try to keep in mind the desirability of dishes that can either be prepared ahead of time or cooked in a few minutes. This is one of the many virtues of the SHRIMP AND CRABMEAT REMICK. In the morning before I go out I cook the seafood, Wine, green pepper, and mushrooms for 7–8 minutes, and while the seafood simmers I prepare the sauce. The seafood in its Wine marinade and the sauce are placed in the refrigerator until about 12 minutes before I need them, either just before my first course or while my company is having a last cocktail. I quickly drain the seafood mixture by lifting it from the Wine with a slotted spoon, put it in individual baking dishes, and spoon the sauce over it. The baking dishes are put in the oven and I return to my guests until the Remick is ready to serve. And in case you are watching the budget, tuna fish is a marvelous substitute for shrimp and crabmeat.

Baked Fish Diablo

1½ cups cooked crabmeat
2 pounds shelled deveined
*   cooked shrimp*
White Wine
Salt and white pepper

4–5-pound red fish or red
*   snapper*
SAUCE DIABLO
1 cup cooked or canned
*   mushrooms, if desired*

About 6 hours before baking fish, cover crabmeat and shrimp with White Wine. Bring to a boil, reduce heat, and let simmer over very low heat 5 minutes. Place in covered container and store in refrigerator until ready to use. Sprinkle salt and pepper over fish lightly (both sides and on inside where fish was cut to be cleaned). Place in roaster. Reserve 1 cup of Sauce Diablo and add 1 cup of White Wine to remainder of sauce. Add mushrooms if desired and pour sauce and Wine mixture over fish. Cover roaster. Bake in 350° F. oven until fish flakes easily (approximately 1¼–1½ hours), basting with sauce from pan every 15 minutes. Just before serving, combine the cup of Sauce Diablo that was reserved with the crabmeat mixture. Heat thoroughly. Place fish on platter and cover with crabmeat mixture. Serve at once.

Serves 8–10.

NOTE: For easier handling of the fish, roaster may be lined with strong aluminum foil and, when fish is baked, aluminum foil may be lifted out of roaster and placed on platter.

Baked Fish Flambé

2 cups minced parsley
2 cups minced celery
¼ teaspoon sweet basil
¼ teaspoon thyme
5–7-pound fish

Salt and white pepper
¼ pound softened butter or
   oleomargarine
1 cup White Wine
¼ cup Brandy

Combine parsley, celery, basil, and thyme, and make bed on shallow baking platter. Sprinkle fish well with salt and pepper on both sides and also on the inside where fish has been cut for cleaning. Cover fish with softened butter and place on herb bed. Bake in 375° F. oven, allowing approximately 12 minutes to the pound—fish should be cooked until flesh flakes easily. Four times while fish is baking baste with ¼ cup of heated White Wine. When fish is baked, remove from oven. Heat Brandy. Sprinkle half of it around fish; ignite remaining Brandy and pour over the celery and herb bed. Serve at once. *Serves 10–12.*

Baked Fish with Marinière Sauce

4 pounds scaled and cleaned
   fish
Salt and white pepper
½ cup water
1 cup dry White Wine
2 tablespoons butter
1 tablespoon finely chopped
   shallots

2 tablespoons sifted flour
1 cup heated breakfast cream
3 egg yolks slightly beaten
1 cup boiled deveined shelled
   shrimp
1 cup sautéed or canned
   mushrooms
Salt and white pepper

Sprinkle fish well, inside and out, with salt and pepper. Place in baking pan; add water and Wine. Bake in 375° F. oven until flesh flakes easily—45–60 minutes—basting from time to

time with liquid in pan. Melt butter and add shallots. Cook until shallots are tender, stirring frequently. Remove from heat and stir in flour. Again return to heat and continue stirring until thickened and smooth. Again remove from heat. Add cream; return to low heat and stir until thick. Add a small amount of hot sauce to egg yolks. Blend and then combine yolk mixture with remainder of sauce. Cook over low heat, constantly stirring, for 3 minutes. Add shrimp, mushrooms, and season to taste with salt and white pepper. Heat thoroughly, still stirring. Place fish on hot platter, cover with sauce, and serve quickly.
Serves 8.

Baked Fish with Oyster Stuffing

4–5-pound bluefish, red fish, trout, or red snapper	*1½ cups dry bread crumbs*
Salt and white pepper	*2 tablespoons dry Sherry*
36 small oysters with liquid	*Salt and pepper*
¼ cup melted butter or oleomargarine	*½ cup minced pickled pork*
¼ cup finely chopped onion	*½ cup minced onion*
¼ cup chopped celery	*½ cup minced celery*
2 tablespoons minced parsley	*½ cup water*
	½ cup dry White Wine
	4 strips bacon

Rub inside and outside of fish with salt and white pepper. Drain oysters, reserving liquid. Heat butter or oleomargarine and cook onion and celery in it until onion is clear. Add minced parsley and oysters and cook only long enough for oysters to puff and edges to curl. Remove from heat and stir in bread crumbs. Sprinkle with Sherry and add just enough of reserved oyster liquid to hold mixture together. Season to taste with salt and pepper. Stuff mixture into fish and sew up opening or skewer it together. Mix pickled pork, onion, and celery. Place a layer of this mixture in the bottom of the baking pan. Place fish in pan. Pour water and Wine over fish and place slices of bacon

on top of fish. Bake 15 minutes in 425° F. oven; reduce heat to 350° and continue baking until fish flakes easily (45–60 minutes).
Serves 8–10.

Broiled Fillet of Sole Marguery

2 *tablespoons butter*
2 *tablespoons flour*
1 *cup fish or chicken stock*
¾ *cup dry White Wine*
Salt and white pepper
2 *egg yolks slightly beaten*
9 *small oysters with their liquid*

18 *medium-size boiled shelled deveined lake shrimp*
3 *broiled fillets of sole, broiled with Wine and lemon juice as directed in recipe for* SKILLET-BROILED FILLETS

Melt butter. When it bubbles, remove from heat and stir in flour that has been measured and then sifted. Return to heat and stir constantly until mixture thickens, but do not brown. Again remove from heat and add stock and Wine slowly, stirring until blended. Return to heat and cook over low heat, stirring constantly until thickened. Season to taste with salt and pepper. Stir a small amount of sauce into slightly beaten yolk and then stir egg yolk into remainder of sauce. Cook oysters[1] until they puff (3–5 minutes) in their own liquid. Drain and add oysters and shrimp to sauce. Heat thoroughly, stirring constantly and gently. Pour hot sauce over hot broiled fish fillets and serve at once.
Serves 3.

[1] If oysters were washed, season liquid lightly with salt before cooking them.

Cold Fish Platter

4–5-pound red fish or red
  snapper
Salt and white pepper
2 cups White Wine
Water
¾ cup SAUTERNE
  MAYONNAISE
3 tablespoons minced sweet
  cucumber pickles
2 thin slices pimiento-stuffed
  olives
1 narrow strip pimiento
1 cup canned green
  asparagus

1 cup cooked cauliflower
  flowerets
Small canned beets well
  drained
3 sliced tomatoes
1 cup sliced cucumbers
4 avocados peeled and cut in
  halves
1 cup chicken, shrimp, or
  crabmeat salad
Romaine, watercress, or
  lettuce
Paprika
Desired salad dressings

Remove eyes from fish and season to taste with salt and white pepper. Boil the fish (which should either be placed on a rack or wrapped in heavy cheese cloth) in the 2 cups of White Wine mixed with water to cover until flesh of fish flakes easily. Remove fish from stock and place on large serving platter. Chill thoroughly in refrigerator. Cover fish with Sauterne Mayonnaise. Sprinkle mayonnaise with minced pickles. Simulate eyes with the thin slices of pimiento-stuffed olive and make the mouth of the fish with the narrow strip of pimiento. Arrange the asparagus, cauliflower, beets, sliced tomatoes, and cucumbers around the fish, leaving room for the avocados. Fill the avocado hollows with the chicken, shrimp, or crabmeat salad and place the avocados on the fish platter. Garnish with the salad greens. Sprinkle fish with paprika. Serve desired salad dressings separately.

Serves 8.

Court Bouillon of Red Fish

2 tablespoons shortening	¼ teaspoon thyme
2 tablespoons sifted flour	¼ teaspoon sweet
3½ cups boiling water	marjoram
2 cups dry White Wine	1 large bay leaf
½ cup minced onion	½ teaspoon allspice
1 minced clove garlic	Salt and Tabasco sauce to
2 cups canned tomatoes	taste
2 tablespoons minced green	4 pounds fish cut in ½-
pepper	pound slices
2 tablespoons minced	Juice of 1 lemon
parsley	3 tablespoons Sherry

Melt shortening in heavy large pan. Stir in flour and stir constantly until smooth and brown. Remove from heat and stir in boiling water. Again stir until smooth over medium heat. Add Wine, onion, garlic, tomatoes, green pepper, parsley, thyme, marjoram, bay leaf, and allspice. Season to taste with salt and Tabasco. Bring to a boil. Reduce heat and allow to simmer for 5 minutes. Add fish, slice by slice, and the juice of a lemon. Again bring to a boil; lower heat and allow to simmer until flesh of fish flakes easily. Add Sherry. Cook 2 minutes more. Remove bay leaf and place fish slices on hot platter. Pour sauce over fish.

Serves 8.

Fillet of Sole or Flounder (Fillet of Sole Thermidor)

8 fillets of sole or flounder	1½ cups boiled lobster cut in
Salt and white pepper	1-inch chunks or boiled
2 cups whipping cream	whole shelled and deveined
¾ cup dry White Wine	shrimp or crawfish
	1 pound seedless white grapes
	in small clusters
	Sweet Sauterne

Sprinkle fillets with salt and pepper. Lay side by side in large shallow pan. Combine cream and ½ cup White Wine and pour over fish. Bring to a boil and cook over very low heat until fish flakes easily (8–10 minutes). Place fillets on heatproof platter and put platter in warm oven. Cook cream and Wine until only about half of original quantity remains. Add remaining ¼ cup of White Wine to lobster, shrimp, or crawfish. Bring to a boil and reduce heat. Cook until seafood is thoroughly heated. Poach grapes in sweet (imported) Sauterne. Lift the hot lobster, shrimp, or crawfish from the Wine with a slotted spoon so that seafood will drain. Arrange the shellfish around the fish platter and cover the fish with the cream and Wine sauce. Place platter 4 inches under broiler unit and cook until sauce is golden brown. Arrange poached grape clusters around platter and serve at once.

Serves 8.

Fillet of Sole Ravigote

1 minced shallot
2 cups CREAM SAUCE
½ cup dry White Wine
⅓ cup whipping cream
Salt and white pepper, if
   desired
8 fillets of sole
Salt and white pepper
⅓ cup butter or
   oleomargarine
   (approximate)

1 tablespoon lemon juice
⅓ cup meat stock or
   bouillon
¼ teaspoon dried tarragon
¼ teaspoon dried chervil
1 tablespoon minced parsley
2 teaspoons tarragon vinegar
2 tablespoons melted butter
Paprika
Parsley sprigs

Add shallot to Cream Sauce and allow to simmer over very low heat for 8 minutes, stirring frequently. Remove from heat and stir in Wine and cream. Stir until blended, and return to heat. Stir constantly for 3 minutes. Check seasoning and, if desired, add salt and white pepper to taste. Set sauce aside.

Rub fillets with salt and pepper. Melt ⅓ cup butter or oleomargarine in pan large enough to hold fillets without overlapping. Add lemon juice. Place fillets in butter or oleomargarine-lemon mixture and cook over very low heat until fish will flake easily, but do not brown. Should more butter or oleomargarine be needed, it may be added. To sauce add: stock or bouillon, herbs, vinegar, and 2 tablespoons melted butter. Allow to cook over low heat, stirring carefully until ingredients are completely blended. When piping hot, place fillets on hot platter. Cover with sauce and sprinkle with paprika. Garnish with parsley.
Serves 8.

Fillets Amandine

¾ cup blanched and slivered almonds	¼ teaspoon rosemary
8 fresh or thawed frozen fish fillets	¼ teaspoon thyme
	½ cup chopped celery
Salt and white pepper	¼ cup minced parsley
⅓ cup softened butter or oleomargarine	½ cup chopped green pepper
3 large thinly sliced firm tomatoes	1 cup whole canned mushrooms
Salt and pepper	½ cup Rosé Wine
¼ teaspoon basil	1 tablespoon lemon juice
	3 tablespoons Rosé Wine

Spread almonds on cooky tray and place in 350°F. oven until golden brown, turning almonds after about 5 minutes so they will brown evenly on all sides. Sprinkle fish on both sides with salt and pepper and cover with softened butter or oleomargarine. Arrange tomato slices in shallow large baking-serving dish. Sprinkle lightly with salt and pepper. Combine basil, rosemary, and thyme and sprinkle over tomato slices. Combine celery, parsley, green pepper, and mushrooms and cover tomato layer. Mix ½ cup Wine and lemon juice and sprinkle half over the vegetables. Cover with fish fillets and sprinkle with remainder of Wine and lemon juice mixture. Bake in 350° F. oven for 10 minutes. Sprinkle fillets with remaining Wine. Continue baking for 10 minutes or until fish flakes easily. Remove from oven and sprinkle almonds over fish. Return to oven and bake for 5 minutes. Serve at once.

Serves 8.

Fish on Bed of Onions, Mushrooms, and Potatoes

8 SKILLET-BROILED FISH
    FILLETS
*⅓ cup butter or
    oleomargarine*
⅓ cup chopped onion
*½ clove minced garlic
    (optional)*
*¾ cup fresh sautéed or
    sliced canned mushrooms*

½ cup diced cooked ham
*1 cup ¾-inch cubes of
    peeled boiled potatoes*
¼ cup dry White Wine
2 tablespoons minced parsley
Salt and pepper, if desired
BÉARNAISE SAUCE

Broil fillets in accordance with recipe for SKILLET-BROILED FISH. Melt butter or oleomargarine and when it bubbles (360° F.) add onion, garlic, if desired, and mushrooms. When onion is clear, add ham and potatoes. Heat thoroughly, stirring gently from time to time. Sprinkle with Wine and parsley. Check seasoning and, if desired, sprinkle with salt and pepper to taste. Make a bed of mixture on a hot platter. Place fish fillets on potato bed and coat fish with BÉARNAISE SAUCE.

Serves 8.

Flounder with Caviar

2 pounds flounder fillets	1 cup of hot stock in which
4 cups dry White Wine	fish was poached
Juice of 1 large lemon	1 cup scalded half-and-half
2 teaspoons salt	(half milk and half cream)
¼ teaspoon white pepper	1 egg yolk well beaten
3 tablespoons butter or	Salt and white pepper
oleomargarine	2 tablespoons red and/or
3 tablespoons sifted flour	black caviar

Poach flounder in White Wine with lemon juice, 2 teaspoons salt and ¼ teaspoon pepper, following recipe for POACHED FISH FILLETS. When flesh flakes easily, lift fish to hot platter and place in warm oven. Melt butter or oleomargarine. Remove from heat when it bubbles and stir in flour; return to low heat and stir constantly until mixture thickens. Do not allow to brown. Again remove from heat and add fish stock and half-and-half. Return to medium heat and cook, continuously stirring until sauce thickens. Add a small amount of sauce to yolk and when completely blended, stir yolk into remainder of sauce. Check seasoning and add salt and pepper to taste. Spread sauce over fish and garnish with the caviar. Serve at once.

Serves 4.

Flounder with Herbs

2 2-pound flounders	¼ teaspoon thyme
Salt and white pepper	2 tablespoons minced parsley
1½ cups dry White Wine	¼ teaspoon sweet basil
1½ tablespoons butter or	1 bay leaf
oleomargarine	½ cup canned mushrooms
2 tablespoons flour	Salt and pepper
¼ teaspoon allspice	

Sprinkle fish with salt and white pepper. Place in baking-serving platter and add Wine. Bake in 375° F. oven for 30 minutes. Remove from oven. Melt butter or oleomargarine. Stir in flour and continue stirring until roux is smooth and thickened. Add liquid in which fish was baked, allspice, herbs, and mushrooms. Cook over low heat, stirring constantly, until sauce thickens. Check seasoning and, if needed, season to taste with salt and pepper. Pour sauce over fish and bake in 375° F. oven until flesh flakes easily (about 15 minutes).
Serves 6.

Poached Fish Fillets

6 fillets of fish	2 teaspoons salt
4 cups dry White Wine	½ teaspoon white pepper
3 tablespoons lemon juice	

Place fillets in wide pan. Combine remaining ingredients and pour over fish. Bring to a boil. Reduce heat and simmer over very low heat until fillets flake easily with a fork. Remove from heat and serve hot or cold.
Serves 6.

Pompano in White Wine

½ cup finely chopped shallots	1½ tablespoons capers with juice
½ cup chopped green pepper	1½ teaspoons Worcestershire sauce
¼ cup butter	Salt and white pepper
2 tablespoons sifted flour	6 fillets of pompano, broiled
1½ cups Moselle Wine	with White Wine and
1 egg yolk well beaten	lemon juice (see recipe for
1 tablespoon chopped pimiento	SKILLET-BROILED FILLETS)

Cook shallots and green pepper in butter over low heat until tender, stirring constantly. Remove from heat and stir in flour.

Return to heat and cook over low heat, continuing to stir until thickened. Again remove from heat and stir in Wine. Return to heat and continue to stir until sauce thickens. Mix a small amount of the sauce with the well-beaten egg yolk until completely blended and then stir yolk mixture into remainder of sauce. Add pimiento, capers, Worcestershire sauce, and salt and white pepper to taste. Place the Broiled Fillets on a heated platter and cover with hot sauce. Serve at once.

Serves 6.

Red Snapper or Red Fish Chambord

1 cup stale bread
White Wine
15 small oysters with liquid
Salt and white pepper
¼ cup minced onion
2 tablespoons minced parsley
1½ tablespoons minced celery
3 tablespoons butter or oleomargarine
4–5-pound red snapper or red fish
Salt and white pepper
Softened butter or oleomargarine
Wine squeezed from bread, plus equal parts Wine and water to make 1 cup

¼ teaspoon allspice
2 tablespoons minced parsley
¼ teaspoon thyme
¼ teaspoon cloves
1 crumbled small bay leaf
3 tablespoons butter or oleomargarine
½ cup chopped onion
½ cup chopped celery
¼ cup minced parsley
¼ cup minced green pepper
4 large peeled chopped tomatoes
Salt and pepper
24 medium-size oysters with their liquid
1 cup whole cooked or canned mushrooms

Sprinkle bread liberally with Wine. Let stand for 30 minutes. Squeeze bread, retaining the Wine which is squeezed from it. Season oyster liquid to taste with salt and pepper, and bring liquid to a boil. Reduce heat and add 15 small oysters. Allow them to simmer until they puff and their edges curl. Cook onion, parsley, and celery in 3 tablespoons of butter or oleomargarine until the onion is clear. Add the bread and 3 tablespoons of the hot oyster liquid. Stir and mash with a fork until the mixture is smooth and there are no lumps of bread in it. Add oysters and check seasoning. If desired, add additional salt and pepper.

Rub inside and outside of fish with salt and pepper. Stuff oyster mixture into fish and sew or skewer fish together. Rub fish with softened butter or oleomargarine. Place in baking pan. Strain Wine in which bread was soaked and then combine with equal parts Wine and water to make 1 cup. Heat and pour over fish.

Combine allspice, 2 tablespoons parsley, thyme, cloves, and the crumbled bay leaf. Remove the skin from a 4-inch-square space on the upper side of the fish. Prick flesh and sprinkle spice and herb mixture over space. Cover pan. Place baking pan in 350° F. oven.

Bake fish for 1–1¼ hours until flesh will flake easily, basting fish from time to time with liquid in roasting pan. Melt 3 tablespoons butter or oleomargarine. Cook ½ cup chopped onion, ½ cup chopped celery, ¼ cup minced parsley, and green pepper until onion is clear. Add tomatoes and season to taste with salt and pepper. Stir until smooth. Cover the baked fish with sauce. Return to 350° F. oven for 10 minutes. Heat 24 medium-size oysters and mushrooms in oyster liquid (if salt is needed, it may be added, but quite often the oyster liquid is salty). Bring to boiling point and reduce heat. Allow to simmer until oysters puff and their edges curl (3–5 minutes). Place fish on platter. Cover with sauce and garnish with oysters and mushrooms.

Serves 8–10.

Sharfe (Stewed Fish)

4–5-pound red snapper or
  other meaty fish
Clove of garlic cut in half
Salt and white pepper
½ cup minced onion
3 tablespoons olive oil
1½ tablespoons flour
2 tablespoons tomato paste

Equal parts water and dry
  White Wine to cover fish
⅛ teaspoon thyme
2 tablespoons minced
  parsley
2 tablespoons minced celery
1 small bay leaf
1 egg yolk well beaten
Salt and pepper, if desired

Slice fish. Rub with cut clove of garlic. Sprinkle well with salt and white pepper. Brown onion in oil. Remove from heat and stir in flour. Return to stove and cook over moderate heat, stirring constantly until brown. Remove from heat again and stir in tomato paste. Again return to stove and cook over moderate heat 2 minutes. Add fish, including head, enough water and Wine mixture to cover, thyme, parsley, celery, and bay leaf. Bring to a boil; reduce heat and allow to simmer over very low heat in an uncovered pan until flesh of fish will flake easily. Remove bay leaf and then place fish slices on hot platter. Stir a small amount of hot sauce into the egg yolk. Add egg mixture to remainder of sauce and stir until blended. Check seasoning and, if needed, add salt and pepper to taste. Heat thoroughly, stirring constantly, and pour over fish. Serve at once. *Serves 8–10.*

Skillet-broiled Fish or Fillets

6 fillets of fish or 6 small
  fish
Salt and white pepper
Kitchen Bouquet

½ cup butter or
  oleomargarine
  (approximate)
¾ cup dry White Wine
2 tablespoons lemon juice
Sprigs of parsley

Sprinkle fillets or small fish well with salt and pepper. Brush lightly on both sides with Kitchen Bouquet. Melt butter or oleomargarine in skillet and when fat bubbles (360° F.), put fish in frying pan, being careful not to let the fillets or the whole fish overlap (if they cannot all be cooked at once, then cook part and keep warm in covered heatproof platter in warm oven). Additional butter or oleomargarine may be used if needed. Cook 8 minutes; turn fish. Sprinkle browned side of each fillet or whole fish with 1 tablespoon Wine and ½ teaspoon lemon juice. Cook 8 minutes more or until flesh is firm, but flakes easily, and turn fish onto platter with the side up that was browned last. Sprinkle each whole fish or fillet with another tablespoon of Wine and ½ teaspoon lemon juice. Garnish with parsley.

Serves 6.

Trout Marguery

4 fillets of trout
Salt and white pepper
2 tablespoons olive oil
½ cup water
1 cup dry White Wine
½ cup butter
4 egg yolks well beaten

¾ cup boiling fish stock
  (prepared in wine)
2 tablespoons lemon juice
16 boiled deveined shelled
  shrimp
½ cup canned or cooked
  mushrooms
Salt and white pepper

Sprinkle fillets with salt and pepper and brush with olive oil. Place in baking pan and add water and White Wine. Bake in 450° F. oven until flesh flakes easily. Melt butter in top of double boiler over hot, not boiling, water. Gradually stir in— and never stop stirring—the well-beaten egg yolks. Then, constantly stirring, gradually add the boiling fish stock. Cook over the hot water, being sure it never reaches the boiling point, just until the mixture starts to thicken. Remove from heat and stir in lemon juice. When blended, add shrimp and mushrooms and season to taste with salt and pepper. Place fish on hot platter and pour sauce over it.

Serves 4.

NOTE: Should sauce start to curdle while being cooked, beat with rotary egg beater as fast as possible.

Crabmeat Croquettes

> *2½ cups cooked crabmeat*
> *Wine-flavored* CREAM SAUCE
>   *very thick, (approximately*
>   *1 cup)*
>
> *Salt and white pepper to*
>   *taste*
> *1 beaten egg*
> *Cracker crumbs*
> *Deep hot fat*

Combine crabmeat with just enough thick Cream Sauce to hold seafood together. Add salt and pepper to taste. Cool in refrigerator for at least 30 minutes. Shape into *6 pyramids.* Dip into slightly beaten egg, then in crumbs. Fry in hot fat, to a depth of 3–4 inches, in a deep skillet at a temperature of 375° F. Turn until golden brown on all sides. Drain on absorbent paper.

Boiled Crabs or Shrimp

> *12 live hard-shelled crabs or*
>   *5 pounds shrimp*
> *2½ quarts boiling water*
>   *(approximate)*
> *2 cups dry White Wine*
> *2 rounded tablespoons salt*
> *¼ teaspoon cayenne or 4*
>   *whole red peppers*
>
> *4 4-inch pieces celery with*
>   *leaves*
> *12 sprigs parsley*
> *1 sliced lemon*
> *¾ teaspoon basil*
> *¼ teaspoon thyme*
> *2 bay leaves*

Rinse crabs or shrimp until water runs clear. Place in boiling water to cover and add Wine, salt, pepper, celery, parsley, lemon, basil, thyme, and bay leaves. Bring to a boil; reduce heat and allow to simmer. Cook shrimp 10–20 minutes (depending on size) until tender or cook crabs 20–25 minutes until shells turn red. Drain and let cool at room temperature. Store in refrigerator until ready to use.

Crabs serve 6–8, depending on size; shrimp serve 8.

Stuffed Crabs

4 1-inch thick slices bread
White Wine or Sherry
¼ cup bacon grease or
*   butter*
3 tablespoons minced
*   onion*
2 tablespoons minced
*   parsley*
2 tablespoons finely chopped
*   celery*
¼ teaspoon cumin
¼ teaspoon turmeric
1 teaspoon monosodium
*   glutamate*

¼ teaspoon basil
1 tablespoon Worcestershire
*   sauce*
¼ teaspoon Tabasco
*   Sauce*
2½ cups cooked crabmeat
1 egg slightly beaten
Salt and pepper
¼ cup toast or bread
*   crumbs*
1 tablespoon butter
1½ tablespoons Parmesan
*   cheese*

Soak bread in Wine. Squeeze out Wine and reserve ¼ cup. Melt bacon grease or butter. Add onions and cook until clear, but do not brown. Stir in bread, parsley, celery, cumin, turmeric, monosodium glutamate, basil, and cook, stirring (over low heat), until bread is browned slightly. Stir in Worcestershire sauce, Tabasco, and crabmeat. Remove from heat. Stir a small amount of mixture into the egg and then stir egg into remainder of mixture. Season to taste with salt and pepper. Return to low heat and stir in ¼ cup Wine squeezed from bread. Stir and mash mixture with a fork so that it is thoroughly blended and

there are no lumps of bread. Let mixture stand until cool. Fill
4 crab shells that have been carefully washed and cleaned, or
4 greased individual baking dishes. Sprinkle mixture with
crumbs, dot with butter, and lightly sprinkle with cheese. Bake
in 375° F. oven for 20 minutes.

Lobster or Crabmeat Bordelaise

*2¼ cups half-and-half
(half milk and half cream)*
*⅓ cup finely chopped
onion*
*⅓ cup scraped and finely
chopped carrot*
*3 tablespoons butter or
oleomargarine*
3 tablespoons flour

1 egg yolk well beaten
*Salt and cayenne pepper to
taste*
*3 cups boiled lobster cut in
small chunks, or cooked
crabmeat*
*3 tablespoons Amontillado
Sherry*

Bring half-and-half to a boil. Add onion and carrot and
reduce heat. Cover pan; cook over low heat until vegetables
are tender. Melt butter or oleomargarine. Remove from heat
and stir in flour. Return to heat and continue stirring over medium heat until thick and smooth. Again remove from heat
and gradually add half-and-half with onion and carrot. Return
to medium heat and cook, stirring continuously, until thickened. Add a small amount of hot sauce to well-beaten yolk and
stir until blended. Add yolk mixture to remainder of sauce and
season to taste with salt and cayenne. Add seafood; cook until
very hot and stir in Sherry. Cook 2 minutes and serve without
delay.
Serves 6.

Lobster, Crabmeat, or Shrimp au Gratin

2 tablespoons butter or
  oleomargarine
2 tablespoons sifted flour
1¾ cups half-and-half
  (half cream and half
  milk)
½ cup grated American
  cheese

½ cup grated Swiss cheese
¼ cup dry Sherry or dry
  White Wine
3 cups cooked lobster
  chunks, crabmeat, or
  shrimp segments
¼ cup bread crumbs
2 teaspoons butter

Melt butter or oleomargarine. Remove from heat and stir in flour. Return to low heat and cook, stirring constantly, until thick and smooth. Heat half-and-half. Remove roux from heat and stir in hot half-and-half. Return to medium heat and cook, continuing to stir, until smooth and thick. Add ¾ of American and Swiss cheese and cook, constantly stirring, until cheese is completely melted. Add Wine and cook 2 minutes. Make a layer of the seafood in baking dish. Cover with layer of cheese sauce and sprinkle with part of remaining grated cheese. Alternate layers of seafood, sauce, and cheese until dish is filled, ending with cheese layer. Cover with crumbs and dot with butter. Bake in 375°F. oven 15 minutes.
Serves 6.

Lobster or Crabmeat Mousse

1 tablespoon gelatine
¼ cup dry White Wine
1 cup hot chicken stock
1½ cups chilled boiled
  lobster chunks or lump
  crabmeat
2 hard-cooked eggs cut in
  small pieces
2 tablespoons chopped
  green pepper
1 tablespoon minced parsley

⅛ teaspoon cumin
1 cup stiffly whipped
  cream
Salt and pepper to taste
3 chilled tomatoes cut in
  quarters
1 cup thinly sliced chilled
  cucumbers
CREAM OF SHRIMP-SHERRY
  DRESSING
Cracked ice

Soak gelatine in Wine. Bring stock to boiling point and pour over gelatine. Stir with wooden spoon until dissolved. Place in refrigerator until mixture reaches consistency of egg white. Combine seafood, eggs, green pepper, parsley, and cumin. Stir into gelatine and then fold in stiffly whipped cream. Check seasoning and fold in salt and pepper to taste. Spoon into oiled molds and let stand in refrigerator. Unmold; garnish with tomato quarters and cucumbers and serve with Cream of Shrimp-Sherry Dressing, which has been spooned into a bowl embedded in cracked ice.

Serves 6.

Lobster Newburg or Crabmeat Newburg

3 cups boiled lobster meat (cut into 1-inch chunks) or lump crabmeat	*½ cup Sherry*
	½ cup breakfast cream
	2 egg yolks slightly beaten
⅓ cup butter melted and bubbling	*Salt and cayenne pepper*
	⅛ teaspoon mace

Add the seafood to the bubbling butter and cook 5 minutes over medium heat, stirring from time to time. Add Sherry and cook 2 minutes. Scald cream and add a small amount to egg yolks. Combine yolks with remainder of cream. Stir in lobster or crabmeat, including butter and Sherry in which seafood was cooked. Season to taste with salt and pepper. Add mace. Cook over hot, not boiling, water in top of double boiler or the inset pan of a chafing dish, stirring constantly—and gently—with a wooden spoon until thickened and thoroughly heated.

Serves 6.

Poached Lobster or Crabmeat or Shrimp

3 cups boiled lobster cut in
   1-inch chunks, or 3 cups
   cooked lump crabmeat, or
   3 cups cooked shelled
   deveined shrimp

½ cup whole canned
   mushrooms
Dry White Wine
6 slices hot toast
6 teaspoons anchovy paste

Combine seafood and mushrooms. Cover with Wine and bring to a boil. Lower heat and cook over very low heat for 5 minutes. Spread toast with anchovy paste. Lift seafood with slotted spoon, so that most of Wine will drain off, and heap on toast. Serve immediately.
Serves 6.

Lobster or Crabmeat Royal

2 medium-size boiled lobsters
   or 3 cups lump crabmeat
2 cups whipping cream
   scalded
½ cup Sherry heated
⅛ teaspoon cayenne
   pepper
¾ cup sliced canned
   mushrooms

1½ tablespoons minced
   pimiento
1½ tablespoons minced
   green pepper
Salt
⅛ teaspoon mace or
   nutmeg
¼ cup toast crumbs
1 tablespoon butter melted

Remove meat from the body and claws of the lobster (claw meat should be kept whole) and cut meat from body and tail into 1-inch chunks, or, if using crabmeat, check to be sure it is free of shells. Place seafood in top of double boiler. Combine cream, Sherry, and cayenne pepper. Pour over seafood. Cook over boiling water until only about ¾ original quantity of liquid remains. Add mushrooms, pimiento, and green pepper. Season to taste with salt, and add mace or nutmeg. If using lobster, fill shell, and, if using crabmeat, fill serving dish. Combine crumbs and butter and sprinkle seafood with mixture. Garnish lobster with claw meat. Serve very hot.

Serves 6.

Lobster Thermidor

2 medium-size or 4 small
   boiled lobsters
2 tablespoons butter
2 tablespoons flour
1½ cups breakfast cream
¼ cup dry White Wine
⅛ teaspoon cayenne
   pepper

⅛ teaspoon turmeric
⅛ teaspoon cumin
Salt to taste
½ cup finely chopped
   canned mushrooms
¼ cup grated Parmesan
   cheese

Split lobsters lengthwise. Remove tail meat and cut into small pieces. Reserve shells. Melt butter. Remove from heat and stir in flour. Return to heat and cook over low heat stirring constantly until thick and smooth. Again remove from heat and gradually stir in cream and Wine. Cook over low heat, continuing to stir until thick. Add pepper, turmeric, cumin, and season to taste with salt. Stir until blended. Add mushrooms and lobster meat. Mix well. Fill lobster shells; sprinkle cheese over lobster-meat mixture and place 4 inches under broiler unit. Cook until golden brown.

Serves 4.

Baked Stuffed Oysters

48 medium-size oysters
3 slices bread
White Wine to cover
3 tablespoons butter or
   bacon grease
½ cup finely minced onion
1 cup minced parsley
2 tablespoons finely minced
   celery
1 egg slightly beaten
¼ teaspoon thyme

1 teaspoon monosodium
   glutamate
¼ teaspoon sweet basil
½ cup sliced canned
   mushrooms
1 tablespoon Worcestershire
   sauce
¼ teaspoon Tabasco sauce
Cracker crumbs
Salt and pepper

Drain oysters and dry between absorbent paper towels for several hours in refrigerator. Soak bread in White Wine for 30 minutes. Squeeze Wine from bread, reserving ¼ cup of Wine. Melt butter or grease in skillet. Add onion and cook until clear. Stir in bread, parsley, and celery, and cook over low heat, stirring constantly for several minutes. Add the ¼ cup of Wine squeezed from the bread and cook, mashing and stirring with a fork, until there are no lumps in the bread. Add oysters and cook only until they puff, stirring from time to time to keep mixture from sticking to bottom of pan. Remove from heat and cool. Stir in, until blended, the egg, thyme, monosodium glutamate, basil, mushrooms, Worcestershire sauce, and Tabasco. Add just enough cracker crumbs to hold the mixture together and season to taste with salt and pepper. Fill 6 greased individual baking dishes with mixture and bake in 375° F. oven for 20 minutes.

Serves 6.

Oysters Bienville

1 tablespoon butter	2 tablespoons very dry
1½ tablespoons sifted flour	White Wine or Sherry
¼ teaspoon salt	¼ cup minced parsley
⅙ teaspoon cayenne	2 slightly beaten egg yolks
pepper	Salt and white pepper to
¼ teaspoon thyme	taste
1 cup whipping cream	36 oysters with shells
2 tablespoons grated	Rock salt
Parmesan cheese	2 tablespoons melted butter
⅓ cup minced boiled	Salt and white pepper
deveined shrimp	

Melt 1 tablespoon butter slowly in a soup plate on a warm spot on stove. Stir in flour, ¼ teaspoon salt, cayenne pepper, and thyme. Continue stirring until smooth. Set mixture aside. Scald cream in top of double boiler and stir it into flour mixture until they are blended. Add cheese, shrimp, Wine, and parsley. Stir a small amount of mixture into slightly beaten yolks and then combine yolks with remainder of mixture. Cook over hot, not boiling, water, stirring constantly until thickened. Check seasoning and add salt and pepper to taste.

Scrub and boil the shells to remove all sand. Place rock salt to a depth of 1 inch in *6 pie pans.* Embed 6 shells on each pan. Bake in 400° F. oven for 15 minutes. Brush inside of shells with melted butter. Place a drained oyster on each shell. Sprinkle lightly with salt and white pepper. Place pie pans about 4 inches under broiler unit and cook for 5 minutes. Cover oysters with sauce and return to broiler. Cook until sauce is lightly browned and serve at once.

Oysters in Brown Sauce with Spaghetti Ring

36 large oysters with liquid
8 ounces uncooked spaghetti
3 quarts boiling water
2 tablespoons salt
2 cups hot Wine-flavored CHEESE SAUCE *(approximate)*
1 egg well beaten
⅓ cup grated American cheese
2 tablespoons butter or oleomargarine

1 tablespoon finely chopped onion
2 tablespoons sifted flour
1 cup hot oyster liquid
¼ cup Sherry
Salt and pepper to taste
1 cup whole canned mushrooms
1 tablespoon minced parsley
Kitchen Bouquet
¼ cup butter or oleomargarine

Drain oysters, reserving 1 cup of liquid. Place oysters on a board covered with several layers of absorbent paper towels. Cover seafood with additional layers of paper towels and store in refrigerator for several hours.

Cook spaghetti in rapidly boiling water, to which 2 table-spoons of salt have been added, for 15 minutes. Drain spaghetti and rinse with cold water. Add just enough hot Cheese Sauce to spaghetti to hold it together. Add a small amount of the spaghetti mixture to the slightly beaten egg and then mix egg with remainder of spaghetti. Cover bottom of well-greased ring mold with the grated American cheese. Cover cheese with spaghetti mixture. Bake in 350° F. oven 40–45 minutes until spaghetti is golden brown on top.

Thirty minutes after the spaghetti has been placed in the oven, melt 2 tablespoons butter or oleomargarine. Add onion and cook until it is clear. Remove from heat and stir in flour. Return to medium heat and stir continuously until roux is a rich brown and smooth. Again remove from heat and stir in hot oyster liquid. Return to medium heat and keep stirring until sauce is thickened. Add Sherry and salt and pepper to taste.

Stir until smooth. Add mushrooms and parsley and cook over low heat, stirring from time to time for 5 minutes. Set sauce aside. Coat oysters very lightly with Kitchen Bouquet. Melt butter or oleomargarine. Cook oysters in it until they puff and edges curl (over medium heat). Drain oysters.

When spaghetti ring is baked, turn it out on serving platter. Heat the Brown Sauce and add oysters. Cook until the oysters are thoroughly heated, stirring gently to keep mixture from sticking to bottom of pan. Fill center of ring with part of oyster mixture and surround the ring with the remainder. *Serves 6.*

Oysters in Sherry Sauce

36 large oysters with liquid	*1 egg yolk slightly beaten*
2 tablespoons butter or	*Salt and pepper to taste*
oleomargarine	*1 cup cooked or canned*
2 tablespoons sifted flour	*mushrooms*
¾ cup heated breakfast	*3 tablespoons Sherry*
cream	*Toast or patty shells*

Scald oysters in oyster liquid until they puff and edges curl (3–5 minutes). Drain oysters, reserving 1 cup of liquid. Melt butter or oleomargarine. Remove from stove and stir in flour. Return to medium heat and continue stirring until smooth and thickened, but do not brown. Heat oyster liquid that was reserved and remove sauce from stove. Stir in hot oyster water and return sauce to heat, continuing to stir until thickened. Again remove from the heat and stir in hot breakfast cream. Allow to simmer over low heat, continuing to stir, until smooth and thick. Add a small amount of hot sauce to egg yolk and then combine egg yolk with remainder of sauce. Season to taste with salt and pepper. Add oysters and mushrooms and cook over low heat until they are piping hot. Stir in Sherry and cook 2 minutes. Serve at once on hot toast or in hot patty shells. *Serves 6.*

Shrimp and Crabmeat Remick

For each serving (multiply quantites below by number of people to be served):

¼ cup cooked lump crabmeat

¼ cup cooked shelled deveined shrimp

Dry White Wine

1 tablespoon chopped green pepper

2 tablespoons whole canned mushrooms

⅛ teaspoon celery salt

⅛ teaspoon dry mustard

⅙ teaspoon paprika

3 tablespoons stiff mayonnaise

4 teaspoons chili sauce

1 teaspoon Worcestershire sauce

1½ teaspoons tarragon vinegar

2 drops Tabasco Sauce

Add crabmeat and shrimp to enough Wine to cover seafood. Mix green pepper and mushrooms. Bring to a boil. Lower heat and let simmer over very low heat for 5 minutes. Cover pan and store in refrigerator for at least 4 hours. Lift seafood out of Wine with slotted spoon, letting Wine drain off the crabmeat and shrimp. Place in greased individual baking dishes. Combine remaining ingredients and cover seafood with sauce. Bake at 450° F. for 8 minutes.

NOTE: ½ cup cooked shrimp, ½ cup cooked crawfish, ½ cup cooked crabmeat, ½ cup drained and washed tuna, or ½ cup cooked lobster may be substituted in the above recipe for the ¼ cup crabmeat combined with the ¼ cup shrimp.

Shrimp Diablo

*3 pounds raw shelled
  deveined shrimp
1 small clove garlic minced
  fine
1 tablespoon oleomargarine
  or butter melted and
  bubbling*

*2½ cups SAUCE DIABLO
½ cup dry White Wine
Salt and pepper to taste
Steamed rice*

Shell and devein shrimp. Cook garlic in bubbling fat until it is tender. Add Sauce Diablo and White Wine. Cook several minutes and add raw shrimp. Season to taste with salt and pepper. Reduce heat and allow to simmer 15–20 minutes until shrimp are tender, depending on size. Serve very hot with steamed rice.
Serves 6.

Shrimp and Olive Casserole

*1½ cups Sherry-flavored
  CREAM SAUCE
2½ cups boiled shelled
  deveined shrimp
2 tablespoons chopped
  pimiento*

*½ cup chopped ripe olives
2 tablespoons grated
  American cheese
2 tablespoons grated Swiss
  cheese*

Combine sauce, shrimp, pimiento, and olives. Heat thoroughly. Pour into a greased baking dish. Combine American and Swiss cheese and top shrimp mixture with grated cheese. Bake in 375° F. oven until golden brown (15–20 minutes).
Serves 6.

Shrimp and Oyster Jambalaya

3 tablespoons shortening
1 small clove minced garlic
⅓ cup finely chopped
  onion
2 tablespoons finely chopped
  celery
3 tablespoons finely chopped
  shallots
¾ pound raw ham, cut in
  1-inch chunks
¾ pound hot spiced small
  sausages
1 cup raw rice
2 cups water

½ cup canned tomatoes
½ cup dry Rosé Wine
1 teaspoon salt
  (approximate)
⅛ teaspoon black pepper
¼ teaspoon thyme
¼ cup minced parsley
¼ teaspoon basil
2 cups cleaned deveined
  shelled raw shrimp
18 small oysters with their
  liquid
¼ teaspoon Tabasco sauce
  (approximate)

Melt shortening. Sauté garlic, onion, celery, and shallots in it. Add ham and sausages. Cook 5 minutes. Add rice and cook and stir until straw colored. Add water, tomatoes, Wine, salt, pepper, thyme, parsley, and basil. Cover pan and lower heat. Allow to simmer for 30 minutes. Add shrimp. Cover and cook 10 minutes. Cook oysters in their own liquid until they puff (3–5 minutes). Add both oysters and liquid to rice mixture. Cook, stirring frequently to prevent sticking, until nearly dry. Stir in Tabasco sauce and cook 5 minutes more, continuing to stir. Check seasoning and, if needed, additional salt and Tabasco may be added.
Serves 6.

Poultry

My family loved to eat quail, but we weren't the "hunting type." It was an unwritten law in Pike County that nobody ate quail unless he shot it. We got around the "code" by making a deal with some impecunious customers of the family store who loved to hunt for sport and food, but couldn't afford the shells. My father gave them ammunition in return for a promise of half their "bag" of quail.

Consequently, we had more quail than anybody else in the county and Daddy enjoyed teasing his friends about it, especially when they returned empty-handed from a hunt. These frustrated sportsmen vowed that if they ever caught the guilty hunters delivering the contraband, they would have them and my father thrown in jail. Fortunately, we were so expert at smuggling the birds into the kitchen that we continued to dine on all the quail we wanted whenever they were in season.

Now I have eaten quail in some of the finest restaurants and found it terribly dry from the broiling. I thought there must be some way to avoid this, so I went home to my kitchen and tried brushing the birds with Wine before cooking, and this brought out the natural flavor, increased juiciness, and made all the difference in the world.

Another favorite poultry recipe of mine is particularly suited to advance preparation for an impressive company dinner: CHICKEN WITH CHABLIS, MADEIRA, AND COINTREAU. I found myself in a predicament on the occasion of a party for my aunt's fiftieth anniversary where I desperately needed just such a dish. I knew I could not be home until 4:30 on the day of the dinner, and that was bad enough, but the coup de grâce was delivered by the New Orleans climate. New Orleans *never* has snow and ice, and is therefore unprepared for it. When a record-breaking cold wave hit, most of the city's pipes burst, and there weren't enough plumbers to cope with the situation. So on the evening of this family celebration we had a frozen drain and couldn't use the sink. The butler who had been hired for the evening couldn't resist tinkering with the plumbing, so when I returned to the kitchen to make last-minute arrangements I found the floor littered with the plungers, buckets, and tools he had managed to collect.

Unbelievable as it may seem, the dinner party was a success in spite of all these handicaps, thanks to advance preparation of the CHICKEN WITH CHABLIS, MADEIRA, AND COINTREAU and other dishes that could be made ahead of time. Perhaps you would like to have this menu as a sample of a dinner which you can present to your guests with pride while you are at the table enjoying it with them. In addition to the food listed below, I served Martinis, hors d'oeuvres, Wine, coffee, and Brandy.

AVOCADO AND GRAPEFRUIT IN LIME GELATINE

Prepared the day before, unmolded, garnished, and refrigerated again on the afternoon of the party.

MADRILENE

Prepared before guests arrived (in just a matter of seconds) and reheated at serving time.

CHICKEN WITH CHABLIS, MADEIRA, AND COINTREAU

Sauce made day before (can be made weeks or even months before using and stored in freezer). Chicken breasts browned and placed in sauce marinade in refrigerator for 12 hours. Put in oven 1 hour before dinner. Garnished with purple grapes and kumquat sprays before serving.

EGGPLANT AND CHICKEN LIVERS

Prepared day before and refrigerated (this can also be prepared weeks ahead and stored in freezer). Baked at same time as chicken.

STUFFED BAKED POTATOES WITH VERMOUTH

Prepared late afternoon of dinner and baked along with chicken and eggplant. In order to cook the chicken, eggplant, and potatoes in oven at the same time, I placed a very large and heavy cooky tray over the roasting pan containing the chicken and then placed the eggplant casserole and potatoes on this tray.

CHOCOLATE BRANDY PIE with Vanilla Ice Cream

Pie made and ice cream prepared on the morning of the day of the party. At serving time, ice cream cut into wedges, placed on top of pie, and sprinkled with chocolate.

Baked Boned Broilers

3 2-pound broilers	Salt and pepper
3 cups fine bread crumbs	¼ teaspoon marjoram
3 tablespoons minced chives	¼ teaspoon basil
2 large chopped truffles	Dry White Wine to hold
½ cup canned mushroom pieces	mixture together
	Salt and pepper
2 tablespoons minced parsley	⅓ cup Brandy
	⅓ cup melted butter
2 tablespoons minced celery	2 teaspoons Kitchen Bouquet
	¼ cup melted butter
1 pound finely chopped chicken livers	2 tablespoons Cognac
	4 tablespoons Sherry

Have bones removed from broilers. Combine crumbs, chives, truffles, mushrooms, parsley, celery, chicken livers, and salt and pepper to taste. Add marjoram, basil, and just enough dry White Wine to hold mixture together. Divide the mixture between the broilers, placing some in the center of each chicken and pulling up the skin. Place the broilers in a shallow large baking pan so that the skin that was brought together on each of the chickens rests on the pan and is thus held. Sprinkle broilers liberally with salt and pepper. Brush each of the chickens first with Brandy and then with butter. Cook 25 minutes in 350° F. oven. Remove pan from oven and combine Kitchen Bouquet with ¼ cup melted butter. Brush broilers with mixture. Return to oven and bake 10 minutes. Remove from oven; place on hot platter and combine Cognac and Sherry. Heat and sprinkle broilers with mixture. Serve at once.

Serves 6.

Boiled Chicken

1 4½–6-pound chilled
    dressed hen
Salt and pepper
Cold water to almost cover

2 cups White or Rosé Wine
5 1-inch pieces celery
3 tablespoons minced parsley
Salt and pepper, if desired

Hen may be disjointed or cooked whole. Sprinkle liberally with salt and pepper and place in heavy deep pan. Almost cover with cold water and add wine. Bring to a boil. Add celery and parsley. Lower heat; cover pan and allow to simmer over low heat for 1 hour. Check seasoning, and if needed, add salt and pepper to taste. Continue cooking in covered pan over low heat until tender (1–2 hours more).

Serves 6–8 people.

Broiled Chicken

½ cup Amontillado Sherry
3 1½–2¼-pound broilers
    cut in halves or quarters
Salt and pepper

¾ cup melted butter or
    oleomargarine
    (approximate)
¼ cup warm Brandy

Six hours before serving, pour Sherry over broilers. Store in refrigerator, turning the chicken 3 or 4 times while it is in marinade. Remove from marinade. Sprinkle liberally with salt and pepper on both sides. Brush both sides with melted butter or oleomargarine. Place on broiler rack 3 inches below heated broiler unit. Cook for 4 minutes on each side. Lower heat and also lower rack until it is as far from heating unit as possible. Cook 23–25 minutes, turning broilers every 7 or 8 minutes and brushing well with melted butter or oleomargarine each time chicken pieces are turned. When chicken is cooked through, sprinkle on both sides with warm Brandy.

Serves 6.

Pan-broiled Chicken Breasts

½ cup Amontillado Sherry
6 chilled dressed breasts of
  spring chickens
Salt and pepper

½ cup butter or
  oleomargarine
¼ cup Sherry

Six hours before serving, pour Amontillado Sherry over breasts. Store in refrigerator, turning chicken 3 or 4 times while it is in marinade. Remove from marinade. Sprinkle liberally on both sides with salt and pepper. Melt butter or oleomargarine in large frying pan and when it bubbles (360° F.), add chicken, being careful not to allow pieces to overlap. When chicken is brown on one side, turn and brown on other side. When both sides are brown, sprinkle chicken with half of Sherry. Reduce heat (230° F.) and cover frying pan. Cook chicken 20–25 minutes until breasts are tender and cooked through. Place chicken on warm platter and sprinkle with remaining Sherry.

Serves 6.

Chicken or Turkey à la King

3 cups boiled hen or turkey, cut into 1-inch chunks[1]

2 tablespoons chopped pimiento

½ cup chopped green pepper

3 hard-cooked eggs coarsely chopped

1 cup cooked or canned peas

1 cup cooked or canned whole mushrooms

2 tablespoons butter or oleomargarine

2 tablespoons flour (sifted after measuring)

1½ cups chicken bouillon or turkey or chicken stock

½ cup White Wine

⅛ teaspoon cumin

⅛ teaspoon turmeric

⅔ cup breakfast cream

Salt and pepper to taste

3 tablespoons Sherry

Hot patty shells or toast

Mix chicken or turkey, pimiento, green pepper, eggs, peas, and mushrooms. Melt butter or oleomargarine in skillet; remove from heat and stir in sifted flour. Return to low heat and cook, stirring constantly, until thickened, but do not brown. Stir in bouillon or stock and White Wine until blended. Add cumin, turmeric, and cream. Return to low heat and cook continuing to stir until thickened. Season to taste with salt and pepper. Stir in chicken or turkey mixture. Cook for 10 minutes, stirring from time to time so that mixture will not stick to bottom of pan. Just before serving stir in Sherry. Cook 2 minutes. Serve in hot patty shells or on toast.

Serves 8.

[1] Leftover baked chicken or turkey may be used.

Chicken à la Maryland

½ cup *Amontillado Sherry*
2 *2½-pound chilled
  dressed spring chickens
  disjointed*
Salt and pepper
1 *cup sifted flour*

2 *eggs slightly beaten*
1½ *cups cracker or Rice
  Krispie crumbs*
½ *cup melted butter*
1½ *cups Wine-flavored*
  CREAM SAUCE

Pour Sherry over chicken and let stand in refrigerator several hours before cooking, turning the chicken at least twice during this period. Remove chicken from marinade. Sprinkle chicken on all sides liberally with salt and pepper. Sift flour into shallow bowl. Dip pieces of chicken in flour, then in egg, and then in cracker or Rice Krispie crumbs, covering the chicken pieces well with the crumbs. Place on rack in roasting pan and bake until tender (about 35–45 minutes) in 350° F. oven, basting 3 or 4 times with the melted butter. Place on hot platter and cover with very hot Wine-flavored Cream Sauce.
Serves 6.

Chicken Breasts with Mushrooms and Hearts of Artichokes

6 *fryer breasts*
2 *tablespoons butter or
  oleomargarine*
1 *tablespoon minced onion*
2 *tablespoons sifted flour*
1 *cup hot chicken stock or
  bouillon*
2 *tablespoons minced parsley*
1 *cup dry White Wine*
⅛ *teaspoon rosemary*

Salt and pepper
3 *tablespoons butter or
  oleomargarine*
1½ *cups whole canned
  mushrooms*
6 *hot boiled artichoke
  hearts from which all
  leaves and chokes have
  been removed*

Prepare fryer breasts according to recipe for PAN-BROILED CHICKEN BREASTS. Melt 2 tablespoons butter or oleomargarine until it bubbles (360° F.). Add onion and cook until clear. Remove from heat and stir in flour until blended. Return to heat and cook until thickened and a rich brown. Add hot stock or bouillon, parsley, and White Wine. Cook until thickened. Stir in rosemary, and salt and pepper to taste. Melt 3 tablespoons butter or oleomargarine. Brown mushrooms. Arrange fryer breasts, mushrooms, and artichoke hearts on platter. Pour sauce over breasts and vegetables and serve at once.

Serves 6.

Chicken-Artichoke-Tomato Casserole

3 2-pound broilers quartered	1 cup scalded whipping
1½ cups dry White Wine	cream
Salt and pepper	1 egg yolk slightly beaten
1 tablespoon minced parsley	Salt and pepper
1 tablespoon minced onion	12 hot canned artichoke
1½ cups water	hearts
2 tablespoons butter	3 medium-size firm
2 tablespoons sifted flour	tomatoes, cut in halves,
1½ cups broth in which	sprinkled with salt and
chicken was cooked	pepper, dotted with
	butter, and grilled

Place broilers in bowl and add White Wine. Store in refrigerator 6–8 hours, turning the chicken in the wine several times during this period. Remove chicken from marinade and sprinkle it well with salt and pepper. Place in a large shallow pan and add marinade, parsley, onion, and water. Bring to a boil; reduce heat, cover pan, and cook over low heat until chicken is tender. Melt butter. Remove from heat; stir in flour. Return to medium heat and continue stirring until roux is thick and smooth. Stir in broth in which chicken was cooked and cook, stirring constantly until thick and smooth. Add scalded whipping cream and again cook, continuing to stir until sauce is thickened. Add a small amount of sauce to egg yolk and stir until completely blended. Then stir the yolk mixture into remainder of sauce. Season to taste with salt and pepper. Arrange chicken, hot artichokes, and hot grilled tomatoes on baking-serving platter. Pour sauce over chicken and vegetables. Place in broiler 4 inches from heating unit and cook until sauce is golden brown.

Serves 6.

NOTE: Two 10-ounce packages frozen cooked and drained broccoli spears may be substituted for the artichoke hearts.

Chicken Cacciatore

3½ pounds fryer breasts, legs, and second joints
Salt and pepper
Kitchen Bouquet
½ cup oleomargarine or butter (approximate)
2 cups Vin Rosé
1 cup raisins
1 large clove garlic finely chopped
⅔ cup chopped onion
½ cup chopped green pepper
½ cup chopped celery

¼ cup canned mushroom pieces
1-pound can tomatoes
2 teaspoons dehydrated parsley
⅛ teaspoon pepper
¾ teaspoon salt
1 teaspoon curry
¼ teaspoon thyme
Salt and pepper to taste, if needed
½ cup toasted almond slivers or pecan pieces

Sprinkle chicken with salt and pepper. Lightly coat fryer pieces on all sides with Kitchen Bouquet. Heat oleomargarine or butter in skillet until it bubbles (360° F.). Add chicken pieces and brown on all sides. Place browned chicken in bowl and add Wine and raisins. Store in refrigerator for at least 6 hours, turning chicken in marinade during this period. Strain and reserve the fat in which chicken was browned. About 1½ hours before serving time, melt and heat the reserved fat. Add garlic, onion, green pepper, celery, and mushrooms. Cook until onion is clear. Remove chicken and raisins from marinade and add the marinade and tomatoes to the onion mixture. Bring to a boil. Cook several minutes over medium heat. Add parsley, pepper, salt, curry, thyme, and raisins. Cook over medium heat 8–10 minutes, stirring from time to time. Check seasoning and, if needed, add salt and pepper to taste. Place chicken in roaster and pour sauce over it. Cover roaster. Bake 1 hour in 350° F. oven. Place chicken and sauce on heated platter and sprinkle with almonds or pecans.

Serves 6.

Chicken with Chablis, Madeira, and Cointreau

2½ cups canned beef bouillon	⅓ cup Cointreau
½ cup Chablis	10 fryer breasts or 5 2–2¼-
10 ounces grape jelly	pound broilers halved or
½ cup orange juice	quartered
Juice and rind of 2 large lemons	Kitchen Bouquet
½ cup Chablis	Salt and pepper
¼ cup Madeira	¾ cup butter or oleomargarine
	(approximate)

Mix bouillon and ½ cup Chablis. Stir in jelly. Cook over low heat 1¼ hours. Combine orange juice, lemon juice, and thin strips of lemon rind, cut from fruit with vegetable parer. Cook juice and rind for 10 minutes over low heat. Add ½ cup Chablis, the Madeira, and Cointreau. Strain and combine with jelly mixture. Cook for an additional 10 minutes over low heat.

Lightly coat chicken with Kitchen Bouquet. Sprinkle chicken pieces with salt and pepper on all sides. Melt ½ cup butter or oleomargarine in skillet and when it bubbles (360° F.), add chicken, being careful not to let pieces overlap. Brown chicken on all sides and continue cooking until all of chicken is browned. Add the additional butter or oleomargarine when needed. Place chicken in large deep bowl and pour grape jelly sauce over it. Let stand in refrigerator for at least 12 hours, turning the pieces in the marinade at least 3 or 4 times during this period. Place chicken in a large baking pan. Cover bottom of pan to a depth of ¼ inch with marinade. Cover roaster pan with aluminum foil. Place in 325° F. oven and cook 1 hour. *Serves 10.*

Chicken with Chablis, Madeira, and Cointreau, Stuffed with Pâté Brandy Stuffing

CHICKEN WITH CHABLIS, MADEIRA AND COINTREAU
PÂTÉ BRANDY STUFFING

Prepare chicken according to preceding recipe. Prepare Pâté Brandy Stuffing. After chicken is removed from marinade fill hollow of each piece with Pâté Brandy Stuffing. Place chicken in large baking pan, skin side down. Cover bottom of pan to a depth of ¼ inch with marinade. Cover roaster pan with aluminum foil. Place in 325° F. oven and cook 1 hour. *Serves 10.*

Chicken or Turkey Florentine

2 cups water
1 rounded teaspoon salt
2 10-ounce packages frozen spinach
¼ cup minced parsley
¼ cup minced celery
Mayonnaise to hold mixture together
Salt and pepper to taste

Curry to taste (¾–1¼ teaspoons)
10 slices baked turkey or 12 slices roast chicken
1 cup hot Wine-flavored CREAM SAUCE
2 tablespoons grated Parmesan cheese

Bring water to a boil and add salt, spinach, parsley, and celery. Again bring to a boil and when spinach is defrosted, cover pan and reduce heat. Cook 4–6 minutes. Drain. Add just enough mayonnaise to hold mixture together and season to taste with salt and pepper. Stir in curry. Cook only until mixture is thoroughly heated. Make bed of spinach on heatproof platter. Arrange turkey or chicken slices on spinach. Cover with hot Cream Sauce and sprinkle with grated cheese. Cook 4 inches under broiler until sauce is golden brown. Serve at once. *Serves 5.*

Chicken Fricassee

1 4–5-pound chilled disjointed hen
Salt and pepper
1 cup sifted flour
1 cup vegetable shortening (approximate)
2 tablespoons butter or oleomargarine
2 tablespoons sifted flour
3½ cups boiling water
1½ cups hot dry White Wine

2 small bay leaves
¼ teaspoon thyme
1 teaspoon basil
3 tablespoons minced parsley
½ cup chopped onion
½ cup chopped celery
1 small clove minced garlic (optional)
Salt and pepper, if desired
½ cup Red Wine

Sprinkle hen with salt and pepper. Roll in flour and fry in hot melted vegetable shortening (360° F.) to a depth of ¾ inch in skillet until chicken is brown on all sides. Drain chicken on absorbent paper. Heat butter or oleomargarine until it bubbles. Remove from stove and stir in the 2 tablespoons flour. Stir until blended and return to medium heat. Continue cooking and stirring until smooth and a rich brown. Gradually add boiling water and hot Wine, stirring as you add. When sauce is smooth, place chicken in a heavy deep saucepan. Cover with sauce. Add bay leaves, thyme, basil, parsley, onion, celery, and, if desired, garlic. Bring to a boil. Lower heat; cover pan and allow to simmer over low heat for 1 hour. Check seasoning and if more salt and/or pepper are desired, add. Continue cooking in covered pan over low heat until chicken is tender (45–60 minutes more). Add Red Wine, heat thoroughly, and serve. *Serves 6.*

Spring Chicken Fricassee

*1 3-pound disjointed chilled
  frying-size chicken
Kitchen Bouquet
Salt and pepper
½ cup butter or
  oleomargarine
½ cup chopped onion
½ cup chopped celery
⅓ cup chopped green
  pepper
¾ cup sliced canned
  mushrooms*

*1½ cups tomato juice or
  canned tomato
¼ cup minced parsley
¼ teaspoon rosemary
¼ teaspoon orégano
¼ teaspoon basil
1 bay leaf
¾ teaspoon salt
White Wine to cover
3 tablespoons Amontillado
  Sherry, if desired
Salt and pepper, if needed*

Lightly brush chicken with Kitchen Bouquet. Sprinkle well with salt and pepper. Heat butter or oleomargarine until it bubbles (360° F.) and brown chicken on all sides in hot fat. Remove chicken and strain grease. Pour the strained fat into a skillet and add onion, celery, green pepper, and mushrooms. Cook only until onion is clear. Add tomato juice or canned tomato, parsley, rosemary, orégano, basil, bay leaf, and salt. Stir until blended. Place chicken in heavy deep saucepan. Add tomato sauce and enough White Wine to cover. Bring to a boil; reduce heat and cook over low heat in a covered pan, stirring from time to time, until tender (40–45 minutes). If desired, add Sherry. Check seasoning and, if needed, add salt and/or pepper. Serve very hot.
Serves 4.

Chicken Mousse

Substitute 1½ cups minced boiled chicken for 1½ cups lobster or crabmeat specified in recipe for LOBSTER OR CRAB-MEAT MOUSSE.

Chicken Paprika

1 3-pound chilled dressed spring chicken disjointed	*¼ cup chopped onion*
½ cup Sherry	*2 tablespoons flour*
Salt and pepper	*3 tablespoons Amontillado Sherry*
½ cup butter or oleomargarine	*1 teaspoon dehydrated parsley flakes*
3 tablespoons Sherry	*2 cups commercial sour cream*
2 tablespoons strained grease (in which chicken was cooked)	*Salt to taste*
	1½ teaspoons paprika

Sprinkle chicken with ½ cup Sherry and let stand in refrigerator for 6–8 hours, turning chicken in Wine several times during this period. Sprinkle chicken with salt and pepper. Heat butter or oleomargarine until it bubbles (360° F.) and brown chicken on all sides. Reduce heat (235° F.), cover skillet, and cook until chicken is tender and cooked through to the bone. Remove chicken to heatproof platter, sprinkle with 3 tablespoons Sherry and place in warm oven. Strain grease in which chicken was cooked and heat 2 tablespoons of it. Add onion and cook only until it is tender. Remove from heat and stir in flour. Return to medium heat and cook, stirring constantly, until smooth and rich brown. Stir in 3 tablespoons Sherry and parsley flakes. Remove from heat and stir in sour cream, salt to taste, and paprika. Cook just long enough to heat the sauce thoroughly. Pour sauce over chicken and serve at once.
Serves 4.

Chicken Pie

1 stewed hen, prepared according to recipe for STEWED CHICKEN,
omitting bay leaf, thyme, and basil
1 cup breakfast cream
Biscuit or pie dough

Follow directions for preparing Stewed Chicken, omitting
bay leaf, thyme, and basil. After seasoning is checked, add
breakfast cream. Add the final cup of Wine as specified in
recipe and cook until chicken is tender. Remove meat in large
pieces from bones and place in large casserole. Pour cream
broth in which the chicken was cooked over hen until it reaches
to 1 inch of the top of the casserole. Prepare biscuit or pie
dough. Roll to ¼-inch thickness. Cut slits in dough so that
the steam can escape. Cover the top of the casserole with the
dough. Bake in 450°F. oven for 15 minutes.
Serves 6–8 if 5–6 pound hen is used.

Chicken and Rice Casserole

*3½ pounds fryer breasts,
legs, and second joints*
½ cup Sherry
Kitchen Bouquet
Salt and pepper
*½ cup butter or
oleomargarine*
½ cup chopped onion
½ cup chopped celery
*½ cup chopped green
pepper*
*½ large minced clove
garlic*

1½ cups chopped tomato
*2 tablespoons minced
parsley*
¼ teaspoon orégano
¼ teaspoon thyme
¼ teaspoon Tabasco sauce
Salt to taste
2 tablespoons salad oil
1 cup uncooked rice
*4 parts chicken bouillon to
1 part White Wine to cover
rice and chicken*
Salt and pepper to taste

Sprinkle chicken with Sherry 6–8 hours before cooking, turning the chicken several times in the marinade during this period. Lightly coat chicken pieces with Kitchen Bouquet and sprinkle liberally with salt and pepper. Heat butter or oleomargarine until it bubbles (360° F.). Add chicken and brown on both sides. Put chicken in large casserole. Strain grease and heat. Cook onion, celery, green pepper, and garlic in grease until onion is clear. Add tomato, parsley, orégano, thyme, Tabasco, and cook, stirring from time to time, over low heat for 5 minutes. Season to taste with salt. Pour tomato sauce over chicken. Heat salad oil. Add rice and cook, stirring constantly, over medium heat until straw brown. Spoon rice into casserole. Mix bouillon and Wine and season mixture to taste with salt and pepper. Pour over rice and chicken until they are covered. Bake in 350° F. oven for 1½ hours.
Serves 6.

Chicken or Turkey Salad with Sour Cream

2 *4-pound hens or 1 8-pound broiler turkey prepared according to recipe for* CHICKEN WITH WINE AND HERBS
3 *hard-cooked eggs cut in small pieces*

1½ *cups sliced ripe olives*
1¼ *cups stiff mayonnaise*
1 *cup commercial sour cream*
1 *teaspoon Worcestershire sauce*
Salt and pepper to taste

When poultry is tender, cool. Remove skin and gristle. Cut meat into ¾-inch chunks. Combine with eggs and ripe olives. Mix mayonnaise and sour cream by folding the cream into the mayonnaise. Fold in Worcestershire sauce and season to taste with salt and pepper. Fold sour cream dressing into the chicken or turkey mixture. Chill.
NOTE: *The above recipe serves 12–14; for family use,* use 1 hen, 2 hard-cooked eggs, ¾ cup sliced olives, ¾ cup mayonnaise, ½ cup commercial sour cream, ½ teaspoon Worcestershire sauce, and salt and pepper to taste.

Chicken with Wine and Herbs

*1 5–6-pound chilled
  dressed hen disjointed
Salt and black pepper
Poultry stock to cover
1 cup White Wine
½ cup coarsely chopped
  celery
⅓ cup thinly sliced onion*

*8 sprigs parsley
⅛ teaspoon sweet marjoram
⅛ teaspoon thyme
1 bay leaf
Salt and black pepper, if
  desired
1 cup Vin Rosé or White
  Wine*

Sprinkle chicken with salt and pepper. Place in deep heavy pan. Cover with stock and add 1 cup Wine. Bring to a boil. Add celery, onion, and parsley. Again bring to a boil. Reduce to low heat, cover pan, and allow to simmer for 1 hour. Add marjoram, thyme, bay leaf, and check seasoning. If desired, add salt and pepper to taste. Cover pan and cook over low heat until chicken is tender (1–2 hours more). Just before serving add 1 cup Vin Rosé or White Wine and heat thoroughly.
Serves 6–8.

Krispy Chicken

*½ cup Sherry
6 breasts of frying-size
  chickens
Salt and pepper*

*½ cup melted butter or
  oleomargarine
1 cup Rice Krispie crumbs*

Pour Sherry over breasts. Let stand in refrigerator for 5 or 6 hours, turning chicken at least 3 or 4 times during this period while it is in marinade. Remove breasts from Sherry and sprinkle them liberally with salt and pepper. Dip the breasts into the melted butter or oleomargarine, letting them stand in the melted

fat long enough to be completely covered with it. Roll breasts
in Rice Krispie crumbs. Place skin side up in shallow pan lined
with aluminum foil. Do not let pieces overlap. Bake in 350° F.
oven 1 hour. Do not cover pan or turn chicken while it is cooking.
Serves 6.

Potted Chicken

*1 4–4½-pound dressed
   chilled hen
Salt and pepper
1½ tablespoons salad oil
½ cup boiling water
½ cup White Wine,
   Sherry, or Vin Rosé*

*1¼ cups whipping cream
¾ cup canned whole
   mushrooms
⅓ cup whipping cream if
   needed*

Split hen down back. Sprinkle liberally on both sides with
salt and pepper. Place hen with breast up in roaster. Brush with
oil. Bring water and Wine to a boil. Pour over hen. Bake in
350° F. oven for 35 minutes. Add 1¼ cups cream and the
mushrooms. Cover roaster and continue cooking until chicken
is tender (1–2 hours more). If necessary, the additional cream
may be added.
Serves 6.

Poulet Sous Cloche

*8 boned fryer breasts
¾ cup Sherry
Salt and cayenne pepper
8 ½-inch slices ham steak*

*⅓ cup Curaçao or Grand
   Marnier
1 cup heavy cream
   (approximate)
4 tablespoons Sherry*

Sprinkle breasts with Sherry and store in refrigerator for 6–8
hours, turning 2 or 3 times during this period. Rub breasts with

salt (liberally) and cayenne (frugally). Trim the ham steaks until they are only slightly larger than the breasts. Brush steaks on both sides with Curaçao or Grand Marnier. Place ham steaks in 8 individual baking dishes with tight bell-shaped glass covers. Arrange the breasts on the ham and pour 2 tablespoons of cream over each breast. Put the glass covers securely in place and bake at 350° F. for 1 hour. If needed, a small additional amount of cream may be poured over the chicken breasts if they appear to be too dry during the baking period. Just before removing from oven, brush each breast with 1½ teaspoons Sherry.

Serves 8.

Roast Hen or Capon

*4–5-pound chilled dressed
    hen or 5-pound chilled
    dressed capon*
Salt and pepper
Desired stuffing

1¼ cups water
*¾ cup White Wine, Vin
    Rosé, or Sherry*
Kitchen Bouquet, if desired

Rub inside and out of hen or capon with salt and pepper. Fill cavity with desired stuffing and skewer or sew the skin together to close opening. Place chicken in roasting pan. Add water and Wine. Cover pan. Cook in 350° F. oven, allowing 35 minutes per pound and basting every 35–40 minutes. When chicken or capon is cooked through, remove cover, and if it is not sufficiently brown, brush lightly with Kitchen Bouquet and bake in uncovered roaster 10 minutes.

Serves 6–8.

Smothered Chicken

*1 3½-pound chilled
   dressed spring chicken
   disjointed
Salt and pepper
Sifted flour*

*½ cup butter or
   oleomargarine
Equal parts water and Vin
   Rosé*

Sprinkle chicken with salt and pepper. Dredge with sifted flour. Heat butter or oleomargarine until it bubbles (360°F.). Add chicken and brown lightly on all sides. Half cover with mixture of water and Wine. Cover skillet; cook over low heat (235°F.) until chicken is tender and most of liquid has cooked into it.
Serves 4.

Smothered Chicken or Capon with Mushrooms

*¾ cup Cream Sherry
1 5-pound chilled dressed
   hen or capon
Salt and pepper
¾ cup ham steak cut in
   small chunks
¾ cup minced celery
⅓ cup chopped green
   pepper
¼ cup minced onion*

*2 tablespoons minced
   parsley
1 slice pickled pork
Equal parts boiling water
   and White Wine
¼ cup tomato juice
½ cup sliced canned
   mushrooms
Salt and pepper if needed*

Pour Cream Sherry over hen or capon 4 or 5 hours before cooking and store in refrigerator. Turn poultry several times during this period. Remove bird from Sherry. Sprinkle well with salt and pepper. Combine ham, celery, green pepper, onion, and parsley. Place pickled pork in bottom of roaster and cover with chicken or capon. Cover chicken or capon breast with ham mixture. Cook over medium heat until pickled pork starts to brown. Add water and Wine mixture to a depth of 2 inches in the pan. Cover pan and cook in 325°F. oven for 2¾ hours. Remove bird and place on warm platter. Add tomato juice and mushrooms to sauce. Check seasoning and, if needed, add salt and pepper to taste. Heat thoroughly and pour over chicken or capon. Serve at once.

Serves 6.

Stewed Chicken

*1 5–6-pound chilled
    dressed hen disjointed
Salt and pepper
½ cup butter or
    oleomargarine
6 cups cold water
1 cup White Wine or Vin
    Rosé
⅔ cup coarsely chopped
    celery*

*3 tablespoons minced
    parsley
Salt and pepper to taste
1 bay leaf
¼ teaspoon basil
¼ teaspoon thyme
1 cup White Wine or Vin
    Rosé*

Sprinkle hen with salt and pepper. Melt butter or oleomargarine, and when it bubbles (360°F.) brown chicken on all sides in hot fat. Drain on absorbent paper. Place chicken in deep heavy pan. Add water and 1 cup Wine. Bring to a boil. Add celery and parsley. Reduce heat and cover pan. Cook over low heat for 1 hour. Check seasoning and, if needed, add salt and pepper to taste. Add bay leaf, basil, and thyme. Again cover and cook over low heat until nearly tender (1–1¾ hours more). Stir in 1 cup White Wine or Vin Rosé and cook until tender.

Serves 6–8.

Stewed Chicken and Dumplings

1 stewed hen, prepared according to preceding recipe for STEWED CHICKEN, *omitting bay leaf, thyme, and basil*
1 cup breakfast cream
1 cup sifted flour
½ teaspoon salt
1¼ teaspoons baking powder

⅛ teaspoon cumin
2 teaspoons dehydrated parsley
1 tablespoon grated American cheese
1 tablespoon grated Parmesan cheese
2 rounded tablespoons vegetable shortening
½ cup milk

Follow recipe for Stewed Chicken, omitting bay leaf, thyme, and basil. After chicken has cooked an hour over low heat and when seasoning is checked, add cream. Cover pan and cook over low heat until nearly tender. Stir in the final cup of Wine specified in Stewed Chicken recipe.

Sift flour; measure; add salt, baking powder, and cumin. Sift. Stir in parsley and grated cheese. Cut in the shortening with two knives or a pastry blender (or use both instruments if you wish) until mixture has the consistency of a coarse meal. Stir in milk. Drop dumplings by teaspoonfuls on chicken, being careful not to drop them on the liquid. Bring liquid to a boil. Cook 10 minutes with pan uncovered and then cover pan tightly and cook an additional 10 minutes. Serve at once.

A 5–6 pound hen serves 6–8.

Virginia Breast of Chicken

1 cup Cream Sherry
6 boned fryer breasts
Salt and pepper
Kitchen Bouquet
½ cup butter or
  oleomargarine

6 thick slices ham
½ cup Napoleon Brandy
1 cup whole canned
  mushrooms
2 cups whipping cream

Pour Sherry over breasts and store in refrigerator for 3–4 hours, turning the breasts 2 or 3 times during this period. Sprinkle breasts with salt and pepper, liberally, and brush lightly with Kitchen Bouquet. Melt butter or oleomargarine and heat until it bubbles (360° F.). Brown chicken in melted fat on both sides, and just before removing from skillet sprinkle 1 tablespoon of Cream Sherry marinade over each breast. Tie a thick slice of ham around each breast and brush with Brandy. Place in baking serving dish. Add mushrooms and cream. Cover baking dish—aluminum foil may be used if dish does not have cover. Bake 1 hour in 350° F. oven.
Serves 6.

Glazed Roast Duck

1 4½–5½-pound chilled
  dressed duck
⅓ cup Sherry
Salt and pepper
Desired stuffing

¼ cup Cognac mixed with
  ¼ cup water
2 tablespoons Cognac
1 tablespoon honey
½ teaspoon meat extract

Wipe inside and out of duck with wet cloth. Pour Sherry over duck 6 hours before cooking. Store in refrigerator and turn duck in the marinade 3 or 4 times during this period. Remove duck from Wine. Rub bird with salt and pepper. Fill cavity with desired stuffing and skewer or sew to close opening. Place duck on rack and put rack in roasting pan. Bake in 325° F. oven. Combine ¼ cup Cognac with ¼ cup of water. Baste bird with the heated mixture of Cognac and water every 20 minutes. Allow 35 minutes per pound for roasting— duck is roasted when leg meat feels soft and legs move easily— and 15 minutes before cooking time elapses, sprinkle with 2 tablespoons Cognac. Combine honey and meat extract and coat duck with mixture. Increase heat to 375° F. Complete cooking and serve whole or sliced.

Serves 6–7.

Duck Hash

2 cups Claret or Burgundy
2 5–6-pound ducks
Salt and pepper
2 medium-size peeled
  onions
2 medium-size unpeeled
  cooking apples
½ cup pan juices
¼ cup boiling bouillon
6 cups water
1½ cups Claret or
  Burgundy
2 small bay leaves
3 small carrots scraped and
  cut in chunks
3 4-inch-long celery stalks
3 tablespoons minced
  parsley
¼ teaspoon basil
¼ teaspoon thyme
3 tablespoons butter or
  oleomargarine
1 tablespoon minced onion
1½ tablespoons chopped
  celery
3 tablespoons sifted flour
2 teaspoons Worcestershire
  sauce
1 teaspoon monosodium
  glutamate
1 cup cooked or canned
  mushrooms
½ cup Claret or Burgundy
Salt and pepper to taste

Pour Claret or Burgundy over ducks and store in refrigerator 6–8 hours, turning ducks in marinade 3 or 4 times during this period. Remove ducks from Wine, reserving the marinade. Rub inside and out of each duck with salt and pepper. Place 1 onion and 1 apple in each duck. Put ducks on rack and place rack in baking pan. Bake in 325° F. oven in uncovered roaster, basting every 15 minutes with the boiling marinade. Allow 35 minutes per pound for roasting time. About 1 hour before cooking time expires, start to spoon off grease from roasting pan and continue to do this from time to time. When the ducks are roasted—meat of leg will feel soft and the leg will give easily when it is moved up and down—remove from pan. Combine pan juices, from which as much of the fat as possible has been removed, with bouillon and with the onions that were cooked in the cavities of the ducks. Liquidize in blender or put through a food mill. Remove skin and gristle from ducks and take meat from bones. Boil bones in water and 1½ cups Claret or Burgundy, adding bay leaves, carrots, celery, parsley, basil, and thyme. Cook until liquid is reduced to 3½ cups. Strain. Melt butter or oleomargarine. Add minced onion and 1½ tablespoons celery and cook until onion is clear. Stir in flour and continue stirring over medium heat until smooth and a rich brown. Stir in strained stock in which bones were cooked and continue cooking over medium heat and stirring until sauce is smooth and thickened. Add liquidized or pureéd onion, Worcestershire sauce, monosodium glutamate, mushrooms, and ½ cup Claret or Burgundy. Season to taste with salt and pepper. Stir in duck meat cut in 1-inch chunks and cook 10 minutes over low heat, stirring from time to time. Serve very hot.

Serves 12–14.

NOTE: *For family meals or for a small group,* follow above recipe, using 1 duck and only ½ of the quantities specified for each of the other ingredients.

Roasted Wild Ducks

2 wild ducks   ½ cup Claret
Salt and pepper   ½ cup water
2 turnips, apples, or peeled
  onions

Pick, singe, and wipe outside of ducks carefully. Draw the ducks, leaving the heads on. The insides of the birds should not be washed, so draw carefully. Cut an opening at the neck of each duck and draw head and neck through opening, letting head emerge at back. Rub inside of ducks lightly with salt and pepper. Place turnip, apple, or onion in each body cavity. Place ducks in baking pan and pour mixture of Claret and water over them. Bake in 425° F. oven for 25 minutes, basting with pan liquid every 8 minutes.
Serves 4.

Ducklings Flambé

2 4–5-pound dressed Long   ¼ cup drippings from pan
  Island ducklings   ¼ cup Sherry
1 cup Sherry   1 teaspoon Kitchen Bouquet
Salt and pepper   1 cup preserved kumquats
APPLE STUFFING   2 tablespoons Cointreau
⅓ cup Brandy or Sherry   ¼ cup Brandy

Wipe out inside of ducklings. Pour Sherry over them 6 hours before cooking. Store in refrigerator and turn birds in marinade 3 or 4 times during this period. Rub inside and out of ducklings with salt and pepper, and stuff. Close body openings with skewers or by sewing. Place ducklings breast up on rack in shallow pan. Roast at 325° F. for 2 hours, basting occasionally with heated ⅓ cup Brandy or Sherry. Drain drippings from pan. Combine ¼ cup of these drippings with ¼ cup Sherry and Kitchen Bouquet. Brush ducklings with this mixture. Return to oven and bake required time—allow 35 minutes per pound for roasting. Bird is done when leg meat is soft and legs move easily. Sprinkle kumquats with Cointreau. Place ducklings on hot platter. Garnish with kumquats. Heat ¼ cup Brandy. Sprinkle 2 tablespoons hot brandy over birds and ignite remainder. Pour burning Spirit over ducklings and serve at once.

Serves 8–10.

Roast Goose

Fat young goose about 12 pounds	*⅓ cup browned melted butter*
Salt and pepper	*2 tablespoons melted goose fat*
APPLE STUFFING	
½ cup chopped onion	*2 tablespoons sifted flour*
¼ cup chopped celery	*1½ cups water*
2 tablespoons minced parsley	*½ cup Vin Rosé*
2 cups water	*Salt and pepper to taste*
2 cups Vin Rosé	

Wipe inside and out of singed dressed goose from which the neck, wings, head, and feet have been cut. Wash inside and out and cover with cold water. Soak 10 minutes in cold water. Drain and pat dry with absorbent paper towels.

Rub inside lightly with salt and pepper and sprinkle the salt and pepper heavily over the breasts and lightly over legs and back. Stuff, and close cavities by sewing or skewering. Place goose, breast side up, on rack in roasting pan. Add onion, celery, and parsley to 2 cups of water and combine with 2 cups of Vin Rosé. Pour mixture over goose. Roast at 325° F., allowing 25 minutes per pound. When Wine and water mixture cooks down, baste every 20 minutes with browned melted but-

ter. Melt and heat goose fat. Remove from heat and stir in flour. Stir until smooth. Return to heat and cook, continuing to stir, until a rich brown. Again remove from heat and add water and Wine. Cook over medium heat, stirring from time to time until thickened. Season to taste with salt and pepper.
Serves 14–16.

Guinea Hens Baked in Cream and Tomatoes

1 cup White Wine
2 2½-pound dressed guinea hens
Salt and pepper
3 tablespoons salad oil
3 tablespoons butter or oleomargarine
½ cup finely chopped shallots
¼ cup minced celery
¼ cup finely chopped green pepper

1 cup breakfast cream
¾ cup canned tomato
½ cup canned whole mushrooms
⅛ teaspoon cayenne pepper
2 tablespoons minced parsley
¼ teaspoon basil
Salt and pepper to taste
3 tablespoons dry White Wine

Pour Wine over hens and let stand in refrigerator for several hours, turning 2 or 3 times during this period. Rub guineas, inside and out, with salt and pepper and coat breasts of hens with salad oil. Place in baking pan and add Wine in which hens were marinated. Roast in 500° F. oven for 10 minutes. Lower heat to 325° F. and cover pan. Cook until hens are tender (about 1½ hours). Remove from pan, reserving pan juices. Cool guineas. Melt butter or oleomargarine and when it bubbles (360° F.), add shallots, celery, and green pepper. Cook until tender. Stir in pan juices and cream and when blended, add remaining ingredients. Bring to a boil. Place guinea hens in baking pan. Pour tomato mixture over them and cook 10 minutes, uncovered, in 350° F. oven.
Serves 6.

Roast Partridge

4 dressed partridges	*½ cup boiling Sherry*
Salt and pepper	*4 slices pickled pork*
¼ cup melted butter	*¼ cup Sherry*

Truss partridges. Rub lightly with salt and pepper. Pour 1 tablespoon of melted butter and 2 tablespoons of boiling Sherry over each partridge, placed side by side in a shallow baking pan. Cover the breasts with pickled pork. Roast in 425° F. oven 30–35 minutes. Remove, place on warm platter. Sprinkle with ¼ cup Sherry.
Serves 4.

Roast Pheasant with Chablis and Bourbon

1 dressed chilled pheasant	*½ peeled and chopped*
2 cups Chablis	*large cooking apple*
½ cup butter or	*2 tablespoons chopped*
oleomargarine	*celery*
2 finely chopped shallots	*1 tablespoon Chablis*
2 tablespoons chopped	*2 slices bacon*
celery	*1 cup whipping cream*
3 tablespoons Bourbon	*1 tablespoon grated*
Salt and pepper	*horse-radish*
1 teaspoon minced parsley	

Cover pheasant with 2 cups Chablis and let stand in refrigerator for 6 to 8 hours, turning bird occasionally in marinade. Lift pheasant from Wine. Heat butter or oleomargarine until it bubbles (360° F.). Put pheasant, shallots, and 2 tablespoons celery in bubbling fat. Brown bird on all sides, and from time to time stir the vegetables. If the vegetables appear to be browning too fast, remove them from skillet. Place pheasant, browned shallots, and celery in shallow roasting pan. Heat Bourbon and pour two thirds of the Spirit over the bird. Ignite remainder of Bourbon and pour over pheasant. When flame dies, sprinkle bird with salt and pepper. Combine parsley, apple, celery, and 1 tablespoon Chablis. Fill cavity in pheasant with apple mixture and tie legs together so as to cover body opening. Pour marinade into roasting pan. Place strips of bacon over breast of bird and cook uncovered for 50 minutes in 350° F. oven, basting frequently with pan juices. Blend cream and horse-radish and pour over pheasant. Continue cooking until tender (leg will give easily when moved—about 25 to 35 minutes), basting with pan gravy every 10 minutes.

Allow ⅔–¾ pound meat for each serving.

Broiled Quail

4 quail
6 tablespoons Sherry
Salt and pepper
¾ cup butter or oleomargarine (approximate)
¼ cup heated Sherry

Draw and pick quail. Wipe with damp cloth. Remove any shot. Split birds down the back; pour 6 tablespoons of Sherry over them and let stand in refrigerator for 6–8 hours, breasts down. From time to time, spoon Sherry marinade over backs of quail. Sprinkle birds with salt and pepper on both sides. Melt butter or oleomargarine in heavy iron skillet and heat until it bubbles (360° F.). Place birds, breasts down, in skillet. Cover with a lid that will fit down into the skillet and then place a heavy weight on lid so that birds will cook through to the bone. Cook over moderate heat. When quail are brown on one side (about 5–7 minutes), turn and brown on other side. Should additional butter or oleomargarine be needed, add it.

When birds are browned on both sides, place on warm platter and sprinkle each quail with 1 tablespoon of warm Sherry.
Serves 4.

Rock Cornish Game Hens Baked in Brandy

2 small peeled apples cored
  and cut into ½-inch
  chunks
¼ cup chopped celery
2 tablespoons minced
  parsley
3 tablespoons Cognac

6 14–16 ounce Rock
  Cornish game hens
Salt and pepper
¾ cup Cognac
½ cup melted butter
1 tablespoon Kitchen
  Bouquet
2 tablespoons melted butter

Combine apples, celery, and parsley, and sprinkle with 3 tablespoons Cognac. Wipe out neck and body cavities of Rock Cornish hens. Sprinkle hens liberally with salt and pepper. Fill cavities with apple mixture. Close body cavity with a single skewer and place each hen on rack in shallow baking pan, tucking skin of neck down on the rack so that the mixture packed into the neck cavity will not fall out. Brush hens first with Cognac and then with melted butter. Bake in 425° F. oven for 15 minutes. Again brush liberally with Cognac and melted butter. Reduce heat to 350° F. Cook 15 minutes and brush with Cognac and butter. Cook 25 minutes. Pour any remaining Cognac and melted butter (from the ¾ cup Cognac and ½ cup butter) over the hens. Combine Kitchen Bouquet with 2 tablespoons melted butter. Brush each hen with mixture. Cook 10 minutes.
Serves 6.

Rock Cornish Game Hens with Kumquats and Wild Rice

6 14–16-ounce Rock Cornish
   game hens
⅓ cup Curaçao
1 tablespoon Cognac
Salt and pepper
½ cup butter or
   oleomargarine
½ cup Grand Marnier or
   ¼ cup Curaçao and
   ¼ cup Cognac

2 tablespoons juice from
   preserved kumquats
½ cup drained preserved
   kumquats
Hot boiled wild rice
¾ cup hot sautéed whole
   mushrooms

Brush hens with mixture of ⅓ cup Curaçao and 1 table-spoon Cognac. Store in refrigerator for several hours. Rub hens inside and out liberally with salt and pepper. Melt butter or oleomargarine and when it bubbles (360° F.), brown hens on all sides. Place hens in baking dish and brush with Grand Marnier or a mixture of Curaçao and Cognac. Bake at 350° F. 50 minutes, brushing birds twice with Grand Marnier or Cura-çao mixture during this period and reserving 2 tablespoons of the Spirit. Combine the kumquat juice with the 2 tablespoons of Grand Marnier or Curaçao and Cognac mixture and brush hens with mixture. Continue baking in 350° F. oven for 15 minutes. Place on warm platter and garnish with kumquats. Combine wild rice and mushrooms and serve with hens.

Serves 6.

Roast Squab

4 squab
6 tablespoons Sherry
Salt and pepper
2 tablespoons butter

2 tablespoons Cognac
4 thin strips bacon
Melted butter
Warm Cognac

Pick, singe, and draw squab. Pour Sherry over them and let stand in refrigerator for 6–8 hours, turning them from time to time in marinade. Sprinkle birds lightly with salt and pepper. Place small piece of butter on inside of each bird. Truss and brush breasts lightly with 2 tablespoons Cognac. Tie strip of bacon over each breast. Roast 10 minutes at 400° F. Reduce heat to 350° F. and roast 20 minutes more, basting every 5 minutes with melted butter and warm Cognac.

Serves 4.

Roast Turkey

1 dressed turkey	*Kitchen Bouquet, if desired*
Salt and pepper	*2 tablespoons browned flour*
PATE BRANDY STUFFING *or other desired stuffing*	*4 tablespoons cold water*
Butter (½ cup for 8–12 pound turkey, ¾ cup for 13–15 pound turkey, 1 cup for 16–20 pound turkey	*¼ cup sliced canned mushrooms*
	1 tablespoon dehydrated parsley
2 cups water	*3 tablespoons Sherry or White Wine*
2 cups dry White Wine or Sherry	*Salt and pepper*

Wipe inside and out of dressed turkey with cloth. Rub both inside and out liberally with salt and pepper. Fill cavities with Pâté Brandy Stuffing or other stuffing, if desired. Cream butter and rub over breast of turkey. Place bird in roaster pan. Add water and Wine. Cover pan.

If turkey weighs 8–10 pounds, cook at 325° F. 3–3½ hours.

If turkey weighs 10–14 pounds, cook at 325° F. for 3½–4 hours.

If turkey weighs 14–18 pounds, cook at 300° F. for 4–4½ hours.

If turkey weighs 18–20 pounds, cook at 300° F. for 4½–5 hours.

If turkey weighs 20 pounds or over, cook at 300° F. for 5–6 hours.

Baste turkey with pan juices every 40 minutes. Fifteen minutes before cooking time expires, remove lid from pan and if turkey is not brown enough, brush lightly with Kitchen Bouquet. Complete baking. Turkey is done when the meat of the leg feels soft and when the legs give very easily when moved up and down.

Combine flour and cold water and beat with fork or rotary egg beater until smooth. Bring pan juices from turkey to a boil. Blend with browned flour mixture and cook over medium heat until smooth. Add mushrooms, parsley, Wine, and season to taste with salt and pepper.

Allow ⅔–¾ pound for each serving.

NOTE: It is suggested that turkey be allowed to stand about 45 minutes before cutting.

Turkey Flambé

8-pound turkey stuffed with PATE BRANDY STUFFING *and roasted according to preceding recipe*
2 tablespoons chopped juniper berries
⅓ cup Gin

Prepare turkey. As soon as it is baked, place on very hot platter and sprinkle with the juniper berries. Heat Gin. Sprinkle all but 1½ tablespoons of the hot Gin over turkey. Ignite the remaining Gin and pour burning Spirit over bird. Serve at once.

Serves 10–11.

Turkey with Truffles and Ham

1½ pounds diced lean ham
½ pound truffles
1 cup large whole canned
   mushrooms
¼ teaspoon nutmeg

⅓ cup Sherry
Salt and pepper, if desired
1 15-pound turkey, to be
   cooked according to ROAST
   TURKEY *recipe*

Heat ham in skillet. Add truffles, mushrooms, nutmeg, Sherry, and salt and pepper, if desired, to taste. Cook over low heat, stirring from time to time, for 8 minutes. Use as stuffing for turkey and cook bird according to Roast Turkey recipe.
Serves 16–18.

Meats

My father ran a general store in Magnolia, where at one time or another we sold everything from pins to coffins. He had a grocery department of which he was very proud, and I loved to help him with it. On one occasion he had bought some large hams that weren't selling too well, so we decided that I would cook one to be sold in small quantities. Those were the days before tenderized hams, so I started by boiling it in Wine with spice and apple slices. Then I baked it with a Wine-flavored butterscotch glaze. My father was so delighted with the ham that I had produced that he served it to the customers who came into the store that day. After two or three people had tasted it, news got around town very quickly and soon they were standing in line to sample it. This experience was quite an exhilarating one for a teen-age cook and has remained vivid in my memory. It probably contributed to my interest in cooking with Spirits, when many years later I started using Wine marinades and brushing meats with Liqueurs.

Your first thought in considering the use of Wines for meat marinades may be that this is expensive cooking, but since inexpensive Wines are quite satisfactory for this purpose, it actually adds very little to the cost of the preparation of a large roast, and you can be confident that the meats you serve will be tender and juicy, with a delightful flavor. Personally, I am more than willing to pay this small insurance, in these days of high-priced meats, so that the roasts I cook will be as nearly perfect as I can make them.

Baked Beefsteak with Vegetables

2½ pounds boneless sirloin
   steak 1¾ inches thick
Dry Gin
3 tablespoons butter or
   oleomargarine
¾ cup sliced onion
½ cup green pepper cut in
   1-inch pieces
½ cup coarsely chopped
   celery
1 cup whole canned
   mushrooms

¼ cup butter or
   oleomargarine
3 large tomatoes cut in
   quarters
1 tablespoon minced parsley
⅓ cup Red Burgundy or
   Claret
Salt and pepper for
   vegetables
Kitchen Bouquet, if needed
Salt and pepper for meat
1½ cups cooked green
   beans well heated

Brush steak liberally on both sides with Gin several hours before cooking and store in refrigerator. Place 3 tablespoons butter or oleomargarine in shallow baking dish and place baking dish in 500° F. oven to melt fat. Add steak. Allow 25 minutes for medium and 18 minutes for rare steak, turning steak twice while it is cooking. Sauté onion, pepper, celery, and mushrooms in ¼ cup melted butter or oleomargarine over medium heat, stirring from time to time. Add tomatoes, parsley, and Burgundy or Claret. Season to taste with salt and pepper. Cook over low heat, stirring gently (so that tomatoes will not be broken into small pieces) from time to time, for 8 minutes. Five minutes before steak reaches desired point of doneness, if it is not a rich brown, brush lightly on both sides with Kitchen Bouquet. When cooking time expires for the steak, remove from oven and sprinkle liberally on both sides with salt and pepper. Place on hot platter and arrange tomato-mushroom mixture on top of steak. Surround steak with hot green beans.

Serves 4.

Beef Stroganoff

2½ pounds tender lean
   beef cut in thin narrow
   short strips
⅘ quart Moselle Wine
Salt and pepper
1½ tablespoons finely
   minced onion
1 tablespoon finely minced
   chives
1 teaspoon dehydrated
   parsley
⅓ cup butter or
   oleomargarine

2 tablespoons flour measured
   and then sifted
1½ cups hot beef stock or
   bouillon
½ cup Moselle Wine
   marinade
¾ teaspoon paprika
½ cup small sautéed
   mushrooms
Salt and pepper to taste
1 cup commercial sour
   cream

Cover beef with Moselle and let stand in refrigerator over-night. Drain meat and reserve ½ cup marinade. Sprinkle beef with salt and pepper. Mix with onion, chives, and parsley. Melt all but 2 tablespoons of butter or oleomargarine in skillet and heat until bubbling (360° F.). Add beef mixture and cook until meat is tender and lightly browned. Set meat aside. Melt remainder of butter or oleomargarine. Remove from heat and stir in flour. Return to stove and cook over low heat, stirring constantly, until thickened but not brown. Again remove from heat and stir in stock or bouillon and marinade until blended. Pour into top of double boiler and add paprika, meat, and mushrooms. Season to taste with salt and pepper. Cook over boiling water, stirring from time to time, until sauce is thick (about 15 minutes). Just before serving, add sour cream and cook only long enough over hot but not boiling water to heat mixture thoroughly.
Serves 6.

Chili

3 tablespoons salad oil	2 cups canned or stewed
3/4 cup finely minced onion	tomatoes
1 1/2 large finely minced	1 cup water
garlic pods	1 cup Red Wine
2 tablespoons minced	3 tablespoons chili powder
parsley	1/8 teaspoon cayenne
1 1/2 pounds ground beef	Salt and black pepper to
	taste

Heat oil in skillet. Cook onion and garlic in bubbling oil
(360° F.) until onion is clear. Add parsley and ground beef.
Continue cooking, stirring occasionally, over medium heat until meat grains stand apart. Add tomatoes, water, and Wine.
Bring to a boil. Add chili powder, cayenne, and salt and black
pepper to taste. Cover pan and cook over very low heat 1 hour,
stirring from time to time.
Serves 4.

Corned Beef or Tongue

5–6-pound corned beef or pickled tongue
1/4 teaspoon black pepper
2 bay leaves
1 cup chopped onion
2 cups White Wine
Water to cover
2 unpeeled, quartered apples, if desired

Wash beef or tongue and, if salty, soak until free of excess
salt. Place meat in a deep heavy skillet. Add pepper, bay leaves,
onion, White Wine, and water to cover. If desired, apples may
be added. Bring to a boil. Cover pan, reduce heat, and allow

to simmer over very low heat for 2¾–3¼ hours until meat or tongue is tender. Remove skin and cut off roots of tongue. Serve hot or cold.
Serves 8–10.

Daube

4–5-pound beef shoulder roast	*1 tablespoon minced parsley*
1 large clove garlic cut in slivers	*1 bay leaf*
	¼ teaspoon thyme
1½ cups Red Wine	*½ cup chopped green pepper*
Salt and pepper	
3 tablespoons bacon grease, butter, or oleomargarine	*½ cup mushroom pieces*
	1 cup boiling water
¾ cup sliced onion	*Marinade*
	Salt and pepper

Make 4 or 5 slits in roast and insert slivers of garlic. Place in bowl and pour Wine over meat. Cover bowl and store in refrigerator for 3 or 4 hours, turning meat in marinade several times. Remove meat and reserve marinade. Sprinkle meat heavily with salt and pepper. Melt bacon grease, butter, or oleomargarine in deep heavy skillet and when fat bubbles (360° F.), sear roast until rich brown on all sides. Remove daube. Lightly brown onions in fat in which meat was seared. Add meat, parsley, bay leaf, thyme, green pepper, mushrooms, water, and marinade. Bring to a boil; lower heat and cover. Allow to simmer until tender. Season gravy to taste with salt and pepper.
Serves 8–10.

Daube with Spaghetti

DAUBE *as prepared in preceding recipe*	*4 cups hot boiled spaghetti*
1 cup canned tomatoes	*⅓ cup grated Parmesan or Romano cheese*
1 crushed pod of garlic	
1 teaspoon sugar	

Prepare Daube according to preceding recipe up to point where salt and pepper to taste are added to gravy after meat is tender. Add tomatoes, garlic, and sugar. Then add the salt and pepper specified in Daube recipe. Place hot Daube on center of a platter. Surround with hot spaghetti. Heat tomato gravy thoroughly and pour over hot spaghetti. Sprinkle with grated cheese.
Serves 8–10.

Jellied Daube

3½–3¾-pounds lean top or bottom beef round
⅘ quart Claret
1 bay leaf
¾ cup sliced onion
⅓ cup chopped celery
1 tablespoon dehydrated parsley flakes
½ teaspoon black pepper
1 clove minced garlic
Salt
¼ cup salad oil
Equal parts marinade and water to cover meat
3¾ cups stock in which meat was cooked

Salt and pepper to taste
5 tablespoons gelatine (unflavored)
2 teaspoons vinegar
3 tablespoons Claret
3 stiffly beaten egg whites
¼ cup cooked carrot slices
6 canned hearts of artichokes halved
¾ cup stiff mayonnaise
½ cup commercial sour cream
Creole or hot prepared mustard to taste

Marinate beef round in mixture of Claret, bay leaf, onion, celery, parsley, black pepper, and garlic, and store in refrigerator in covered container for 12 hours. Turn meat in Wine several times during this period. Remove meat and bay leaf from marinade. Sprinkle meat well with salt. Heat salad oil in skillet until it bubbles (360° F.) and sear meat on all sides in hot oil. Place round in deep heavy saucepan (iron preferred). Add equal parts of marinade and water to cover meat. Bring to a boil. Reduce to low heat and cover pan securely. Allow meat to simmer until tender (approximately 2¾–3¼ hours). Remove meat from stock and strain the stock. Chill both the meat and stock in the refrigerator. When stock is cold remove fat. Sprinkle 3¾ cups of stock, seasoned to taste with salt and pepper, with gelatine. Add vinegar and 3 tablespoons Claret. Cook over medium heat, stirring constantly, until gelatine is completely dissolved. Add egg whites and cook over low heat, folding the eggs into the stock until it comes to a boiling point. Strain through a damp cloth into a bowl. Place bowl in a pan of ice and stir gelatine until it starts to set. Pour ¾ inch of the aspic into an oiled large shallow rectangular mold. Slice meat and arrange slices on the aspic. Decorate with carrot slices and hearts of artichokes. Cover meat with remainder of aspic. Refrigerate until firm. Unmold. Combine mayonnaise and sour cream. Season to taste with Creole mustard. Serve the mayonnaise-sour cream sauce with the Jellied Daube. *Serves 6–8.*

Ground Meat with Tomatoes and Corn

2½ pounds ground beef	*1 tablespoon minced celery*
¼ cup Claret	*2 cups canned corn niblets*
Salt and pepper	*4 large tomatoes cut in*
2 tablespoons minced	*thick slices*
parsley	*Salt and pepper*
¼ teaspoon cumin	*¼ teaspoon rosemary*
1 tablespoon minced onion	

Combine meat and Wine. Sprinkle with salt and pepper. Mix in parsley, cumin, onion, and celery. Place layer of ground beef mixture in bottom of greased baking dish. Cover with corn and top with tomato slices. Sprinkle tomatoes with salt, pepper, and rosemary. Alternate layers of the meat, niblets, and tomatoes, sprinkling each tomato layer with salt, pepper, and rosemary. Bake for 40 minutes in 350° F. oven. *Serves 4.*

Hamburger with Wine

1 pound ground beef
2 tablespoons Red
   Burgundy

Butter or oleomargarine
Salt and pepper

An hour before cooking, combine beef and Wine and shape into 4 patties. Store in refrigerator. Rub butter or oleomargarine over skillet until it is well greased and heat (if skillet is equipped with thermostat, set at 360° F.). Cook patties over medium heat 3–5 minutes, depending on degree of rareness desired. Turn and sprinkle cooked side with salt and pepper. Cook 3–5 minutes more. Turn patties and sprinkle liberally with salt and pepper.
Serves 4.

Pot Roast

6-pound bottom round of
   beef
⅘ quart Claret or Red
   Burgundy
Salt and pepper
Flour, if desired
½ cup bacon grease,
   butter, or oleomargarine
½ cup diced carrots
⅔ cup coarsely chopped
   celery
¼ cup minced parsley
¼ cup mushroom pieces
¼ cup chopped onion
½ small clove garlic
   (optional)

1 cup canned or stewed
   tomatoes or 1 cup beef
   bouillon
¾ cup marinade
⅓ cup bouillon
Salt and pepper
1 cup small white cooked or
   canned onions
1 cup partially boiled small
   potato balls
1 tablespoon browned flour,
   if needed
2 tablespoons cold water, if
   needed
¼ cup marinade
Salt and pepper to taste

Cover meat with Wine about 6 hours before ready to cook. Let stand in refrigerator, turning roast several times during this period. Remove meat and reserve 1 cup of marinade. Sprinkle round with salt and pepper liberally and, if desired, dredge with flour. Heat bacon grease, butter, or oleomargarine until it bubbles (360° F.). Brown roast on all sides in the hot fat and place in deep heavy iron skillet or Dutch oven (with lid). Strain fat and reheat. Add carrots, celery, parsley, mushroom pieces, chopped onion, and, if desired, garlic. Cook only until the onion is clear. Add tomato or 1 cup beef bouillon, ¾ cup marinade, and ⅓ cup bouillon. Season to taste with salt and pepper. Cook over very low heat 5 minutes. Pour over meat. Cover pan tightly and cook over low heat until almost tender (3¾–4½ hours). Add onions and potato balls. Continue cooking until potato balls can be easily pierced with a fork and meat is tender. If gravy is too thin, stir flour into cold water and beat with fork or rotary egg beater until smooth. Stir some of hot gravy into flour mixture and when blended, stir into remainder of gravy. Add ¼ cup of marinade and season to taste with salt and pepper.

Serves 12–14.

Quick Meat Sauce

3 tablespoons salad oil	*½ cup Red or White Wine*
1 pound ground beef	*Salt and pepper to taste*
2 cups SAUCE DIABLO	

Heat salad oil until bubbling (360° F.). Add beef and cook until meat grains stand apart (about 8 minutes). Combine with Sauce Diablo, Wine, and season to taste with salt and pepper. Cook over very low heat for 20 minutes. Serve piping hot.

Serves 4.

Ragout of Beef

2½ pounds top or bottom round of beef cut in chunks
Claret to cover
Salt and pepper
Flour
⅓ cup bacon grease, butter, or oleomargarine
1 tablespoon flour sifted
1½ cups beef stock or bouillon
Marinade
2 scraped carrots cut in slices

2 tablespoons chopped onion
¼ cup minced parsley
¼ cup minced celery
⅓ cup canned mushroom pieces
Salt and pepper
⅛ teaspoon thyme
⅛ teaspoon rosemary
⅛ teaspoon basil
⅛ teaspoon tarragon
2 tablespoons Ruby Port
2 teaspoons Champagne Cognac

Cover meat with Claret and let stand in refrigerator at least 4 hours. Drain marinade from beef, reserving the Claret. Sprinkle meat with salt and pepper and dredge with flour. Heat bacon grease, butter, or oleomargarine until it bubbles (360° F.) and add meat. Brown on all sides. Place meat in deep heavy saucepan and strain grease. Return strained grease to skillet. Heat until it bubbles. Remove from stove and stir in 1 tablespoon sifted flour. Return to stove and cook over medium heat until roux is brown and smooth. Again remove from heat and add stock or bouillon and marinade. Bring to a boil, stirring constantly, and pour over meat. Add carrots, onion, parsley, celery, mushroom pieces, and cook over low heat, covered, 15 minutes. Season to taste with salt and pepper. Add thyme, rosemary, basil, and tarragon. Allow to simmer over low heat until meat is tender (about 45 minutes) in covered pan. Add Port and Cognac and cook over very low heat 5 minutes. Serve very hot.

Serves 6.

Roast Beef

Standing rib, top or bottom
  round, boned or rolled
  beef roast
⅘ quart Claret or Red
  Burgundy
½ cup coarsely chopped
  celery

¼ cup minced parsley
1 scraped carrot cut in
  chunks
Salt and pepper
Kitchen Bouquet

The night before beef is to be roasted, place in a large bowl. Pour Claret or Red Burgundy (an inexpensive Wine may be used for this purpose) over meat until it is almost covered. Add celery, parsley, and carrot. Cover bowl and store in refrigerator until ready to use, turning beef 3 or 4 times while it is in marinade. When ready to roast, remove meat from marinade. Drain and pat dry. Wine may be strained and reserved to be used in gravy.

Sprinkle meat liberally with salt and pepper. Insert meat thermometer in center of thickest part of meat, but do not let thermometer rest in fat or touch the bone. Place meat with fat side up on rack. Roast in uncovered shallow pan in 325° F. oven, in accordance with the following:

	APPROXIMATE TIME MIN. PER POUND	INTERNAL TEMPERATURE AS SHOWN ON MEAT THERMOMETER
Standing Rib		
Rare	26	140° F.
Medium	30	160° F.
Well Done	35	170° F.
Top or Bottom Round		
Rare	15–18	140° F.
Medium	20–24	160° F.
Well Done	26–30	170° F.

	APPROXIMATE TIME MIN. PER POUND	INTERNAL TEMPERATURE AS SHOWN ON MEAT THERMOMETER
Boned or Rolled		
Rare	28	140° F.
Medium	32	160° F.
Well Done	38	170° F.

If a rich brown roast is desired, brush roast with Kitchen Bouquet 15 minutes before cooking time expires. It is suggested that beef be served "au jus," but if gravy is desired, see recipe for PAN-BROWN GRAVY.

Allow ½–⅔ pound per serving for the standing rib roasts and ⅓–½ pound per serving for the top or bottom round or the boned or rolled roasts.

Sauerbraten

5 pounds bottom or top round
1½ tablespoons salt
¾ teaspoon black pepper
1 cup vinegar
⅘ quart Burgundy Wine
Water to cover
2 small bay leaves
6 cloves
¾ cup chopped onion
1 tablespoon dehydrated parsley
¼ cup bacon grease

2 tablespoons sifted flour
8 small gingersnaps crushed
Salt and pepper to taste, if needed
Sugar to taste (1½–2½ tablespoons)
¼ cup Red Burgundy Wine
Water or sugar or vinegar to taste, if needed
⅔ cup commercial sour cream

Wipe beef round and trim off gristle. Sprinkle meat with 1½ tablespoons salt and ¾ teaspoon black pepper. Place in earthenware or glass bowl. Add vinegar, Wine, water to cover, bay leaves, cloves, onion, and parsley. Cover bowl and place in refrigerator for 48 hours, turning 2 or 3 times each day. Remove meat from marinade and strain, reserving 2 cups. Brown meat in hot bacon grease on all sides and then place it in roasting pan. Strain grease and then heat to bubbling (360° F.). Remove from heat and stir in flour. When blended, return to medium heat and cook, constantly stirring, until rich brown. Add marinade and stir until smooth. Add gingersnaps, salt and pepper, if needed, and sugar (all three of the last ingredients are to be added to taste). Stir until thickened and smooth. Pour over roast. Bake in 350° F. oven, basting with sauce from pan every 30 minutes. Allow 28 minutes per pound for roasting. Thirty minutes before cooking time elapses, pour ¼ cup Wine over meat and blend with gravy. Check gravy and if too thick, stir in water; if too sour, stir in sugar and/or water to taste, and if not sour enough, add vinegar to taste. Place meat on heated platter. Bring gravy to boiling point. Stir in sour cream and serve at once.

Serves 10–12.

Steak with Roquefort

Large thick steak	*Kitchen Bouquet*
6 tablespoons Roquefort	*Salt and pepper*
cheese	*⅓ cup Burgundy or Claret*
1 tablespoon dry Sherry	*Parsley sprigs*

Make incisions about 2½ inches apart and about ¾ inch deep in thick large beefsteak. Combine cheese and Sherry. Pack 2 teaspoons of Roquefort-Sherry mixture in each incision. Heat broiler grid for 10 minutes—it must be very hot. Coat 1 side of steak with Kitchen Bouquet and place on grid, which should be about 3 inches below heating unit, coated side up. Cook in accordance with chart in STEAK WITH SHERRY recipe and when time for one side has elapsed, sprinkle liberally with salt and pepper. Turn steak and coat uncooked side with Kitchen Bouquet. Complete broiling steak and sprinkle unseasoned side with salt and pepper liberally. Place steak on hot platter. Stir Burgundy or Claret into juices in broiling pan. Mix well and pour over steak. Garnish with parsley and serve at once.

Allow ½–⅔ pound per serving for steak with bone and ⅓–½ pound per serving for boneless steak.

Steak with Sherry

Thick large steak	*⅔ cup hot Sherry*
Sherry	*Thin slices lemon*
Vegetable oil	*Parsley sprigs*
Salt and pepper	

Several hours before cooking, coat steak on both sides with Sherry. Store in refrigerator until ready to use. Heat broiler grids for 10 minutes—they must be very hot. Immerse steak in oil for 5 minutes. Drain. Place on grid 3 inches under heating unit and broil in accordance with the following:

TOTAL TIME EACH SIDE IN MINUTES

	RARE	MEDIUM	WELL DONE
Porterhouse, Tenderloin, Rib, Fillet, T-Bone, Sirloin, and Club			
1 inch	4	6	10
1½ inches	6	10	12
2 inches	10	14	20

When cooking time for one side has expired, turn steak. Sprinkle cooked side liberally with salt and pepper. Cook required time in accordance with above chart. Sprinkle unseasoned side with salt and pepper. Place steak on heated platter immediately. Pour ⅔ cup hot Sherry into broiler pan, stirring so as to thoroughly mix pan juices with Sherry. Pour over steak. Garnish with lemon slices and parsley sprigs. Serve at once.

Allow ½–⅔ pound per serving for steak with bone and ⅓–½ pound per serving for boneless steak.

Crown Roast of Lamb

2 lamb loins containing ribs
Thin slices of fat pickled pork
Salt and pepper
¾ cup Sauterne
¼ cup water
4 cups cooked green peas (approximate)
¼ cup butter

Scrape the meat from the ribs and trim off backbone. Trim the ends of the bones so that they are short and even. Shape each loin in a semicircle, with the ribs outside, and then sew the two loins together with strong thread to form a crown. Wrap a thin slice of fat pickled pork around the end of each bone to prevent it from burning. Sprinkle roast liberally with salt and pepper. Place on rack in shallow pan. Brown in 500° F. oven. Reduce temperature as soon as meat is browned, to 300° F. Add Sauterne to water and bring to a boil. Pour over roast. Allow 45 minutes per pound for baking (including time meat was browned at 500°), basting with pan juices every 20 minutes. When done, remove pork fat from bones. Heat peas, drain, and add butter. Fill crown with peas.

Allow ½–⅔ pound per serving.

Lamb Chops Flambé

6 1½-inch-thick lamb
   chops
Salt and pepper
Butter
6 large slices canned
   pineapple
¼ cup dry White Wine or
   Cointreau

6 maraschino cherries, which
   have been soaked at least
   12 hours in equal parts of
   their own juice and
   Maraschino Liqueur
¼ cup Rum

Sprinkle chops with salt and pepper. Rub heavy skillet lightly with butter, and heat. Add chops. Cook 9 minutes on each side over medium heat. Arrange chops on serving baking platter. Top each chop with slice of pineapple and spoon Wine or Cointreau over fruit. Place cherry in center of each slice of pineapple. Bake in 375° F. oven for 8 minutes. Heat Rum and pour ⅔ of it over chops. Ignite remainder of Spirit and pour burning Rum over chops. Serve at once.

Serves 6.

Lamb Stew

2½ pounds lamb from
   shoulder and neck cut in
   small pieces
Salt and pepper
⅓ cup bacon grease,
   butter, or oleomargarine
⅓ cup chopped onion
Boiling water
White Wine
Salt and pepper
1 bay leaf

2 tablespoons chopped
   parsley
3 tablespoons chopped
   celery
¼ cup sliced canned
   mushrooms
¼ teaspoon basil
¼ teaspoon rosemary
¾ cup scraped diced
   carrots
1 cup potato balls

Sprinkle lamb with salt and pepper. Heat grease, butter, or oleomargarine in skillet until it bubbles (360° F.). Brown meat and onion in hot fat. Place in deep heavy saucepan and add an equal mixture of boiling water and Wine to cover. Bring to a boil. Lower heat and allow to simmer until meat is almost tender. Season to taste with salt and pepper. Add bay leaf, parsley, celery, mushrooms, basil, rosemary, carrots, and potato balls. Bring to a boil. Reduce heat and cook until carrots and potatoes can be easily pierced with a fork. Serve very hot. *Serves 6.*

Roast Lamb

Leg, shoulder, or boned and rolled shoulder of lamb
White Crème de Menthe
Salt and pepper
Kitchen Bouquet, if desired

Six hours before roasting lamb, brush meat liberally with white Crème de Menthe and let stand in refrigerator until roasting time. Sprinkle meat liberally with salt and pepper. Insert meat thermometer in center of thickest part of meat, but do not let thermometer rest in fat or touch the bone. Place meat with fat side up on rack. Roast in uncovered shallow pan in 325° F. oven, in accordance with the following:

	APPROXIMATE TIME MIN. PER POUND	INTERNAL TEMPERATURE SHOWN ON MEAT THERMOMETER
Leg		
Medium	35	175° F.
Well Done	40	180° F.
Shoulder, Well Done	35	180° F.
Shoulder, Boned and		
Rolled	40	180° F.

If a rich brown roast is desired, brush roast with Kitchen Bouquet 15 minutes before cooking time expires. If gravy is desired, see recipe for PAN-BROWN GRAVY.

Allow ½–⅔ pound per serving for lamb with bone, and ⅓–½ pound per serving for boneless roast.

Barbecued Spareribs

3 pounds meaty spareribs
⅘ quart Burgundy or Claret
Salt and pepper
1½ cups sliced onion
⅔ cup catsup
1 cup marinade
½ teaspoon chili powder

¼ teaspoon basil
2 tablespoons minced parsley
½ teaspoon English mustard
2 teaspoons brown sugar
Tabasco sauce to taste
Salt and pepper to taste

Marinate spareribs in Wine for at least 4 hours, storing in refrigerator during this period. Remove meat from Wine, reserving 1 cup of the marinade for the sauce. Sprinkle spareribs on both sides with salt and pepper. Place layer of the spareribs in deep casserole with a cover. Arrange layer of sliced onions over meat and alternate layers of spareribs and onions until dish is ⅔ filled, ending with a layer of onions. Prepare sauce by combining remaining ingredients. Pour sauce over meat and onions and cover casserole. Bake in 325° F. oven for 1½–2 hours until meat is almost tender. Remove cover and complete cooking meat until tender (about 30 minutes).

Serves 6.

Flaming Stuffed Pork Chops

8 thick pork chops	Salt and pepper
Salt and pepper	Kitchen Bouquet
¾ cup soft bread crumbs	¾ cup butter or
1 cup mincemeat	oleomargarine
⅓ cup finely chopped	(approximate)
peeled apple	⅓ cup White Wine
2 tablespoons Brandy	8 canned apricot halves,
2 tablespoons melted	heated in their own juice
oleomargarine or butter	¼ cup Brandy

Cut pocket in each chop. Sprinkle chop with salt and pepper. Combine crumbs, mincemeat, apple, Brandy, 2 tablespoons melted oleomargarine or butter, and salt and pepper to taste. Stuff pockets with mixture and then sew pockets to meat with heavy thread. Lightly brush chops on both sides with Kitchen Bouquet. Melt ½ cup butter or oleomargarine and heat in skillet until it bubbles (360° F.). Brown 4 chops on both sides and place them in baking serving dish large enough to hold the 8 chops without their overlapping. Add as much of the remaining butter or oleomargarine as is needed to brown the remaining chops on both sides. When these chops are browned, place in baking dish. Pour White Wine over chops. Cover baking dish with aluminum foil and place in 350° F. oven. Bake 55 minutes. Heat apricot halves in their own juice and drain. Arrange hot apricots around chops. Heat Brandy. Pour ⅔ hot Brandy over chops. Ignite remainder of Brandy and pour burning Spirit over meat. Serve at once.

Serves 8.

Fresh Pork Roast

Pork leg, rib and loin, shoulder (picnic), shoulder (boned and rolled), shoulder (butt)
Rum
⅘ quart Sauterne
2 cooking apples cut in quarters
Salt and pepper
Kitchen Bouquet, if desired

Six hours before roasting, brush meat liberally with Rum. Store in refrigerator. Two hours later, place meat in large bowl. Pour Sauterne over it and add apples. Keep in refrigerator until ready to use, turning the pork in the marinade several times during this period. When ready to roast, remove meat from marinade. Drain and pat dry. Wine may be strained and reserved to be used in gravy.

Sprinkle meat liberally with salt and pepper. Insert meat thermometer in center of thickest part of meat, but do not let the thermometer rest in fat or touch the bone. Place meat with fat side up on rack. Roast in uncovered shallow pan in 325°F. oven in accordance with the following:

	APPROXIMATE TIME MIN. PER POUND	INTERNAL TEMPERATURE AS SHOWN ON MEAT THERMOMETER
Leg	45–50	185°F.
Rib and Loin	35–40	185°F.
Shoulder, Picnic	40	185°F.
Shoulder, Boned and Rolled	55	185°F.
Shoulder, Butt	40–50	185°F.

If a rich brown roast is desired, brush roast with Kitchen Bouquet 15 minutes before cooking time expires. If gravy is desired, see recipe for PAN-BROWN GRAVY.

Allow ⅓–½ pound for boned meat and ½–⅔ pound for meat with bone per serving.

Pork Chops Flambé

Salt and pepper	*½ cup dark brown sugar*
4 1¼-inch thick pork chops	*1 tablespoon grated orange rind*
Kitchen Bouquet	*⅛ teaspoon nutmeg*
½ cup melted butter or oleomargarine	*⅛ teaspoon cardamon, if desired*
4 large sliced cored peeled cooking apples	*¼ cup Sauterne*
	⅓ cup Rum

Sprinkle salt and pepper over chops on both sides and coat them with Kitchen Bouquet. Heat butter or oleomargarine in skillet until it bubbles (360° F.). Brown chops on both sides. Put in baking dish. Place sliced apples on chops. Combine sugar, orange rind, nutmeg, and, if desired, cardamon. Cover apples with this mixture and sprinkle with Sauterne. Bake in 350° F. oven for 45 minutes. Heat Rum and sprinkle half of it over the chops. Ignite the remainder and pour at once over chops. Serve immediately.

Serves 4.

Pork Chops with Wine

See recipe for VEAL CHOPS WITH WINE.

Baked Ham Steak with Raisin Sauce

1 cup Sauterne
1 cup seedless raisins coarsely chopped
2-inch-thick slice tenderized ham steak
1 cup water
½ cup sugar
2 teaspoons lemon juice

Pour Wine over raisins and ham and let stand in refrigerator 6 hours, turning the ham in the Wine several times during this period. Place ham in shallow baking dish. Combine raisins and Wine in which they were soaked with water. Cook over very low heat for 10 minutes. Stir in sugar and continue cooking over low heat 5 minutes more. Add lemon juice and pour syrup with raisins over ham. Bake in 350° F. oven for 1 hour.
Allow ⅓–½ pound per serving.

Baked Ham Steak with Pineapple Juice and Cointreau

1½-inch-thick tenderized ham steak
⅓ cup brown sugar
¼ cup pineapple juice
¼ cup Cointreau

Place steak in large shallow baking dish. Sprinkle with brown sugar and pour juice and Cointreau over ham. Bake in 350° F. oven for 1 hour, basting with the Cointreau syrup every 15 minutes.
Allow ⅓–½ pound for each serving.

Ham Olympus (with Cherry-Madeira-Cointreau Glaze)

Pretenderized ham
4 Delicious apples
⅘ quart Sauterne
½ teaspoon cinnamon
½ teaspoon cardamon
12 cloves
1 cup Rum
½ cup Apricot Brandy

1 pound, 1 ounce can Bing
* cherries*
¾ cup liquid from cherries
2 tablespoons cornstarch
½ cup Madeira
¼ cup Cointreau
¼ cup light corn syrup
1 tablespoon lemon juice
Cloves

Place ham in large deep bowl. Cut apples into slices about 1½ inches thick. Attach apple slices to ham with wooden toothpicks. Slowly pour Sauterne over ham and place bowl in refrigerator for 1 hour. Remove apple slices and picks and turn ham. Attach apples to upper side of ham with picks. Add cinnamon, cardamon, and cloves to Rum. Pour spiced Rum over ham very slowly and return to refrigerator for 1 hour. Again turn ham, attaching apple slices to top, and pour Apricot Brandy over ham. Return to refrigerator and let stand in marinade at least 12 hours, turning the ham—putting apples on upper side whenever it is turned—at least 4 times during this period. Cover shallow baking pan with aluminum foil. Place rack on foil. Place ham with apples attached on rack. Cook in 325° F. oven, allowing 20 minutes to the pound. Baste with marinade every 30 minutes during baking period; 20 minutes before cooking time expires, remove ham from oven; remove apples and picks.

Drain cherries and reserve ¾ cup of liquid. Combine a small amount of the reserved juice with the cornstarch and stir until smooth. Gradually add remainder of the liquid, continuing to stir. Add Madeira, Cointreau, and corn syrup. Bring to a boil over medium heat and stir constantly while cooking. Add lemon juice and continue cooking and stirring until mixture thickens and is almost clear. Use 1 cup of mixture for glaze and reserve remainder for sauce.

Carefully remove the rind from the ham. Score the fat with a sharp pointed knife into diamond or square pattern. Insert a clove in the center of each diamond or square. Spread ½ cup of glaze over ham. Bake in 450° F. oven 10 minutes. Remove from oven. Spread on another ½ cup of glaze and cook 10 minutes more in 450° F. oven. Let stand at least 20 minutes before slicing.

Add cherries to remaining cherry juice mixture. Just before serving, cook on low heat and serve as sauce with ham. Sauce may be kept warm in inset pan placed in water jacket of chafing dish while ham is served.

Allow ½–⅔ pound for each serving.

NOTE: Precooked ham may be prepared in same manner, but should only be cooked 45 minutes in 325° F. oven before first coat of cherry glaze is applied. Then continue cooking in same manner as directed for pretenderized ham.

Picnic Ham with Wine

Picnic ham
Cold water if ham is salty
2 cups dry White Wine
Water to cover
4 unpeeled cooking apples
2 2-inch sticks cinnamon
10 cloves
2 small bay leaves
1 teaspoon basil

Rum
Cloves
⅔ cup orange marmalade
¾ cup dark corn syrup
1 tablespoon Brandy and
* 1 tablespoon Curaçao*
* or 2 tablespoons' Grand*
Marnier

Cut small sliver from bottom of picnic ham. If very salty, soak ham for 1 hour in cold water. Place ham in deep large pan. Add Wine, water to cover, apples, cut in halves, cinnamon, 10 cloves, bay leaves, and basil. Bring to a boil. Lower heat and allow to simmer for 1 hour. Place ham in deep bowl. Cover with the liquid, spice, herbs, and apples with which it was cooked. Cover bowl and place in refrigerator. Let stand overnight. Place ham on rack; attach apples with which it was boiled to ham with wooden toothpicks. Place rack in shallow uncovered pan and insert thermometer into ham, being careful not to let thermometer rest in fat or let it touch bone. Cook in 325° F. oven, basting every 20 minutes with Rum. (Total cooking time will be approximately 30 minutes per pound for 5–7 pound ham and 25 minutes per pound for larger picnic hams). When thermometer registers 165° F.—about 20 minutes before baking time expires—remove ham from stove. Remove apples and picks.

Remove rind carefully and score fat with sharp pointed knife into diamond or square pattern. Insert a clove in the center of each diamond or square. Combine marmalade, corn syrup, Brandy and Curaçao, or Grand Marnier. Spread half of mixture over ham. Bake ham in 450° F. oven for 10 minutes. Remove ham from oven; spread remaining glaze over it and bake 10 minutes more at same temperature. Let ham stand 20 minutes before slicing it.

Allow ½–⅔ pound per serving.

Grillades (Veal Steaks)

3 pounds veal round cut in thin slices
Salt and pepper
1½ tablespoons oleomargarine or butter
1 clove minced garlic
2 tablespoons chopped onion
1 tablespoon finely chopped celery
1 tablespoon flour measured and then sifted
3 medium-size peeled and sliced tomatoes or 1 cup canned tomatoes
1 tablespoon minced parsley
3 tablespoons vegetable oil
1½ teaspoons vinegar
½ cup very hot Red Wine
½ cup boiling water
1 small bay leaf
¼ teaspoon orégano
Salt and pepper to taste
Hot steamed rice or boiled spaghetti

Pound veal until tender. Sprinkle on both sides with salt and pepper. Heat oleomargarine or butter until it bubbles (360° F.) and add garlic, onion, and celery. Cook until onion is clear. Remove from heat; stir in flour and return to medium heat. Stir constantly until a rich brown. Add tomatoes and parsley and allow to simmer over very low heat, stirring from time to time, for 5 minutes. Heat vegetable oil until it bubbles (360° F.) and brown grillades on both sides in hot oil. Place meat in tomato sauce. Add vinegar, Wine, water, bay leaf, orégano, and stir until blended. Bring to a boil. Reduce to low heat, cover pan, and allow to simmer for 20 minutes. Season to taste with salt and pepper and cook over low heat an additional 10 minutes. Serve with hot steamed rice or boiled spaghetti. *Serves 8.*

Ragout of Veal

⅘ quart Vin Rosé	2 tablespoons chopped celery
2½ pounds veal cut in 1½-inch squares	1 bay leaf
Salt and pepper	¼ teaspoon thyme
Flour	½ cup coarsely chopped onion
⅓ cup bacon grease, butter, or oleomargarine	½ cup canned mushroom pieces
Marinade	Salt and pepper
1 cup water	
2 tablespoons chopped parsley	

Pour Wine over meat and store in refrigerator at least 4 hours. Drain and reserve marinade. Sprinkle veal with salt and pepper. Dredge with flour. Heat grease until it bubbles (360° F.) and brown meat on all sides in hot grease. Place meat in deep heavy saucepan. Add marinade, water, parsley, celery, bay leaf, thyme, onion, and mushrooms. Bring to a boil. Reduce to low heat and cover pan. Cook 30 minutes and season to taste with salt and pepper. Continue cooking over low heat in covered pan until meat is tender (about 20 minutes). Serve piping hot. *Serves 6.*

Roast Veal

Leg, loin, shoulder, or	*⅓ cup minced parsley*
boneless shoulder of veal	*Salt and pepper*
⅘ quart Vin Rosé	*Kitchen Bouquet, if desired*

The night before veal is to be roasted, place in large bowl. Pour Vin Rosé (an inexpensive Wine may be used for this purpose) over meat. Add parsley. Cover bowl and store in refrigerator until ready to use, turning veal 3 or 4 times while it is in marinade. When ready to roast, remove meat from marinade. Drain and pat dry. Wine may be strained and reserved for gravy.

Sprinkle meat liberally with salt and pepper. Insert meat thermometer in center of thickest part of meat, but do not let thermometer rest in fat or touch the bone. Place meat with fat side up on rack. Roast in uncovered shallow pan in 325° F. oven, in accordance with the following:

	APPROXIMATE TIME MIN. PER POUND	INTERNAL TEMPERATURE AS SHOWN ON MEAT THERMOMETER
Leg	35–40	175° F.
Loin	35	175° F.
Shoulder	40	175° F.
Boneless Shoulder	55	175° F.

If a rich brown roast is desired, brush roast with Kitchen Bouquet 15 minutes before cooking time expires. If gravy is desired, see recipe for PAN-BROWN GRAVY.

Allow ½–⅔ pound per serving for veal with bone, and ⅓–½ pound per serving for boneless roast.

Veal Chops with Wine

6¾-inch-thick veal chops
Salt and pepper
Kitchen Bouquet
½ cup butter or
  oleomargarine
½ cup Sherry or White
  Wine

¼ cup water
1 tablespoon minced parsley
1 tablespoon minced celery
¼ cup sliced canned
  mushrooms
¼ teaspoon sweet basil

Sprinkle chops with salt and pepper. Brush one side lightly with Kitchen Bouquet. Heat butter or oleomargarine until it bubbles (360° F.). Place chops, coated side down, in skillet. Cook 8 minutes. Coat side that is up with Kitchen Bouquet. Turn chops and cook 8 minutes. Stir in Sherry or White Wine, water, parsley, celery, mushrooms, and basil. Bring to boiling point. Reduce to very low heat (about 230° F.). Cover pan and cook 20–35 minutes, depending on size of chops.
Serves 6.

Veal Roasted in Barbecue Sauce

3½–4-pound rolled
  shoulder of veal
Salt and black pepper
⅔ cup tomato catsup
¾ cup Claret or Red
  Burgundy

1 tablespoon Worcestershire
  sauce
¼ teaspoon Tabasco sauce
2 tablespoons vinegar
1½ teaspoons celery seed
¾ teaspoon dry mustard

Rub roast with salt and pepper. Mix remaining ingredients. Place meat in roaster. Pour catsup mixture over roast. Cover pan. Bake in 325° F. oven, basting with barbecue sauce every 30 minutes until meat is tender and cooked through (approximately 3½ hours).
Serves 6–8.

NOTE: If desired, ¾ cup of Claret or Red Burgundy may be poured over meat 6–8 hours before baking. Roast should be stored in refrigerator. When ready to cook, drain wine from meat and follow above recipe, using marinade where the ¾ cup Claret or Red Burgundy is specified.

Croquettes

2 cups cooked meat
Thick Wine-flavored
   CREAM SAUCE
Salt and pepper to taste

Cracker meal
1 slightly beaten egg
Deep fat

Pass meat through coarse blade of meat grinder. Combine with just enough Cream Sauce to hold meat together and season to taste with salt and pepper. Chill for 1 hour. Shape into pyramids and return to refrigerator for another hour. Dip pyramids in meal, then in egg and again in meal. Cook until golden brown on all sides in 375° F. fat to a depth of 3–4 inches. Drain on absorbent paper.
Makes 6 croquettes.

Hash

2 cups cubed cooked beef,
   veal, or lamb, from which
   bones and gristle have
   been removed
2 tablespoons butter or
   oleomargarine
2 tablespoons sifted flour
¾ cup meat stock
   (approximate)

⅓ cup Red Wine
1¾ cups raw potatoes cut
   in small cubes
2 tablespoons minced
   parsley
1 tablespoon minced onion
Salt and pepper

Cut meat in 1-inch cubes. Melt butter or oleomargarine until it bubbles (360° F.). Remove from heat. Stir in sifted flour.

Return to medium heat. Stir constantly and cook until a rich brown and smooth. Add stock and Wine. Cook until thickened and very smooth. Then add meat, potatoes, parsley, and onion. Cook for 10 minutes over low heat and add salt and pepper to taste. Continue cooking until potatoes can be easily pierced with a fork. Stir occasionally while cooking so that hash will not stick in bottom of pan, and if necessary, add additional stock. *Serves 6.*

Swedish Meat Balls with Sour Cream

⅓ *pound ground veal*
½ *pound ground beef*
¼ *pound ground pork*
1½ *cups soft bread crumbs*
⅓ *cup half-and-half (half milk and half cream)*
2 *tablespoons Sherry*
2 *tablespoons butter or oleomargarine*
½ *cup onion minced fine*
¾ *teaspoon poultry seasoning*
¼ *teaspoon dry mustard*

2 *eggs well beaten*
Salt and pepper to taste
½ *cup butter or oleomargarine (approximate)*
2 *tablespoons sifted flour*
⅔ *cup hot canned bouillon (not diluted)*
⅔ *cup hot water*
⅔ *cup hot White Wine*
1 *cup commercial sour cream*
Salt and pepper to taste

Grind meats together. Soak bread in half-and-half and Sherry for 30 minutes. Squeeze bread until nearly dry and combine with the ground meat. Heat 2 tablespoons butter or oleomargarine until it bubbles (360°F.). Cook onion in hot fat until it is clear. Combine onion, poultry seasoning, mustard, and eggs with meat mixture. Season to taste with salt and pepper. Roll into 50 small balls. Melt part of the ½ cup butter or oleomargarine and heat to 360°F. Brown 10–12 balls on all sides. Store on hot platter in warm oven. Continue browning the meat balls, 10 or 12 at a time, being careful never to crowd the skillet and using additional butter or oleomargarine as needed. Place the meat balls in the oven as they are browned. When all the meat is cooked, strain fat from skillet. Return 2 tablespoons of fat to the skillet and heat until it bubbles (360° F.). Remove from heat and stir in flour until blended. Again return to heat and continue to stir until thick and smooth. Add bouillon, water, and Wine, and stir until thickened. Add meat balls. Cook 4–5 minutes. When ready to serve, heat, stir in sour cream, and season gravy to taste with salt and pepper. *Makes 50 small meat balls.*

Liver, Bacon, and Onions

½ *pound bacon cut in thin slices*
1½ *pounds young calves' liver cut in ¼-inch-thick slices*
Salt and pepper
Flour
Bacon grease
3 *tablespoons butter or oleomargarine*

½ *cup onion cut in thin strips*
2 *tablespoons minced parsley*
½ *cup boiling water*
¼ *cup dry White Wine*
Salt and pepper

Fry bacon over low heat. Wrap in absorbent paper towels and keep in warm oven. Remove membranes from liver slices. Sprinkle well with salt and pepper and sift flour lightly over both sides of liver slices. Heat enough bacon grease to cover bottom of skillet. Place liver in hot grease and cook until browned on both sides. Reduce heat until it is very low and cook 4 minutes more. Put liver on hot platter and keep in warm oven.

Drain bacon grease from skillet. Melt butter or oleomargarine. Add onion and parsley and cook until onion is very lightly browned, stirring constantly. Add water and Wine. Bring to a boil and reduce heat. Cook over low heat until liquid is reduced to approximately one half of original quantity. Season to taste with salt and pepper. Pour sauce over liver and garnish with crisp bacon.

Serves 6.

Irish Stew

3 pounds mutton, beef, or veal cut into 2–3-inch chunks	*Marinade*
	Water to cover
	Salt and pepper
1 cup Red or White Wine	*4 small Irish potatoes cut in small chunks*
Salt and pepper	
½ cup butter or oleomargarine	*3 small carrots scraped and cut in thin slices*
⅓ cup chopped onion	*2 teaspoons Worcestershire sauce*
2 tablespoons chopped celery	
2 tablespoons minced parsley	*¼ cup dry White or Red Wine*

Four hours before cooking, sprinkle meat with 1 cup Wine and store in refrigerator. Turn meat in marinade several times during this period. Remove meat from Wine, reserving the marinade. Sprinkle meat well with salt and pepper. Melt butter or oleomargarine until it bubbles (360° F.). Brown meat in hot fat and place in deep heavy saucepan (preferably iron). Cook onion in fat until clear. Add onion, celery, parsley and marinade to meat, and water to cover. Bring to a boil. Reduce heat and cover pan. Cook over very low heat for 45 minutes.

Season to taste with salt and pepper. Cook, covered, for 30 minutes more. Add potatoes, carrots, and Worcestershire sauce. Cover and let simmer until potatoes and carrots can be easily pierced with a fork (about 15 minutes) and meat is tender. Add ¼ cup Wine and bring mixture to a boil. Serve very hot.
Serves 8.

Creamed Sweetbreads

1¼ pounds sweetbreads	*1½ cups Wine-flavored*
Cold water	CREAM SAUCE
2 cups water	*½ cup canned button*
1 teaspoon salt	*mushrooms*
2 teaspoons vinegar or lemon	*2 tablespoons finely chopped*
juice	*green pepper*
	4 large pieces toast

Soak sweetbreads in cold water for 10 minutes. Bring to a boil water, salt, and vinegar or lemon juice. Add sweetbreads and reduce heat. Cook over very low heat for 20 minutes. Drain and separate into small pieces. Combine sweetbreads, Cream Sauce, mushrooms, and green pepper. Heat thoroughly and serve on toast.
Serves 4.
NOTE: Most markets sell sweetbreads from which pipes and membranes have been removed and which have been frozen. In the event that fresh sweetbreads are obtained, with the pipes and membranes, follow above recipe up to the point where the sweetbreads are cooked and drained. Immediately place in cold water and remove membranes and pipes. Separate into small pieces.

Sweetbreads and Artichokes

1½ pounds cooked
    sweetbreads (see recipe for
    CREAMED SWEETBREADS)
1 cup scalded whipping
    cream
3 tablespoons Cream Sherry

Salt and pepper to taste
6 large hot fresh boiled
    artichoke hearts from which
    leaves and chokes have
    been removed

Place sweetbreads in a shallow pan. Combine cream and Sherry and pour over sweetbreads. Bring to a boil; turn down heat and cook over low heat until cream mixture is reduced to ¾ original quantity. Season to taste with salt and pepper. Place artichoke hearts on warm platter and arrange sweetbreads on and around the artichoke hearts. Pour cream-Sherry mixture over them.
Serves 6.

Sweetbread Croquettes

1½ pounds cooked
    sweetbreads (see recipe for
    CREAMED SWEETBREADS)
½ cup canned mushroom
    pieces
Thick Sherry-flavored CREAM
    SAUCE

Salt and pepper, if desired
Cracker meal or bread crumbs
1 egg slightly beaten
Deep fat

Chop cooked sweetbreads and mushrooms into very small pieces. Add just enough Cream Sauce to mixture to hold it together and season to taste with salt and pepper. Heat thoroughly and then place in refrigerator for 1 hour. Form into 6 small pyramids. Return to refrigerator for 1 hour. Dip pyramids in meal or crumbs, then in egg and again in meal or crumbs. Let stand 30 minutes. Fry in 375° F. fat to a depth of 3–4 inches in a deep skillet until golden brown on all sides. Drain on absorbent paper.

Serves 6.

Jellied Tongue

Large tongue
3 cups Vin Rosé or White Wine
5 cups water
4 teaspoons salt
½ teaspoon black pepper
½ cup sliced onion
¼ cup scraped diced carrot
¼ cup minced parsley

¼ cup chopped celery
1 tablespoon gelatine
½ cup cold stock
1 cup boiling stock
Salt and pepper to taste
⅓ cup sliced pimiento-stuffed olives
Plum tomatoes or wedges of tomato
Endive or watercress

To the tongue add Wine, water, salt, and pepper. Bring to a boil. Add onion, carrot, parsley, and celery. Again bring to a boil and reduce heat. Cover pan and cook over low heat until tongue is tender. Remove from stock. Cut off roots and remove skin of tongue. Place in refrigerator to chill. Strain stock and reserve.

When tongue is chilled, sprinkle gelatine on cold stock. Pour boiling stock over gelatine and, if needed, add salt and pepper to taste. Store in refrigerator until gelatine is almost set. Slice tongue. Pour a ⅜-inch layer of aspic into an oiled loaf pan. Arrange layer of meat slices and olives on aspic. Cover with another layer of aspic. Alternate layers of tongue and olives with layers of gelatine, ending with gelatine layer. Place in refrigerator to congeal. Unmold. Garnish with tomatoes and salad greens.

Allow ⅓–½ pound tongue per serving.

Stewed Tripe

2 *pounds tripe*
3 *tablespoons butter or*
   oleomargarine
1 *tablespoon flour measured*
   and then sifted
1 *cup boiling water*
1 *cup stewed or canned*
   tomatoes
¾ *cup Red Burgundy*

1 *bay leaf*
⅛ *teaspoon basil*
⅛ *teaspoon thyme*
⅛ *teaspoon marjoram*
¼ *cup minced onion*
3 *tablespoons minced parsley*
¼ *cup canned mushroom*
   pieces
Salt and pepper to taste

Scald and clean tripe well. Cut in narrow strips about 2 inches long. Melt butter or oleomargarine in skillet and when it bubbles (360° F.), brown tripe in melted fat. Remove tripe to saucepan. Strain grease and return it to skillet. Heat and stir in flour. Continue stirring until brown and smooth. Add water, tomatoes, and Wine. When blended, cook over low heat, continuing to stir, until thickened. Add remaining ingredients and pour sauce over tripe. Cook in covered pan over low heat until tripe is tender.

Serves 6.

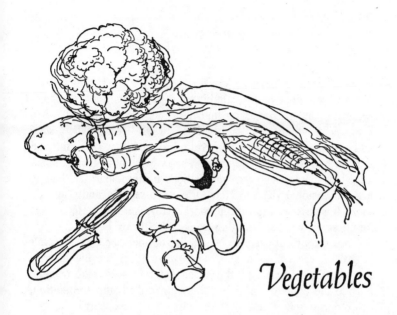

Vegetables

I can never think of the combination of Spirits and vegetables without recalling something that happened long years ago when I was very young. Mississippi has always been a "dry" state and anyone who wanted to entertain his friends by offering them a drink had to keep a supply of Whisky brought in from Louisiana. Uncle Leo, who was my father's business partner, had to make occasional visits to New Orleans to see his family and do some business in the cotton market for the store. He always found some way of bringing back a bottle or two.

Once on a return trip to Magnolia, he met one of the town's judges on the train—a man who was known for his severity as well as his fairness on the bench, but who was quite friendly outside the courtroom. When the train pulled into the station, the judge asked if he couldn't help Uncle Leo carry the two large vegetable baskets he had with him. My uncle handed him one.

Since there was very little entertainment in Magnolia in those days, people often went down to the station to watch the train come in, so there was a sizable number of the judge's constituents on hand as he got off the train carrying a basketful of Whisky and Beer thinly concealed by a layer of vegetables. Uncle Leo carried the basket that contained only vegetables.

The judge, incidentally, went to his grave unaware of his conspiracy in smuggling.

Of all the vegetables I serve, the two that have caused the most comment from my guests are SWEET POTATOES FLAMBÉ and EGGPLANT AND CHICKEN LIVERS. While we don't ordinarily think of a vegetable as being spectacular, SWEET POTATOES FLAMBÉ is a spectacular in technicolor with its rounds of orange sweet potatoes topped with golden rings of pineapple, which

are, in turn, topped with brilliant red maraschino cherries, all
surrounded by dancing blue Rum flames. And it's as delicious
as it is beautiful!

When I serve the EGGPLANT AND CHICKEN LIVERS, my
guests always say, "I've never tasted anything like this," and
then they say, "What is in it?" and finally most of them ask
for the recipe. Since it is part of my Magnolia upbringing to
share recipes, of course they get it.

A "quickie" with an exciting flavor is BUTTER BEANS WITH
HOT SAUTERNE MAYONNAISE SAUCE. The tender beans blend
superbly with the hot sauce, which can be prepared in a matter
of a very few minutes, and the result is a dish worthy of the
finest chef.

Since I have lived in New Orleans for so many years, no
recipe collection of mine would be complete without one for
red beans. It is perhaps a little strange that in a city where
the art of haute cuisine is so highly appreciated, one of the
most popular dishes is made with the red bean. A really sat-
isfying meal for a family of six—if you don't have six in the
family, the cooked beans can be put away for another day in
the refrigerator or freezer without any sacrifice in flavor—can
be prepared at an astonishingly low cost. It's a meal that the
children in the family will love. In fact, many New Orleans
children when asked what they want for their birthday dinners
will answer without hesitation, "red beans and rice." So I suggest that you seek out some dried red beans (sometimes known
as kidney beans) and serve your family DRIED RED BEANS
cooked with Wine and pickled pork, steamed rice, a green salad,
and a simple dessert such as FRUIT WITH COINTREAU-CURACAO
GELATINE, WINE GELATINE or BAKED CUSTARD WITH GRAND
MARNIER-BUTTERSCOTCH TOPPING.

Artichoke Hearts with Chicken and Ham

8 boiled artichoke hearts
from which leaves and
chokes have been removed
¼ cup bread crumbs
1 tablespoon dry White Wine
2 teaspoons chopped chives
1 tablespoon minced parsley
2 tablespoons canned
minced mushrooms
⅓ cup finely chopped boiled
ham

½ cup finely chopped
chicken
Melted butter
Salt and pepper to taste
¾ cup dry White Wine
⅛ teaspoon minced thyme
1 small bay leaf crumbled
1 tablespoon butter
1 tablespoon sifted flour
½ cup dry White Wine
Salt and pepper to taste

Place boiled artichoke hearts in shallow wide pan. Mix bread crumbs, 1 tablespoon Wine, chives, parsley, mushrooms, ham, chicken, and just enough melted butter to hold mixture together. Season to taste with salt and pepper. Fill the artichoke hearts with mixture. Combine ¾ cup Wine with thyme and bay leaf. Pour around artichokes. Cover pan tightly (if no cover is available, use aluminum foil). Cook over very low heat for 15 minutes. Place artichoke hearts on hot platter and store in warm oven. Melt the tablespoon butter. Remove from heat and stir in flour. Return to medium heat and cook, constantly stirring, until smooth and thickened. Stir in ½ cup White Wine (if desired, liquid in which artichoke hearts were cooked may be used and, if needed, additional Wine to make ½ cup may be added). Continue cooking, stirring constantly, until blended. Season to taste with salt and pepper. Pour over hot artichokes and serve at once.

Serves 8.

Stuffed Artichokes

6 small artichokes
3½ cups bread crumbs
¼ cup White Wine
1 tablespoon very finely
  minced or grated onion
¼ cup canned minced
  mushrooms
¼ teaspoon thyme
¾ cup finely minced ham
2 teaspoons finely minced
  celery

2 tablespoons minced parsley
2 tablespoons Parmesan
  cheese
⅛ teaspoon cayenne pepper
Salt to taste
⅓ cup olive oil
3 cups water (approximate)
1 cup White Wine
2 teaspoons salt

Wash artichokes and open out leaves. Sprinkle crumbs with ¼ cup Wine and then add onion, mushrooms, thyme, ham, celery, parsley, cheese, cayenne pepper, and salt to taste. Pack mixture between artichoke leaves and tightly fit the artichokes into pan. Pour olive oil between the leaves. Combine water, 1 cup Wine, and 2 teaspoons salt, and fill pan to a depth of 2½ inches with the mixture—additional water may be added if needed. Cover with lid that fits tightly on pan or with aluminum foil and cook over low heat until a leaf can be easily pulled from artichoke (45–55 minutes). Serve hot or cold.
Serves 6.

Artichokes with Truffle Stuffing

6 slices bread
White Wine to cover
½ cup butter
1 cup button mushrooms
4 ounces truffles
¼ cup minced boiled ham
¼ cup Wine squeezed from
  bread

2 tablespoons tomato juice
⅛ teaspoon thyme
2 tablespoons Sherry
Salt and pepper to taste
8 hot boiled artichoke
  hearts from which chokes
  and leaves have been
  removed

Soak bread in Wine for 30 minutes. Squeeze bread and then mash it with a fork so that there are no lumps. Reserve ¼ cup White Wine squeezed from bread. Melt butter in skillet until it bubbles (360° F.). Sauté mushrooms and truffles. Add bread, ham, ¼ cup Wine squeezed from bread, and cook over medium heat, stirring until blended. Add tomato juice, thyme, Sherry, and season to taste with salt and pepper. Arrange hot boiled artichoke hearts on platter. Fill each heart with truffle mixture and serve at once.

Serves 8.

Asparagus with Sherry-flavored Cream or Cheese Sauce

> *2 pounds hot cooked asparagus (fresh, canned, or frozen)*
> *1 cup hot Sherry-flavored* CREAM SAUCE *or 1 cup hot Sherry-flavored* CHEESE SAUCE

Drain hot cooked asparagus and place in serving dish. Pour hot Cream or Cheese Sauce over vegetable.

Serves 6.

Boston Baked Beans

> *1 quart navy or pea beans*
> *Water in which to soak beans*
> *Water to cook beans*
> *½ teaspoon soda*
> *⅓ cup molasses*
> *½ cup sliced onion*
>
> *1 teaspoon dried mustard*
> *1 tablespoon salt*
> *½ teaspoon black pepper*
> *⅔ pound pickled pork*
> *4 parts water to 1 part White Wine*
> *Salt and pepper, if desired*

Soak beans in cold water 8–10 hours. Drain and rinse. Place beans in a large heavy pan and cover with water. Add soda and cook over medium heat until skins are loose (approximately 2¼–2¾ hours). Drain and rinse with cold water. Mix beans, molasses, onion, mustard, salt, and pepper. Place the pickled pork in the bottom of the bean pot or baking dish. Add beans and cover with a mixture of 4 parts water to 1 part Wine. Place top on bean pot or baking dish. Bake in 250° F. oven for a minimum of 5 hours—for best results beans should be cooked 10 hours. As water and Wine cook away, additional water and Wine mixed in the ratio of 4 to 1 may be added. Remove cover and check seasoning. If needed, add salt and pepper to taste. Gently pull pork to top of beans 1¼ hours before cooking time expires and bake uncovered remainder of time.

Serves 8–9.

Butter or Lima Beans with Hot Sauterne Mayonnaise

½ cup stiff mayonnaise
2 tablespoons sweet Sauterne
⅙–¼ teaspoon cayenne
*   pepper (to taste)*

2 cups hot cooked and
*   drained (frozen, fresh, or*
*   canned) butter or lima*
*   beans*
1 tablespoon minced parsley

Combine mayonnaise, Wine, and cayenne. Heat over boiling water, stirring constantly. Place beans in serving dish and as soon as sauce is heated, pour over beans. Sprinkle parsley over sauce.

Serves 6.

Dried Red or Lima Beans or Black-eyed Peas

1 pound dried beans or peas
1 pound pickled pork
4 cups water
1 cup White Wine or Vin Rosé
3 tablespoons minced parsley
⅔ cup minced onion

½ cup chopped celery
½ teaspoon sweet basil
2 small bay leaves
¼ teaspoon marjoram
¼ teaspoon Tabasco sauce
Salt and pepper
Steamed rice

Soak beans or peas overnight in water. Drain and wash. Place pickled pork in a deep heavy saucepan and add water and Wine. Bring to a boil. Add beans, parsley, onion, and celery. Again bring to a boil. Lower heat and cover pan. Cook over low heat 1 hour. Add basil, bay leaves, marjoram, Tabasco, and season to taste with salt and pepper. Cook until beans or peas are tender (approximately 30 minutes more for peas and 1 hour longer for beans) over low heat in covered pan. Stir from time to time to prevent beans or peas from sticking to bottom of pan. Mash a few of the peas or beans in gravy to thicken it. Serve very hot with steamed rice.

Serves 6.

Red Cabbage with Raisins and Chestnuts

½ cup raisins
Sweet Sauterne to cover
1 head red cabbage
Boiling water
3 tablespoons bacon grease
Salt and pepper

½ cup boiled chopped chestnuts
1 tablespoon dark brown sugar
¾ cup water
¼ cup sweet Sauterne marinade

The night before cooking cabbage, cover raisins with sweet Sauterne. Shred cabbage and place in colander. Pour boiling water over vegetable and then steam over boiling water for 12 minutes. Heat bacon grease until it bubbles (360° F.). Add steamed cabbage and brown over medium heat, stirring from time to time. Add salt and pepper to taste, chestnuts, sugar, water, raisins, and ¼ cup marinade. Cover and cook over low heat for 10 minutes, stirring occasionally to prevent sticking to pan. Serve hot.
Serves 6.

Eggplant and Chicken Livers

½ pound chicken livers cut in small pieces	*2 tablespoons parsley*
Salt and pepper	*¼ teaspoon thyme*
4 tablespoons butter or oleomargarine	*¼ cup Cream Sherry*
⅓ cup finely chopped onion	*Salt and pepper*
⅓ cup chopped celery	*2 tablespoons bread crumbs or Rice Krispie crumbs*
2½ cups boiled eggplant mashed with fork until smooth	*2 teaspoons butter or oleomargarine*

Sprinkle livers with salt and pepper. Heat butter or oleomargarine until it bubbles (360° F.). Add livers and cook 3 minutes over medium heat. Add onion and celery and cook until onion is clear, stirring mixture from time to time. Mash approximately half of livers with a fork. Add eggplant, parsley, thyme, Sherry, and season to taste with salt and pepper. Cook 5 minutes, stirring constantly. Place in baking-serving dish or individual baking dishes. Sprinkle with the crumbs and dot with butter. Bake 20 minutes in 350° F. oven.
Serves 8.

Stuffed Eggplant, Squash, or Vegetable Pears
(with Shrimp, Crabmeat, and Ham)

2 medium-size eggplants or
8 small white squash or 4
vegetable pears boiled
whole
4 slices bread
White Wine
¼ cup butter, oleomargarine,
or bacon grease
2 tablespoons chopped onion
2 tablespoons chopped celery
1 cup chopped deveined
cooked shrimp
1 cup cooked crabmeat

½ cup chopped tenderized
ham
¼ teaspoon thyme
¼ teaspoon basil
¼ cup minced parsley
1 teaspoon monosodium
glutamate
2 slightly beaten eggs
Salt and pepper
¼ cup bread, cracker, or
Rice Krispie crumbs
1 tablespoon butter or
oleomargarine

Cut eggplants or vegetable pears in halves or cut a thin slice from the stem end of each squash. Scoop out pulp. Soak bread in White Wine. Squeeze and reserve 3 tablespoons of Wine in which bread was soaked. Melt ¼ cup butter, oleomargarine, or bacon grease. Add onion and celery and cook until onion is clear. Add bread and vegetable pulp and fry until slightly brown, mashing with a fork so that there are no lumps in the mixture. Add Wine that was reserved, shrimp, crabmeat, ham, thyme, basil, parsley, monosodium glutamate, and cook over medium heat, stirring constantly, for 5 minutes. Set aside to cool. When cool, blend in eggs and season to taste with salt and pepper. Stuff mixture into vegetable shells or spoon into a greased baking dish. Cover tops with crumbs and dot with butter or oleomargarine. Bake in 350°F. oven for 20 minutes.

Serves 8.

NOTE: The above is often used with a salad and a dessert as a "meal in one dish."

French Mushrooms

1 pound mushrooms
½ cup butter or oleomargarine
1½ tablespoons sifted flour
½ cup dry White Wine
1⅓ cups breakfast cream
Salt and pepper

Wash and pat mushrooms dry. Pare only if skins are coarse. Melt butter or oleomargarine until it bubbles (360° F.). Add mushrooms and cook for 5 minutes, stirring constantly, over medium heat. Remove mushrooms to top of double boiler. Strain fat in which they were cooked and return 2 tablespoons of it to skillet. Heat until bubbling; remove from heat and stir in flour until smooth. Remove roux from heat and stir in Wine, cream, and salt and pepper. Cook over low heat, continuing to stir, until sauce is smooth. Pour sauce over mushrooms and cook over boiling water 10 minutes, stirring from time to time. Serve very hot.
Serves 4 generously.

Madeira Mushrooms

⅔ pound mushrooms
½ cup butter or
*   oleomargarine*
1 cup sliced onion
2 tablespoons sifted flour

1½ cups beef or chicken
*   bouillon*
2 tablespoons minced parsley
1 bay leaf
Salt and pepper
3 tablespoons Madeira

Wash and pat mushrooms dry. Pare only if skins are coarse. Melt butter or oleomargarine and heat until it bubbles

(360° F.). Add onion and cook until clear. Remove from heat. Stir in flour until blended. Return to low heat and cook until thickened and a rich brown, continuing to stir. Add bouillon, parsley, bay leaf, and season to taste with salt and pepper. Add mushrooms. Cook over low heat, stirring from time to time, until mushrooms are tender. Two minutes before removing from heat, stir in Madeira until completely blended. Remove bay leaf and serve.

Serves 4.

Stuffed Baked Potato with Vermouth

6 large baking potatoes
2 tablespoons butter
¼ cup heated breakfast
   cream (approximate)
1 teaspoon dehydrated
   parsley

6 tablespoons French
   Vermouth
Salt and pepper
Paprika

Bake potatoes in 400° F. oven for 45–60 minutes until they can be easily pierced with a fork. Cut potatoes in halves and scoop out pulp, being careful not to break the shells. Add butter, cream, parsley, and Vermouth. Season to taste with salt and pepper. Beat with a fork until free of lumps and fluffy. If additional cream is needed to make mixture fluffy, add, but add slowly and cautiously so that potatoes will not be watery. Fill 8 of the shells and sprinkle lightly with paprika. Bake 30 minutes in 425° F. oven.

Serves 8.

Stuffed Baked Potato with Vermouth and Cheese

ONE:

Follow recipe for STUFFED BAKED POTATO WITH VERMOUTH and, when Vermouth is added, add ½ cup grated American cheese. Omit paprika and sprinkle potatoes, after they have been stuffed back into shells, with grated Parmesan cheese.
Serves 8.

TWO:

Follow above recipe, using 3 tablespoons instead of ¼ cup hot cream and adding 1 slightly beaten egg when Vermouth is added.
Serves 8.

Candied Sweet Potatoes

1 cup water (approximate)
⅞ cup sweet Sauterne
2 tablespoons Cointreau
2 cups sugar
¼ teaspoon salt
4 large or 6 medium-size raw sweet potatoes peeled and cut in ½-inch slices

1 tablespoon grated orange rind
¼ teaspoon cinnamon
¼ teaspoon cloves
¼ teaspoon cardamon, if desired

Boil water, Sauterne, and Cointreau with sugar to make a thin syrup. Add remaining ingredients and cook over very low heat until potatoes can be easily pierced with a fork. In the event that syrup cooks away too quickly before potatoes are tender, add a small quantity of water.
Serves 6.

Sweet Potatoes Flambé

4 well-shaped sweet potatoes
(about 3 inches thick and
3–4 inches long)
8 cups water
4 teaspoons salt
½ cup Rum or Cointreau
⅔ cup brown sugar
2 tablespoons grated orange
rind
¼ teaspoon cinnamon
⅛ teaspoon nutmeg
⅛ teaspoon cloves

⅛ teaspoon cardamon, if
desired
12 canned pineapple rings
⅓ cup chopped or broken
filberts or pecans
12 maraschino cherries that
have been soaked
overnight in equal parts of
their own juice and
Maraschino Liqueur
⅓ cup Rum

Wash potatoes and boil in water to which salt has been added until they can be easily pierced with a fork. Remove from water. Chill thoroughly and peel. Cut in 1½-inch slices, crosswise. Place slices of sweet potato in large shallow baking dish. Sprinkle with ¼ cup of Rum or Cointreau. Combine sugar, rind, and spices. Sprinkle ½ of mixture over sweet potato rounds. Top with pineapple rings. Fill ring centers with chopped or broken nuts. Sprinkle pineapple and nuts with ¼ cup Rum or Cointreau and remaining sugar and spice. Place cherry in center of each ring. Bake in 375° F. oven for 15 minutes. Remove from oven. Heat ⅓ cup Rum. Pour all but 1½ tablespoons Rum over potatoes and pineapple. Ignite remainder of Rum and pour lighted Spirit over pineapple. Serve at once.

Serves 12.

NOTE: In the event that potatoes of the desired thickness cannot be obtained, use smaller potatoes, but use pineapple as first layer and do not fill the centers of the rings with nuts. Use potato as second layer and sprinkle nuts over sugar mixture.

Sweet Potato Pudding

3 cups boiled mashed sweet
    potato
2 tablespoons melted butter
⅓ cup white or brown
    sugar (approximate)
1 well-beaten egg
¼ cup Benedictine, Rum, or
    Sherry

¼ teaspoon nutmeg
¼ teaspoon cloves
½ teaspoon cinnamon
¼ teaspoon cardamon, if
    desired
Salt to taste
Marshmallows

Combine all ingredients except marshmallows. If desired, additional sugar may be added to taste. Place in deep greased baking dish and bake in 350° F. oven for 20 minutes. Adjust oven temperature to 450° F. and cover top of pudding with marshmallows (either large or small). Bake until marshmallows are golden brown.

Serves 8.

NOTE: In the event that there is no space in oven for cooking pudding, follow above recipe up to point where pudding is put in deep greased baking dish. Put mixture into top of double boiler and heat thoroughly over boiling water. Just before serving, prepare following sauce:

50 large marshmallows
¼ cup Napoleon Brandy

Place marshmallows in top of double boiler and pour Brandy over them. Melt over boiling water, stirring until well blended.

Place pudding in large deep serving dish, cover with marshmallow-Brandy sauce, and sprinkle heavily with ½ cup toasted almond slivers. Serve at once.

Squash Pudding

24 ounces defrosted frozen
   yellow block squash
Salt and pepper to taste
2 tablespoons Bourbon
   Whisky
2 tablespoons Peach Brandy

¼ teaspoon nutmeg
¼ teaspoon cinnamon
¼ teaspoon cloves
⅓ cup dark brown sugar
Nutmeg

Mix squash, salt and pepper to taste, Whisky, Brandy, ¼ teaspoon nutmeg, cinnamon, cloves, and brown sugar. Spoon into well-greased casserole or individual baking dishes. Sprinkle top(s) with nutmeg. Bake in 375° F. oven for 20 minutes. *Serves 6.*

Baked Stuffed Tomato

6 medium-size tomatoes
Salt
3 slices bread
White Wine
1 tablespoon minced onion
1 tablespoon minced parsley
1 tablespoon minced celery
2 tablespoons bacon grease,
   butter, or oleomargarine

⅛ teaspoon thyme
⅛ teaspoon marjoram
¼ teaspoon basil
1 egg slightly beaten
Salt and pepper to taste
2 tablespoons bread or
   cracker crumbs
2 teaspoons butter

Cut slice from stem end of each tomato. Scoop out pulp. Sprinkle inside lightly with salt and turn tomato cup upside down to drain. Soak bread in Wine. Let stand 15 minutes. Squeeze. Combine onion, parsley, and celery. Heat bacon grease, butter, or oleomargarine until it bubbles (360° F.). Add onion mixture and cook only until onion is clear. Add bread and cook until slightly browned, stirring and mashing with a fork until there are no lumps of bread left. Add herbs and tomato pulp. Stir a small amount of hot mixture into egg and then mix egg with remainder of mixture. Season to taste with salt and pepper. Stuff mixture into tomato cups. Top with bread or cracker crumbs and dot with very small pieces of butter. Bake in 375° F. oven for 20 minutes.

Serves 6.

NOTE: If desired, 1 tablespoon grated Parmesan cheese may be added to crumbs before they are sprinkled on tomato.

Tomatoes Grilled with White Wine and Cheese

6 large firm tomatoes
6 tablespoons Sauterne
Salt and pepper

18 paper-thin slices of
   American or Swiss cheese
   (cut with vegetable parer)
   1×2½ inches
Worcestershire sauce

Cut tomatoes in halves. Carefully pour 1½ teaspoons Sauterne over the cut surface of each half. Place in baking dish and bake for 5 minutes in 400° F. oven. Remove from oven. Sprinkle cut surfaces with salt and pepper and cover with the paper-thin slices of cheese. Sprinkle Worcestershire sauce (allowing 2 dashes to each half) over cheese. Place 4 inches under broiler heating unit and cook until cheese is melted. Serve at once.

Serves 6.

Cooked Fruits

I like to serve fruit with poultry or meat, not only because they go together, but because the fruit makes such a beautiful garnish. As far as I am concerned, food prepared by the world's finest chef but slopped on a plate and served without garnish is hardly worth eating.

Quite often I make a cup of an orange or grapefruit by scooping out the pulp and then I fill the basket thus made with Spirit-flavored preserves, jam, or APPLE or CRANBERRY SAUCE, flavored with Cointreau or Kirsch. I place the cup in the center of a platter of sliced meats or poultry and add a garnish of grapes and sprigs of parsley or watercress. If I am serving a whole roast or bird, I use a border of small orange cups or lemon cups filled with SPIRIT-FLAVORED JAM, preserves, or sauce.

Sometimes I use a border of spiced fruit, fried apple rings, CRYSTALLIZED CITRUS FRUIT PEEL, POACHED GRAPES, STUFFED GREENGAGE PLUMS, SAUTEED CANNED FRUIT, STEWED PEACHES or PEARS, BAKED APPLES, BAKED PEACHES or BAKED PEARS, whole preserved kumquats, or brandied fruit.

For very special occasions I surround the meat or poultry with BANANAS FLAMBE.

PICKLED PINEAPPLE or PICKLED WATERMELON RIND may be used either as a border for the platter or to fill the citrus cups.

Most of these fruits may be used as simple desserts, as well as compotes, and when I say "simple," I mean easy to prepare, because the Spirits make these fruits very special.

Applesauce

8 tart firm apples peeled and
  cored
1 cup sugar
⅜ cup water
2 tablespoons Rum
⅛ teaspoon salt

1 2-inch stick cinnamon
  broken in small pieces
⅛ teaspoon nutmeg
⅛ teaspoon cardamon, if
  desired
2 tablespoons Kirsch or
  Cointreau

Cut apples in small pieces. Combine sugar, water, Rum, and
salt. Bring to a boil and cook until syrup spins a thread. Add
apples, cinnamon, nutmeg, and, if desired, cardamon. Again
bring to a boil. Reduce heat and cook over very low heat until
apples are very tender. Drain and chill in refrigerator. Again
drain so that apples are almost free of liquid. Mash and beat
until apples are smooth and free of lumps. Stir in Kirsch or
Cointreau. Store in refrigerator.
Serves 6–7 depending on size of apples.

Baked Apples

6 tart red apples cored
1 cup sugar
½ teaspoon cinnamon
¼ teaspoon cloves
½ teaspoon nutmeg

Equal parts water and sweet
  Sauterne
2 tablespoons Rum or
  Cointreau

Place unpeeled, cored apples in shallow baking dish. Combine sugar, cinnamon, cloves, and nutmeg. Fill apple centers
with mixture. Cover bottom of pan with equal parts of water
and Sauterne. Bake in 350° F. oven until apples are tender,
basting with pan juices every 10 or 15 minutes during baking
period. Remove from oven. Place on serving dish. Pour 1 teaspoon Rum or Cointreau over each of the baked apples. Chill.
Serves 6.

Spiced Apple Rings

9 small tart firm apples
  peeled and cored
2¾ cups sugar (approximate)
½ cup water
½ cup sweet Sauterne
½ cup vinegar (approximate)

1 2-inch stick cinnamon
  broken in small pieces
10 cloves
3–4 drops red vegetable
  coloring
Rum or Cointreau

Slice apples in ⅔ inch rings. Combine sugar, water, Wine, vinegar, cinnamon, cloves and coloring. Bring to a boil and lower heat. Allow to simmer until syrup will spin a thread (230° F.). Check sweetness and tartness, and if needed, add sugar or vinegar to taste. Drop rings, being careful not to crowd pan, into syrup. Cook over low heat until tender. Place rings in a shallow dish and lightly sprinkle each ring with Rum or Cointreau. When rings are all cooked, pour syrup over them. Chill in refrigerator.

Serves 6–8 depending on size of apples.

NOTE: If desired, spices and coloring may be omitted and 1½ tablespoons Red Cinnamon Candy may be substituted.

Stewed Apples

8 tart firm apples peeled and
  cored
⅓ cup butter or
  oleomargarine
⅔ cup sugar (approximate)
1 tablespoon lemon juice
2 tablespoons Rum

⅓ cup water
½ cup sweet Sauterne
⅛ teaspoon salt
1 2-inch stick cinnamon
  broken in small pieces
10 cloves

Cut apples into eighths. Heat butter or oleomargarine until it bubbles (360° F.) and add apples. Sauté apple slices, turning gently after about 3 minutes, until they are a very light golden brown (about 6 minutes). Sprinkle with sugar, lemon juice, and Rum. Combine water, Wine, and salt, and pour over fruit. Add cinnamon and cloves. Bring to a boil; reduce heat, cover, and cook over very low heat until apples are tender (15–20 minutes). Do not overcook, so the slices will remain whole. Just before apples are removed from heat, check sweetness and, if needed, add additional sugar to taste.

Serves 6–8, depending on size of apples.

Baked Bananas

10 slightly green-tipped	*Sugar*
peeled bananas	*2 teaspoons butter*
Rum	*Rum*

Cut bananas in halves lengthwise. Place in baking serving dish and lightly sprinkle with Rum. Sprinkle fruit heavily with sugar and dot with butter. Bake in 350° F. oven until bananas are golden brown. Lightly sprinkle Rum over the cooked fruit.

Serves 6–8, depending on size of bananas.

Bananas Flambé

8 firm slightly green-tipped	*Brown sugar*
peeled bananas	*⅓ cup Rum*
6 tablespoons butter	
(approximate)	

Cut the bananas crosswise into halves. Melt ¼ cup butter in skillet and when it bubbles (360° F.), add bananas. Reduce heat and cook banana halves slowly (a few at a time, so skillet is not crowded). Add additional butter when and if needed. Turn bananas from time to time until they are a light golden brown on all sides. Place on heated platter (keep fried bananas in warm oven until all the fruit is cooked). Sprinkle with brown sugar. Heat the Rum and pour all but 1½ tablespoons of it over bananas. Ignite remainder of Spirit and pour burning Rum over bananas. Serve at once.

Serves 6–8, depending on size of bananas.

Sautéed Canned Fruits

8 peach or pear halves, 16 apricot halves, or 8 pineapple slices (canned)
¼ cup Cointreau or Kirsch or Rum

⅓ cup butter, bacon, or ham grease
3 tablespoons Cointreau, Kirsch, or Rum

Drain fruit. Brush with ¼ cup Cointreau, Kirsch, or Rum. Melt and heat fat until it bubbles (360° F.). Add fruit and sauté over medium heat until lightly browned on all sides. Sprinkle sautéed fruit with 3 tablespoons of Spirit.

Serves 8.

Brandied Cherries

See recipe for BRANDIED PEACHES, and substitute 6 pounds of cherries for 6 pounds of peaches.

Cranberry Sauce

1½ cups water
½ cup sweet Sauterne
2¼ cups sugar

1 quart washed and stemmed cranberries
2 tablespoons Cointreau or Kirsch (approximate)

Boil water, Wine, and sugar together until syrup will spin a thread (230° F.). Add berries to syrup. Reduce heat, cover pan, and cook 5 minutes over medium heat. Remove cover and continue cooking, without stirring, until skins of berries are soft enough to pop (6–10 minutes). Cool and chill. Stir in Cointreau or Kirsch. Check and, if desired, add additional Spirit to taste.

Makes approximately 4⅔ cups.

Crystallized Citrus Fruit Peel

Rind of 2 grapefruit, 5
  oranges, or 8 lemons
Water
Sugar
Rum, Sherry, or White Wine

Water
Vegetable coloring, if
  desired
Sugar

Cut rind with a vegetable parer from grapefruit, oranges, or lemons. Scrape white membrane from peel and cut peel into thin strips. Put in heavy saucepan and cover with cold water. Bring to boiling point, drain, and cover with cold water. Again bring to boiling point and drain. Repeat covering with cold water, bringing to boiling point, and draining operations 3 times more. Measure peel and measure an equal quantity of sugar. Place peel and sugar in heavy saucepan. Cover with mixture made up of equal parts of Rum and water or equal parts of White Wine or Sherry and water, or ¼ part White Wine, ¼ part Rum, and ½ part water. Bring to a boil. Lower temperature and cook over very low heat until rind is transparent. If green or red rinds are desired, add vegetable coloring just before removing rinds from heat. Let rind stand in syrup for 2 minutes. Lift rinds out with fork, letting each piece drain for a moment. Roll in granulated sugar.

Quantity will depend on size and type of fruit.

NOTE: Five medium-size oranges should have enough rind to make the ¾ cup crystallized peel specified in CHOCOLATE SIPS OF SPIRITS recipe.

Spirit-flavored Fruit Preserves or Jam

1 cup fruit preserves or jam
1 tablespoon Kirsch, Cointreau, or Brandy

Combine preserves or jam with Spirit. Chill.

Poached Grapes

Dessert Sherry, sweet Sauterne, or Vin Rosé
1½ pounds white seedless grapes in small bunches

Bring Wine, enough to cover grapes, to a boil. Place grapes
in Wine. Lower heat and cook 5 minutes over very low heat.
Lift grapes from Wine and chill.
Serves 4.

Baked Peaches

8 peaches
½ cup sugar
Equal parts water and Dessert Sherry or sweet Sauterne

Wash peaches, but do not peel. Rub off fuzz. Place fruit in
baking dish. Combine sugar and enough water and Wine to
cover the bottom of baking dish. Bring sugar mixture to a boil
and pour over peaches. Bake in 375° F. oven until tender, basting with syrup from time to time.
Serves 8.

Brandied Peaches

6 pounds (approximately 18) firm freestone peaches
3 cups water
6 pounds sugar
80-proof Brandy

Select firm freestone peaches and rub off down. Combine water and sugar. Bring to a boil and add fruit. Reduce heat and cook over medium heat until peaches are tender enough to pierce with a straw. Remove peaches with slotted spoon so that most of syrup will be drained from the fruit. Place peaches in hot sterilized jars. Continue cooking syrup until it is very thick. Combine 2 parts of syrup with 1 part of Brandy. Bring to a boil, cook until completely blended and thickened. Pour over fruit until syrup reaches top of jar. Seal securely.
Serves 9.

Stewed Peaches

12 peaches   *¾ cup Dessert Sherry or*
4 cups sugar   *sweet Sauterne*
                                      1¼ cups water

Select firm and preferably freestone peaches. Combine sugar, Wine, and water, and pour over fruit. Cook over medium heat until syrup will spin a thread (230° F.). Add peaches. Bring to a boil. Lower heat and allow to simmer until peaches are tender. If desired, slip skins off peaches. Chill.
Serves 6.

Baked Pears

8 unpeeled cooking pears   ⅓ cup Rum
1 cup sugar   Equal parts water and sweet
½ teaspoon nutmeg or mace   Sauterne
½ teaspoon cinnamon

Wash pears. Cut in halves and remove cores. Place fruit in shallow baking dish; combine sugar and spice and sprinkle each pear half with 1 tablespoon sugar and spice. Sprinkle fruit with Rum and cover bottom of baking dish with a mixture of equal parts of water and Sweet Sauterne. Bake in 375° F. oven until tender, basting with pan juice every 15 minutes. Chill.
Serves 8.

Brandied Pears

See recipe for BRANDIED PEACHES and substitute 6 pounds firm peeled pears (approximately 15), which have been cut into quarters or halves, for the peaches. Add rind and juice of 3 lemons when pears are cooked in sugar syrup.

Stewed Pears

4 cups sugar   8 cooking pears peeled
3¾ cups water   Rum or Cointreau
¼ cup Rum or Cointreau

Boil sugar, water, and ¼ cup Rum or Cointreau until syrup spins a thread (230° F.). Cut pears in halves and remove cores. Add pears to syrup. Lower heat and allow to simmer until fruit is tender. Remove pears from syrup. Sprinkle halves on both sides with Rum or Cointreau. Pour syrup over fruit and chill.

Serves 8.

Brandied Plums

See recipe for BRANDIED PEACHES and substitute 6 pounds of plums (approximately 40 small or 24 greengage) for the 6 pounds of peaches.

Stuffed Greengage Plums

18 firm greengage plums
1 tablespoon butter
1 cup sifted powdered sugar
1 tablespoon Anisette, Cointreau, Rum, or Napoleon Brandy
36 pecan halves
⅓ cup Kirsch

Cut half through plum so that stone can be removed but plum remains in one piece. Cream butter and beat in sugar and 1 tablespoon of Spirit. With the Spirit icing, cement 2 pecan halves together and then cover with the icing. Continue until all the pecans are iced with the Spirit butter cream. Stuff centers of plums with iced pecans and sprinkle fruit with Kirsch. Chill thoroughly before serving.

Serves 6–9, depending on size of plums.

Pickled Pineapple

2½ cups canned pineapple
  chunks
Juice from canned pineapple,
  plus enough canned
  unsweetened pineapple
  juice to make 1⅔ cups
¾ cup wine vinegar
  (approximate)
¼ cup Rum

1½ cups sugar (approximate)
¼ teaspoon salt
10 whole cloves
1 2-inch cinnamon stick,
  broken in pieces
¼ teaspoon nutmeg
⅛ teaspoon cardamon, if
  desired

Drain juice from pineapple chunks and add enough unsweetened pineapple juice to make 1⅔ cups. Combine juice with vinegar, Rum, sugar, salt, and spices. Bring to a boil. Lower heat and allow to simmer until syrup will spin a thread (230° F.). Check sweetness and tartness and, if desired, add sugar or vinegar to taste. Add pineapple and bring to a boil. Lower heat and allow fruit to simmer over very low heat for 5 minutes. Cool, place in sterilized jar or plastic container, and store in refrigerator.

Serves 6.

Pickled Watermelon Rind

Rind of large watermelon
Lime water to cover rind
  (using 1 tablespoon lime
  for each gallon water)
Cold water
2 cups water
6½ cups red wine vinegar
½ cup distilled vinegar
½ cup Sauterne
½ cup Triple Sec
4 cups sugar

10 cups sugar
1 teaspoon mace
1 teaspoon cinnamon
⅛ teaspoon cardamon, if
  desired
10 whole cloves
Sugar, if desired
Distilled vinegar, if desired
Kirsch or Triple Sec, if
  desired

Trim peeling and pulp from watermelon. Cut rind into small pieces. Soak in enough lime water to cover for 24 hours. Rinse rind in cold water. Drain. Combine 2 cups water, wine vinegar, ½ cup distilled vinegar, Sauterne, Triple Sec, and 4 cups sugar. Bring to a boil and add rind. Cook over low heat for 25 minutes. Remove from heat and let stand 5 minutes. Stir in 10 cups sugar and spices. Return to stove and cook over low heat for 30 minutes. Check sweetness and tartness and, if desired, add sugar or vinegar to taste. Cook until watermelon rind is clear (approximately 3½ hours for whole cooking process). Pack rind in hot sterilized jars. Cover with hot syrup. Seal and store. If desired, when ready to serve, remove rind from syrup and sprinkle lightly with Kirsch or Triple Sec. Chill for at least 3 hours before serving.

NOTE: Due to variations in sizes of watermelons, as well as differences in thicknesses of the rinds, different amounts of the pickled rind will be obtained from time to time. There should, however, be between *4–6 pints of pickled rind*.

Sauces,
Salad Dressings,
and Stuffings

A Wine-flavored CREAM SAUCE was my first experience with Spirit cooking. I was about fourteen and had read about great chefs using Wines in their sauces. I was making CHICKEN A LA KING and decided I would try adding some of our homemade (slightly sweet, but in those days I honestly didn't know the difference) Wine to the sauce just to see what would happen. My family loved the Chicken à la King, so from that day on I have never made a CREAM, WHITE, or BROWN SAUCE without Wine. After Prohibition, when good dry White Wines, Sherry, Claret, and Burgundy were again available, I was able to substitute them for the homemade Wines I had been using, and there was, as you can guess, a decided improvement in my cooking.

My favorite sauce is SAUCE DIABLO because I can do so much with it. I usually keep some in a large covered container in my refrigerator, where it can be stored perfectly for weeks. Among the many dishes I prepare with SAUCE DIABLO as a base are: SOUP DIABLO, a hearty and delicious soup that is wonderful for cold days and can be made in 15 minutes; SPANISH OMELET; SPANISH EGGS; BAKED FISH DIABLO, which is fit to set before a king or your most dearly beloved; SHRIMP DIABLO, and QUICK MEAT SAUCE. In an emergency, I sprinkle a large disjointed fryer with salt and pepper, brown the pieces, cover them with SAUCE DIABLO, and then cook them in a covered pan over low heat. In 45 minutes I am ready to serve an excellent main course for a company dinner, arranged on the spur of the moment. When I have SAUCE DIABLO in the refrigerator, I am sure that a good meal for unexpected guests can be worked out with a minimum of trouble.

I have also included some of the Wine-flavored salad dressings, and this is another case where the Spirits add delightful flavor. The SHERRY-ROQUEFORT DRESSING or the SAUTERNE MAYONNAISE, both prepared with commercial dressings as their respective bases, can be made in just a couple of minutes, which is far less time than your family or guests will spend talking about them.

Cream Sauce

2 tablespoons butter or oleomargarine	1 egg yolk well beaten
2 tablespoons sifted flour	¼ cup White Wine or 3 tablespoons Sherry
2 cups hot half-and-half (half milk and half cream)	Salt and pepper to taste

Melt butter or oleomargarine. Remove from heat and stir in flour. Return to medium heat, stirring constantly, until thick. Remove from stove and stir in half-and-half gradually. Cook over medium heat until thick and smooth. Stir a small amount of sauce into egg yolk and, when blended, stir the yolk into the remainder of the sauce. Blend in Wine and salt and pepper to taste. Cook over low heat 3 minutes.

Approximately 1½ cups sauce.

NOTE: In those recipes where a Cream Sauce is specified and Wine is added to the sauce itself in the recipe, omit Wine from the above recipe and substitute ¼ cup half-and-half. This also applies to variations of Cream Sauce.

White Sauce (Thick or Thin)

INGREDIENTS FOR THIN SAUCE

2 tablespoons butter or oleomargarine
2 tablespoons sifted flour
2 cups heated milk, meat, poultry, or fish stock, or 1 cup milk
    and 1 cup stock
¼ cup White Wine or 3 tablespoons Sherry
Salt and pepper to taste

Approximately 1½ cups.

INGREDIENTS FOR THICK SAUCE

4 tablespoons butter or oleomargarine
4 tablespoons sifted flour
1⅞ cups hot milk, meat, poultry, or fish stock, or 1 cup milk
    and ⅞ cup stock
¼ cup White Wine or 3 tablespoons Sherry
Salt and pepper to taste

Approximately 1⅔ cups.

NOTE: For a slightly different flavor, substitute ¼ cup Burgundy (Red) for White Wine or Sherry.

MIXING THE SAUCE: Melt butter or oleomargarine until it bubbles. Remove from heat and stir in flour. Return to medium heat and stir continuously until smooth but not brown. Remove from heat and gradually blend in milk and/or stock. Cook over medium heat, stirring until smooth and thickened. Add Wine and salt and pepper to taste. Cook over low heat until blended.

NOTE: In those recipes where a White Sauce is specified and Wine is also specified to be added to the recipe itself, omit Wine in above recipes and add in its place ¼ cup cream. This also applies to variations of White and Cream Sauce such as Cheese, Asparagus, Mustard, Egg, Shrimp and Mushroom, Oyster, Tomato and Caper Sauce.

Asparagus Sauce

¾ cup puréed cooked or canned asparagus
1½ cups hot Wine-flavored WHITE *or* CREAM SAUCE
Salt and pepper to taste

Combine ingredients and heat thoroughly.

Barbecue Sauce for Chicken or Meat

1¼ cups butter	*Juice and rind of large*
1 small minced clove garlic	*lemon*
⅓ cup chopped onion	*1½ teaspoons brown sugar*
1 tablespoon minced chives	*1 tablespoon dehydrated*
1½ cups water	*parsley*
½ cup Red Wine	*1 tablespoon celery flakes*
1½ cups wine vinegar	*3 tablespoons Worcestershire*
1¾ cups tomato catsup	*sauce*
¼ cup chili sauce	*Tabasco sauce to taste*
	Salt to taste

Melt butter and cook garlic and onion in bubbling fat
(360° F.) until they are clear. Do not let butter or vegetables
brown. Stir in remaining ingredients. Bring to a boil and reduce
heat. Cover pan, cook over low heat, stirring from time to
time, for 20 minutes.
Makes approximately 1½ quarts sauce.

Béarnaise Sauce

2 tablespoons minced shallots
  or chives
2 tablespoons tarragon
  vinegar
2 tablespoons White Wine
¼ cup butter

4 egg yolks
¼ cup boiling White Wine
Salt and pepper to taste
¼ teaspoon fresh tarragon,
  if desired

Combine shallots or chives with vinegar and 2 tablespoons
White Wine. Bring to a boil. Reduce to medium heat and cook
until only 1 tablespoon of liquid remains. Strain and cool.
Melt butter over hot but not boiling water to the depth of 1
inch. Add 1 egg yolk to vinegar mixture and beat until light
and fluffy. Add other 3 yolks and beat until thick and lemon
colored. Slowly add the yolk mixture to the melted butter in
the top of the double boiler, stirring constantly. Be very careful that water in bottom of double boiler does not reach boiling point at any time. Gradually stir in boiling White Wine.
Cook only until mixture begins to thicken. Remove from stove.
Season to taste with salt and pepper and, if desired, add tarragon. Béarnaise should be served as quickly as possible, but
if it is necessary to hold for a short time, cover top of double
boiler and keep it over the hot water in the bottom of the
boiler.
  Makes ¾ cup.

Bordelaise Sauce

¼ cup minced onion
2 tablespoons butter
1¼ cups beef bouillon
1 cup Claret or Red
  Burgundy
2 tablespoons minced parsley

2 tablespoons finely chopped
  canned mushrooms
1 tablespoon browned flour
2 tablespoons cold White
  Wine
Salt and pepper to taste

Cook onion in melted and bubbling butter (360° F.) until lightly browned, stirring constantly. Add bouillon, Claret or Burgundy, parsley, and mushrooms. Allow to simmer over low heat 5 minutes. Dissolve flour in White Wine and beat with fork until smooth. Remove onion mixture from heat and stir in flour paste. Continue stirring until smooth, and cook over low heat until thickened. Season to taste with salt and pepper.
Serves 6.

Brown Sauce

2 tablespoons butter, lard, oleomargarine, or bacon grease
2 teaspoons minced onion
2 tablespoons flour measured and then sifted

1½ cups fish, meat, poultry, or vegetable stock (*hot*)
3 tablespoons Sherry or ¼ cup White or Red Wine
Salt and pepper

Heat fat until it bubbles (around 360° F.). Add onion and cook only until clear. Remove from heat and stir in flour. Return to medium heat and cook, stirring constantly, until thickened and a rich brown. Remove from heat and gradually add stock. Cook over low heat, continuing to stir, until thick and smooth. Add Wine and season to taste with salt and pepper.
Makes about 1⅓ cups.
NOTE: In those recipes where a Brown Sauce is specified and Wine is also specified to be added to the recipe itself, omit Wine from above and add in its place 3 tablespoons stock.

Burgundy Sauce for Steak

1 very small clove garlic
2 tablespoons olive oil
¼ teaspoon black pepper
¼ teaspoon salt
2 tablespoons butter
1 tablespoon minced shallot
¼ cup minced mushrooms

½ teaspoon chives
¾ cup whole button
  mushrooms
⅔ cup Red Burgundy Wine
½ cup tomato juice
Salt and pepper to taste

One hour before cooking steak, cut clove of garlic into 2 pieces and rub wooden bowl with cut clove. Combine oil, pepper, and salt, and pour into the bowl. Cover and let stand. Ten minutes before cooking steak, melt butter and, when it sizzles, add shallot. Cook until tender, stirring constantly. Add minced mushrooms, chives, mushrooms, and Wine. Cook over low heat until mixture boils. Reduce to very low heat and let simmer 2 minutes. Add tomato juice and again bring to a boil. Season to taste with salt and pepper. Reduce heat and allow to simmer until ready to use. Pour oil mixture over very hot steak and then pour hot BURGUNDY SAUCE over the meat. Serve at once. *Serves 4.*

Caper Sauce

2½ cups thin Wine-flavored
  WHITE SAUCE prepared
  without salt
3 tablespoons capers

1 tablespoon caper liquid
Anchovy paste to taste
Salt, if needed

Combine ingredients and stir until well blended. Heat thoroughly.

Cheese Sauce

1½ cups thin hot Wine-flavored WHITE *or* CREAM SAUCE
⅔ cup grated Cheddar cheese
2 tablespoons Worcestershire sauce

Combine White or Cream Sauce and cheese. Cook over medium heat, stirring constantly until cheese is melted and completely blended into sauce. Add Worcestershire sauce and heat thoroughly.

Egg Sauce

1½ cups hot thin Wine-flavored WHITE *or* CREAM SAUCE
4 coarsely chopped hard-cooked eggs
2 tablespoons chopped green pepper
⅔ cup canned button mushrooms
⅛ teaspoon turmeric
Salt and pepper to taste

Combine ingredients and heat thoroughly.

Gin 'n' Sauce

¾ cup commercially prepared tartar sauce
¼ cup tomato catsup
2 tablespoons Gin

Combine ingredients and spoon into bowl. Embed bowl in finely chopped ice and serve at once.
Makes about 1 cup.

Pan-brown Gravy

WITH PAN BROWN:

*1½ cups boiling bouillon or
    water
Pan brown*

*¼ cup desired Wine
Salt and pepper to taste*

Pour boiling bouillon or water over pan brown. Stir until thoroughly combined. Add Wine and salt and pepper to taste. Heat thoroughly.

Makes 1¾ cups gravy.

WITH PAN JUICES:

*1 tablespoon browned flour
2 tablespoons cold water
Pan juices*

*¼ cup Red or White Wine if
    pan juices were not
    prepared with a Spirit
Salt and pepper*

Blend flour with cold water and beat until smooth with fork. Add hot pan juices to flour mixture gradually. If Wine was not used in cooking meat, poultry, or fish to make the pan juices, add ¼ cup Wine. Season to taste with salt and pepper. Heat thoroughly.

Maître d'Hôtel Sauce

*1½ tablespoons butter
1½ tablespoons sifted flour
1¾ cups hot clear meat or
    vegetable stock
¼ cup heated dry White
    Wine*

*1 tablespoon lemon juice
1½ tablespoons finely
    minced parsley
1 egg yolk slightly beaten
Salt and pepper to taste*

Melt butter. Remove from heat and stir in flour. Return to stove and cook over very low heat, stirring constantly, until thickened. Remove from stove. Stir in stock and Wine slowly. Cook over low heat, stirring continuously, until smooth and thickened. Stir in lemon juice and parsley. Cook over very low heat for 10 minutes, stirring from time to time. Stir a small quantity of the sauce into the egg yolk and when blended, stir yolk into remainder of sauce. Season to taste with salt and pepper.

Makes about 1⅓ cups.

Marchand de Vin

⅔ *cup chopped mushrooms*   *2 tablespoons minced onion*
⅔ *cup chopped ham steak*   *2 teaspoons browned flour*
¾ *cup bouillon or*   *4 teaspoons cold White Wine*
  consommé   ⅓ *cup Red Wine*
3 tablespoons minced shallots *Salt and pepper to taste*

Combine mushrooms, ham, bouillon or consommé, shallots, and onion. Dissolve flour in White Wine and beat with a fork until smooth. Add paste to mushroom mixture and stir until blended. Add Red Wine. Bring to a boil. Reduce heat and cook over very low heat for 25 minutes. Season to taste with salt and pepper.

Serves 4.

Mustard Sauce

1⅔ *cups thick hot Wine-flavored* WHITE SAUCE
1 tablespoon prepared mustard
¼ *teaspoon turmeric*

Combine sauce, mustard, and turmeric, and heat thoroughly.

Oyster Sauce

1 teaspoon minced chives
1 teaspoon minced parsley
Salt and pepper to taste
12 small oysters with liquid
1½ cups hot Wine-flavored CREAM *or* BROWN SAUCE
⅓ cup canned button mushrooms

Add chives, parsley, salt and pepper to taste to oysters with their liquid. Cook over low heat, never permitting the liquid to boil, until oysters puff and edges curl (3–5 minutes). Drain oysters and add them to hot sauce. Stir in mushrooms and heat thoroughly. Serve at once.
Makes about 2 cups.

Sauce Diablo

2 cups canned or cooked
   tomatoes
¾ cup tomato catsup
¼ cup Sherry or Vin Rosé or
   White Wine
¾ cup water
½ cup chopped onion
½ cup chopped celery
¼ cup minced parsley
⅛ teaspoon cayenne pepper

1 chopped green pepper
1 teaspoon chili powder
¼ teaspoon orégano
¼ teaspoon basil
2 small bay leaves
¼ teaspoon marjoram
¼ teaspoon thyme
¼ teaspoon rosemary
6 drops Tabasco sauce
¾ teaspoon salt

Combine ingredients. Bring to a boil. Reduce heat and cook over low heat for 25 minutes.
Makes about 3 pints.

Shrimp and Mushroom Sauce

1½ cups hot Wine-flavored
    WHITE *or* CREAM SAUCE
⅜ cup coarsely chopped
    boiled deveined shelled
    shrimp
1 teaspoon minced chives

2 teaspoons minced parsley
⅓ cup canned button
    mushrooms
⅛ teaspoon cumin
⅛ teaspoon turmeric

Combine ingredients and heat thoroughly.
Makes about 2 cups.

Tomato Cream Sauce

1½ cups thin hot Wine-
    flavored WHITE SAUCE
1 cup canned tomatoes
2 tablespoons chopped onion
½ bay leaf

1 tablespoon minced green
    pepper
⅛ teaspoon soda
1 tablespoon minced parsley
¼ teaspoon sugar
Salt and pepper to taste

Prepare White Sauce. Cook tomatoes, onion, bay leaf, green pepper, soda, parsley, sugar, and salt and pepper to taste for 10 minutes. Strain. Stir strained tomato sauce into the White Sauce and heat thoroughly.
Makes about 2¼ cups.

Tomato-Mayonnaise-Gin Sauce

3 tablespoons chili sauce
1 teaspoon Worcestershire
    sauce
1 teaspoon lemon juice

1¼ cups very stiff
    mayonnaise
2 tablespoons Gin
⅓ cup stiffly whipped cream
Salt and cayenne pepper

Fold chili sauce, Worcestershire, and lemon juice into mayonnaise, and then fold in Gin and whipped cream. Season to taste with salt and pepper. Spoon sauce into sauce bowl and embed bowl in bed of finely chopped ice.
Serves 8.

Tomato Sauce

2 tablespoons butter or oleomargarine or vegetable shortening	2 tablespoons chopped celery
2 tablespoons minced onion	1 tablespoon minced parsley
2 tablespoons sifted flour	3 tablespoons chopped green pepper
1½ cups boiling tomato juice	¼ teaspoon orégano
⅓ cup White or Red Wine	¼ teaspoon thyme
	Salt and pepper to taste

Melt fat and when it bubbles (360° F.), add onion. Cook until onion is clear. Remove from heat and stir in flour. Return to medium heat and continue stirring until brown, smooth, and thickened. Again remove from heat and stir in tomato juice, Wine, celery, parsley, green pepper, orégano, and thyme. Return to medium heat and cook, stirring constantly, until thickened and smooth. Season to taste with salt and pepper.
Makes about 1½ cups.

Cream of Shrimp-Sherry Dressing

10 ounces frozen cream of shrimp soup thawed	¼ teaspoon Tabasco sauce
3 ounces processed cream cheese (softened)	¼ cup Sherry
	1 teaspoon lemon juice
	2 tablespoons chili sauce

Combine ingredients and beat with wooden spoon until well blended. Chill thoroughly.
Makes about 1⅔ cups.

Curry Dressing with Wine

1 cup FRENCH DRESSING WITH WINE
¼–½ teaspoon curry (to taste)
Riced yolks 2 hard cooked eggs, if desired

Combine ingredients. Chill. Shake vigorously before serving.
If egg is used, makes about 1⅓ cups.

French Dressing with Wine

⅓ cup vinegar plus enough dry White or Red Wine to make ½
  cup
1 cup salad or olive oil
1 teaspoon sugar
Salt and pepper to taste
⅛ teaspoon paprika

Combine ingredients and beat until thick. Chill and, before
serving, shake vigorously.
Makes about 1½ cups.

Sauterne Mayonnaise

2 tablespoons sweet Sauterne
1 cup stiff mayonnaise
⅙ teaspoon cayenne pepper

Fold Wine into mayonnaise and then gently stir in pepper.
Chill thoroughly.
Makes about 1 cup.

Sherry Roquefort Dressing

1 cup commercially prepared Roquefort or Roca-Bleu dressing
2 tablespoons Sherry

Combine dressing and Sherry. Chill.
Makes about 1 cup.

Apple Stuffing

⅔ cup sausage meat
⅔ cup peeled chopped
  cooking apples
1 cup very fine bread crumbs
½ teaspoon onion juice
⅓ cup chopped celery

Salt and pepper to taste
5 tablespoons hot Red Wine
2 tablespoons boiling stock
  or bouillon (may be made
  from cube)

Mix ingredients thoroughly and stuff into poultry, game, or meat before starting to roast.
Makes about 2½ cups.

Bread Stuffing

8 thin slices stale bread
White Wine
¼ cup minced parsley
⅓ cup coarsely chopped
  celery
¼ cup mushroom pieces, if
  desired
¼ cup minced onion

3 tablespoons bacon grease,
  butter, or oleomargarine
  (approximate)
⅓ cup meat, vegetable, fish,
  or poultry stock
1 egg slightly beaten
Salt and pepper to taste

Soak bread in Wine. Squeeze and reserve 3 tablespoons of Wine. Combine bread with parsley, celery, and, if desired, with mushroom pieces. Cook onion in bubbling fat (360°F.) until clear but not brown. Add bread mixture and cook, stirring constantly, until bread begins to brown. Should additional fat be needed, it may be added at this time. Add 3 tablespoons Wine that was reserved when bread was squeezed and the stock. Cook over low heat until liquid is absorbed, stirring and mashing with a fork so there will be no lumps of bread in the mixture. Remove from stove and cool. Beat egg slightly and stir into stuffing. Season to taste with salt and pepper.

Makes about 2½ cups.

Chestnut Stuffing

2 cups fine bread crumbs
¼ cup dry White Wine
5 tablespoons butter or
  oleomargarine
⅓ cup minced onion
⅓ cup chopped celery
2 tablespoons minced parsley

1½ cups boiled chopped
  chestnuts
⅛ teaspoon black pepper
Salt to taste
¾ cup hot Cognac or
  Cointreau (approximate)

Sprinkle crumbs with Wine and let stand for at least 30 minutes. Melt butter or oleomargarine and heat until it bubbles (360°F.). Add onion and celery and cook until onion is clear. Stir in parsley, chestnuts, bread crumbs, pepper, and salt to taste. Remove from heat and add just enough hot Cognac or Cointreau to moisten mixture and hold it together.

Makes about 3 cups.

Giblet Stuffing

See recipe for BREAD STUFFING and add chopped, boiled fowl giblets when bread is added.

Ham-Rice-Tomato Stuffing for Fish

1¾ cups cooked rice	⅔ cup tomato juice
2 tablespoons minced parsley	1 teaspoon Worcestershire
½ cup ham steak cut into	sauce
small pieces	1 tablespoon dehydrated
¼ cup Sherry or dry White	celery flakes
Wine	Tabasco sauce to taste
2 teaspoons minced chives	Salt to taste
¼ cup canned mushroom	
pieces	

Combine rice, parsley, and ham. Bring Wine, chives, mushroom pieces, tomato juice, Worcestershire sauce, celery, and Tabasco sauce to a boil. Cook over medium heat 5 minutes. Season to taste with salt, and pour over rice. When cool, stuff mixture into fish.

Makes 2½ cups.

Nut Stuffing

See recipe for BREAD STUFFING and add 1½ cups chopped filberts or pecans, broken in small pieces, when egg is added.

Pâté Brandy Stuffing

STEP 1:

4 cups water	2 3-inch stalks celery
2 teaspoons salt	Turkey, goose, duck, or
⅛ teaspoon pepper	chicken liver, gizzard,
1 large bay leaf	heart, and neck
6 sprigs of parsley	

Bring water to a boil. Add salt, pepper, bay leaf, parsley, celery, neck, and giblets. Reduce heat. After 30 minutes check liver and, if tender, remove. If not tender, continue cooking until it can be easily pierced with a fork. Cook neck and remaining giblets until tender (1–2 hours). When tender, drain and reserve ⅓ cup of stock. Cool. Cut meat from neck and chop giblets into small pieces. Grind meat and giblets and combine with reserved stock or put stock in a blender, add meat and giblets, and liquidize on high speed for 30 seconds.

STEP 2:

9 slices stale bread	½ teaspoon basil
White Wine	¼ teaspoon thyme
½ cup butter or	⅛ teaspoon cumin
oleomargarine	¼ teaspoon marjoram
1 pound chicken livers cut in	¼ teaspoon rosemary
small pieces	Ground or liquidized neck
Salt and pepper	meat or giblets
½ cup finely chopped onion	2 teaspoons monosodium
1 cup coarsely chopped	glutamate
celery	½ cup Brandy
⅓ cup minced parsley	1 egg well beaten
⅓ cup cooked or canned	Salt and pepper to taste
mushroom pieces	

Soak bread in Wine for 30 minutes. Squeeze and retain ¼ cup Wine squeezed from bread. Melt butter or oleomargarine until it bubbles (360° F.). Sprinkle livers with salt and pepper. Broil livers for 4 minutes in fat, and add onion, celery, parsley, and mushrooms. Cook until onion is clear, mashing half the livers, while they are cooking, into bits. Reduce heat and add bread, ¼ cup Wine reserved when bread was squeezed, basil, thyme, cumin, marjoram, rosemary, ground or liquidized neck meat and giblets, and monosodium glutamate. Cook, stirring and mashing with a fork, until there are no lumps of bread in mixture. When bread begins to brown, stir in Brandy and continue cooking over low heat, stirring constantly, until Brandy is blended with rest of mixture. Remove from heat and, when cool, stir in egg and season to taste with salt and pepper.

Makes about 2½ quarts of stuffing (quantity will vary slightly because of variations in necks and giblets of poultry). NOTE: The above recipe will provide a sufficient quantity of stuffing for a large turkey or goose. If small turkey or duck or chicken is to be stuffed, use only half the quantities specified under Step 2, or the full quantities may be used and the extra stuffing frozen for later use.

Pâté Brandy-Oyster Stuffing

PÂTÉ BRANDY STUFFING
18 medium-size or 24 small oysters with their liquid
Salt and pepper

Follow recipe for Pâté Brandy Stuffing. Drain oysters. Season liquid to taste with salt and pepper, and bring to a boil. Add oysters; immediately reduce heat and allow to simmer over low heat until oysters puff and edges curl (3–5 minutes). Drain oysters and stir into stuffing when egg is added.

Makes about 2¾ quarts.

Oyster Stuffing

BREAD STUFFING
12 medium-size or 16 small oysters with their liquid
Salt and pepper

¼ teaspoon thyme, if desired
¼ teaspoon sweet basil, if desired

Prepare Bread Stuffing. Drain oysters and season liquid to taste with salt and pepper. Bring to a boil. Reduce heat and add oysters. Cook until oysters puff and edges curl (3–5 minutes). Add the drained oysters to dressing when egg is added. If desired, thyme and/or basil may be added at same time. *Makes about 3¼ cups.*

Sage Stuffing

See recipe for BREAD STUFFING and add 1½ teaspoons sage when salt and pepper are added.

Wild Rice Stuffing

1 egg
2 tablespoons Sherry
4 cups hot cooked wild rice
⅔ pound goose or chicken livers cut in small pieces
Salt and pepper
¼ cup butter
⅓ cup chopped onion
¼ cup chopped celery
¾ cup sliced canned mushrooms

1 teaspoon dehydrated parsley flakes
1½ tablespoons butter or oleomargarine
1 tablespoon sifted flour
⅜ cup boiling beef bouillon
¼ cup hot dry White Wine
Salt and pepper to taste

Beat egg until light and beat in Sherry. Add a small amount of the hot rice to the egg and then stir egg into remainder of rice. Set aside. Sprinkle livers with salt and pepper. Melt butter and heat until it bubbles (360° F.). Add livers and cook 4 minutes over medium heat, mashing half of livers into small pieces with a fork. Add onion, celery, and mushrooms, and cook just until onion is clear. Stir in parsley flakes and set liver mixture aside. Melt 1½ tablespoons butter or oleomargarine. Remove from heat and stir in flour. Return to medium heat and cook until smooth and rich brown. Again remove from heat and stir in boiling bouillon gradually. When blended, add Wine and return to heat. Cook over medium heat, still stirring, until slightly thickened. Add liver mixture. Heat thoroughly and stir in rice mixture. Remove from heat and season to taste with salt and pepper.

Makes about 5¼ cups.

Cakes, Tortes,
and Cookies

I was having tea with a friend in the Vieux Carré (the old French quarter in New Orleans) several years ago. She ordered some small chocolate cakes and after she tasted one she raved over the combination of Rum flavoring and chocolate, and mentioned that there were also tiny bits of orange peel in the cake. A few days later, I decided I was going to make some cakes of this type, although I didn't think the results I wanted could be obtained by baking the flavoring into the cakes. Instead, I planned to pour various Spirits—that is, one to a cake—over them after they were baked. I also decided I would use both pecan pieces and small bits of orange rind crystallized in Rum and Sauterne in the cakes. I selected a chocolate cake recipe, which incidentally was for layers, and went to work. The first trial was a success, but small pieces crumbled from the moist cakes when they were iced, and although this really didn't make a great deal of difference when the tops were covered with frosting, I just wasn't satisfied. Also, I had used a plain chocolate icing when I really wanted a Brandy-flavored one. I gradually worked out the changes, and the final result is cakes that don't crumble when iced but are equal in flavor and texture to those made on the first trial, frosted with the Brandy-flavored icing that does them justice. These CHOCOLATE SIPS OF SPIRITS with their twenty-two flavors take time and care, so I reserve them for special occasions, or for friends to whom I wish to pay some unusual attention.

The evolution of the JAM CAKE came about in a different manner. This recipe was given to me years ago in Magnolia, and I followed its original form until I became interested in Spirit cooking and flavoring. Then, working with pencil and paper, I changed the recipe, and for the last two or three years have used it with great success. In Magnolia I had baked the cake as a loaf. When I changed the recipe I made it in layers, and it was only after this book was in the publisher's hands that I decided I should try to make individual JAM CAKES. I did not change the batter or the icing, but I baked it in small muffin cups and changed the temperature of the oven from 335° F. to 400° F. Now I am in a quandary; I don't know whether I like the large cake or the small ones better. I only know that, large or small, this feather-light, spicy cake with its Kirsch or Cointreau flavor, iced with Cherry Heering, Curaçao, Almond Cream Marsala or Brandy-flavored BUTTER-CREAM FROSTING will be something for you to brag about when you bake it.

As you have probably surmised, I am a sentimental soul, and this is clearly demonstrated each year when I bake my FRUIT CAKE OF THE TWELVE SPIRITS. For this cake, and only this cake, is mixed in an earthenware bowl that was given to me by a very old lady when I was a very little girl. Her mother had done her cake mixing in the bowl, and when my friend was married her mother gave her the bowl, so she, too, had used it for her cake making. This is sentiment, however, and not superstition. I am sure that when you bake the FRUIT CAKE OF THE TWELVE SPIRITS you will be successful whether your mixing bowl is old or new, just as long as it's big enough to hold all the batter after the fruits and nuts have been added.

And since I have started the subject of success, regardless of what bowl you use to make a cake, this would be a good time to tell you the whole truth about Angel-Food Cakes. They are probably easier and quicker to mix than any other cake. There are, however, a few simple rules to follow. Sift your flour and sugar mixture six times—and this really doesn't take long. You can separate the egg whites from the yolks while they are still chilled, but don't start to beat the whites until they are room temperature. When you do beat them, don't overbeat. Just beat until a soft peak that bends is formed when the beaters are lifted from the whites. Never use a rotary egg beater because it makes the whites too stiff. Add the sugar and sugar-flour mixture gradually. Use a tube pan that has never been greased, and, after the batter has been spooned into the pan, cut through the batter at least three times to let the air bubbles escape. Start the cake baking in a 250° F. oven and cook for 15 minutes; increase the heat to 300° F. and cook 15 minutes more; then increase the heat to 325° F. and cook 30 minutes. At the end of the hour remove the cake from the stove and invert the pan. Let the cake hang until cool, so that the cells may expand. Read these directions over and I am sure you will agree that there really is nothing complicated about making an angel food, but "cross my heart" that's all the secrets there are for making a fine one, which, in a covered container (and iced), will stay fresh for a week or ten days. And please don't believe those old wives' tales that you must tiptoe when the cake is in the oven. They are absolutely untrue!

Now to go back to the subjects of sentiment and experimenting. The only thing my grandmother ever knew how to cook, insofar as I have been able to find out, was LEBKUCHEN. For years my mother has talked about these wonderful Lebkuchen, and none other suited her—they were too spongy or too crispy; they had too much chocolate or not enough. There was always something wrong or something missing. Knowing that my mother was sentimental about her mother's one great success in the kitchen, I decided that I had better not attempt to make the Lebkuchen. Then several years ago I read in a newspaper an Austrian recipe that sounded rather good to me. I gathered up my courage and tried it. After thoughtfully tasting one from the first batch, Mother told me that I was on the right track, but it still wasn't exactly like what Grandmother used to make. By this time it was almost a point of honor with me to make a Lebkuchen as good or better than my grandmother had made. I had some vague specifications, and since my mother never learned to cook, they were indeed vague, so I really sweated over this one. It was a happy day when Mother at last started telling her friends and family that I made Lebkuchen just like those Grandmother used to make fifty years ago.

Chocolate Sips of Spirits

½ cup butter or
  oleomargarine
1½ cups sugar
3½ squares unsweetened
  baking chocolate
3 eggs separated
1 teaspoon vanilla
¾ cup broken pecans
¾ cup crystallized orange
  peel made according to
  recipe for CRYSTALLIZED
  CITRUS FRUIT PEEL
2⅛ cups sifted cake flour
2 teaspoons baking powder
½ teaspoon salt
1¼ cups milk
¼ cup sugar
CHOCOLATE BRANDY FROSTING

*Any one or any number of
the following Spirits:*
  *Rum, Napoleon Brandy,
  Maraschino, Crème de
  Menthe (green or white)
  Grand Marnier, Sherry,
  Curaçao, Cointreau,
  Apricot Brandy, Anisette,
  Blackberry Brandy, Peach
  Brandy with equal
  quantity of Whisky,
  Benedictine, Kirsch,
  Kummel, Champagne
  Cognac, Triple Sec, Sweet
  Vermouth, Crème de
  Cassis, Cherry Heering,
  Applejack, Almond Cream
  Marsala*

PREPARATION: *Twenty-four hours or more* (as long as 2 or 3 weeks, if desired) before baking prepare crystallized orange peel. When peel is cooled, brush off as much sugar as possible and cut strips into pieces about ½×⅛×⅛ inch. Store in covered container in refrigerator. *Just before baking* let butter or oleomargarine, eggs, and milk stand until room temperature (in very hot weather use cold eggs and milk). Grease small muffin cups with vegetable shortening. Sift flour, measure and sift with baking powder and salt. Melt chocolate over hot, but not boiling, water, and, when melted, allow to cool slightly. Separate whites of eggs from yolks.

MIXING AND BAKING: Cream butter or oleomargarine just until it is fluffy. Do not overbeat. Add 1½ cups sugar by spoonfuls, beating after each addition until blended. Beat for 1 minute after all sugar has been added. Blend in melted chocolate, scraping pan in which it was melted, and egg yolks. Beat 2 minutes. If cake is being made in mixer all of the foregoing is done on the ⁸/₁₀ maximum speed (or speed recommended for creaming butter and sugar), and the following is done on the lowest possible mixer speed. Add vanilla and beat only until blended with batter. Mix pecans and orange peel with flour mixture. Add flour mixture alternately with milk, a small quantity of each at a time, starting and ending with flour. Beat only long enough after each addition to blend the milk and flour with the batter.

Beat egg whites to soft-peak stage with rotary egg beater or on speed recommended for particular mixer being used. Add ¼ cup sugar gradually, continuing to beat until whites are stiff enough to cling to bowl when it is turned upside down. Gently fold the meringue into the batter with a wooden or silver spoon until batter is smooth. Half fill the greased muffin cups and bake in 400° F. oven 12–14 minutes until cake tester inserted in cake comes out clean. Let stand in muffin cups 6–8 minutes. Turn out on racks and then turn right side up. Immediately pour—slowly and carefully so that there is no waste of Spirit—2 teaspoons of any one Spirit included in the list of ingredients above on each cake. This recipe *makes 55 small cakes*, so, if desired, the cakes may be flavored with all of the 22 Spirits listed above. Let cakes stand on racks until cool. Then frost tops with CHOCOLATE BRANDY FROSTING and place each cake in colored fluted baking cup. Store cakes in covered container, and it is suggested that they be kept at least 24 hours before being used.

NOTE 1: If it is desirable to be able to identify the flavor of each cake, this can be done by preparing the following icing and using this icing to write on the top of each cake with a decorating tube the first letter of the name of the alcoholic beverage with which the cake is flavored. In those cases where several Spirits start with the same letter use the first 2 letters of the name, or if there are 2 parts to the name use the first initial of each part. Examples: "Rum" use "R"; Champagne Cognac use "CC"; and Cointreau use "Co."

Icing for Lettering

1 tablespoon vegetable shortening
1 cup sifted confectioners' sugar
Brandy or White Crème de Menthe

Beat shortening until fluffy and beat in sugar. Add just enough Brandy or Crème de Menthe to make an icing that can be put through a decorating tube.

NOTE 2: If after 7 or 8 days the cakes should become a little dry, take out of paper cups and gently turn upside down. In the event that the cakes are marked with identifying letters, slowly and carefully pour over bottom of each 1 teaspoon of same Spirit that was originally used to flavor cake. In the event that cakes are not marked, use 1 teaspoon of Brandy to pour over bottom of each, as the Brandy will blend beautifully with the other flavors and will restore cakes to original freshness. Place cakes, after letting them stand about 30 minutes, in fresh fluted paper cups and store in covered containers.

The Fruit Cake of the Twelve Spirits

1 pound butter or
oleomargarine
1 pound sugar
1 quart figs preserved in
heavy syrup
12 eggs
1 cup Bourbon Whisky
¼ cup Sherry
¼ cup Maraschino
Liqueur
1 pound all-purpose flour
1 tablespoon nutmeg
1 tablespoon cinnamon
1 tablespoon cloves
1 cup molasses
1 teaspoon soda
1 pound pecans broken in
small pieces

2 pounds seedless raisins
2 pounds dried currants
6 ounces candied orange peel
6 ounces candied lemon peel
6 ounces candied citron
1 pound candied cherries
1 pound candied pineapple
½ pound candied mixed
fruit
All-purpose flour to coat the
nuts and fruit
Kirsch, Curaçao, Cointreau,
Napoleon Brandy,
Maraschino Liqueur, Rum,
Sherry, Madeira, Crème de
Cassis, Bourbon Whisky,
Apricot Brandy,
Benedictine

PREPARATION: 72 HOURS BEFORE BAKING: Drain figs. Put through food grinder and combine with ¼ cup Kirsch. Store in refrigerator. Cut orange peel, lemon peel, citron, pineapple, and mixed fruit into pieces about ¼ × ⅛ × ⅛ inch. Cut cherries into ⅓-inch-thick slices.

> Marinate orange peel in Curaçao
> Marinate lemon peel in Cointreau
> Marinate citron in Napoleon Brandy
> Marinade cherries in Maraschino Liqueur
> Marinate pineapple in Rum
> Marinate mixed candied fruit in Sherry

Fruit should be covered by Spirit in which it is marinated. Store marinated fruits in covered containers in refrigerator.

NOTE: If desired, the marinating of the fruits may be started 3 or 4 weeks before the cakes are baked.

PREPARATIONS: DAY BEFORE BAKING: Place raisins and currants in large plastic containers with secure covers so that containers may be turned upside down and liquid in them will not spill. Sprinkle the raisins liberally with Madeira and sprinkle the currants liberally with Crème de Cassis. Cover containers and store in refrigerator. After several hours, turn containers upside down and let stand in that way for 2 or 3 hours; then turn the containers right side up. Reverse the position of the containers at least 4 or 5 times during the period that they are stored in refrigerator.

PREPARATION: DAY OF BAKING: Drain candied and dried fruits, reserving separately the liquids in which they were marinated. Cut brown paper to fit bottoms of 2 10-inch tube pans, 2 8×4×3-inch loaf pans, and 1 5×3×3-inch loaf pan. Grease inside of pans well with vegetable shortening. Place the paper cut to fit on bottoms of pans and grease paper well with vegetable shortening. Let butter or oleomargarine and eggs stand until room temperature. Combine ¼ cup of Sherry drained from the mixed fruits and ¼ cup Maraschino Liqueur drained from cherries. Combine nuts, raisins, currants, fruit peel, citron, cherries, pineapple, and mixed fruits. Sift flour over fruit and nuts so that each piece is lightly coated. Add spices to 1 pound of flour and sift. Add soda to molasses and mix well (soda will cause the molasses to bubble and foam, so the molasses and soda should be mixed in a container large enough to avoid spilling).

Cream butter or oleomargarine. Add sugar by spoonfuls, creaming after each addition. When all sugar is added, beat 1 minute. Add fig preserves and beat 1 minute. Add eggs, 1 at a time, beating 45 seconds after each addition. If using mixer, the foregoing is all done on "creaming speed." At this point the batter must be spooned into a very large bowl. Stir in Whisky, Maraschino Liqueur, and Sherry mixture. Beat until blended. Fold in the pound of flour and the spices alternately with the molasses mixture, starting and ending with the flour— a small amount of each mixture at a time. Beat with a wooden spoon after each addition until blended. Add floured fruits and nuts by handfuls, mixing well with the hands so the fruit is mixed throughout the batter. Spoon the dough into the prepared baking pans until the pans are ⅔ filled with the dough. Place biscuit pan filled with hot water in the bottom of a 250° F. oven. Place oven rack in middle of the oven and place cake pans on rack—leaving a little space between the pans. (It may be necessary to do 2 bakings, but dough will not be injured by standing 5 or 6 hours). Bake until cakes come away from sides of pans and dough does not cling to cake tester when it is inserted in one of the cakes. Hot water may be added to the water in the biscuit pan if it is needed, due to evaporation. Cakes baked in 10-inch tube pans will take approximately 4½–5½ hours, and the smaller cakes will take 3½–4½ hours for baking. When cakes are done remove from oven. Let stand 10 minutes and turn out of pans. Remove paper. While cakes are still warm spoon the following Spirits, which were drained from fruits, over the cakes at 10 minute intervals:

> 1st the Curaçao
> 2nd the Cointreau
> 3rd the Napoleon Brandy
> 4th the Rum

Let cakes stand 2 hours. Pour 2 or 3 tablespoons of Bourbon Whisky over each cake. Let stand another hour and brush tops and sides with Apricot Brandy. At the end of another hour brush tops and sides of cakes with Benedictine. Let cakes stand until cold and until all the Spirits have been absorbed in them. Wrap in aluminum foil and plastic wrap.

NOTE: Each month brush remaining cakes with Apricot or Napoleon Brandy, alternating the Brandies. Let stand for an hour or so after brushing and then rewrap in aluminum foil and plastic wrap and store.

Jam Cake

1⅓ cups butter or oleomargarine	1¼ teaspoons cinnamon
1⅓ cups sugar	1¼ teaspoons allspice
1⅓ cups blackberry jam or preserves (seedless preferred)	1¼ teaspoons cloves
	½ cup sour milk or buttermilk
4 eggs	1½ teaspoons soda
2⅔ cups sifted cake flour	Kirsch or Cointreau

Sift flour, measure, and add spices. Spoon into sifter. Let butter or oleomargarine and eggs stand until room temperature (in very hot weather use cold eggs). Combine sour milk or buttermilk and soda (in a container large enough so that they will not spill when milk bubbles up) and stir with a spoon. Grease 2 9-inch round layer pans and line bottom of pans with wax paper, cut just slightly smaller than pan. Grease paper. Also grease 6 small muffin cups. This is based on an old Mississippi recipe that was used in the days when a few extra tablespoons of dough were made to provide "samples" for the children of the family. If the samples are not made, there will be too much dough in the layer tins.

Cream butter or oleomargarine just until fluffy. Add sugar gradually, beating as it is added. Beat for 1 minute after all sugar has been added. Beat in jam or preserves and beat 1 minute. Add eggs and beat 2 minutes. If cake is being made on mixer, foregoing should be done on 9⁄10 maximum speed or "creaming speed." Sift flour and spices and add, alternately with milk, on lowest possible speed of mixer or with a spoon. Spoon dough into 2 layer pans and half fill the 6 small muffin cups. Bake layers in 335° F. oven until cake tester inserted in layer comes out clean. When layers are baked, bake "samples" in 400° F. oven 12–14 minutes. The layers will take 45–55 minutes to bake. Remove cakes from oven; let stand in pans 10 minutes. Turn out on racks and immediately brush layers liberally with Kirsch or Cointreau. Let stand until cold. (If desired, 1 teaspoon Kirsch or Cointreau may be poured over each of the samples.) Put layers together and ice with desired frosting.

RECOMMENDATION: It is suggested that this cake be iced with BUTTER-CREAM FROSTING flavored with Cherry Heering, Curaçao, Almond Cream Marsala, or Brandy.

Jam Cakes (Individual)

Prepare JAM CAKE batter according to preceding recipe. Grease 55 small muffin cups with vegetable shortening. Half fill cups with batter and place muffin tins in 400° F. oven. Bake 12–14 minutes until cake tester inserted in cakes comes out clean. Remove from oven and let stand 8 minutes. Turn out on racks, right side up. Pour 2 teaspoons Cointreau or 1½ teaspoons Kirsch over each cake, carefully so as not to waste the Spirit. Let stand until cold. Frost tops with desired icing and place each cake in a fluted paper baking cup. Store in covered container.

Rum Ring

1 cup candied citron or mixed
  candied fruit cut in small
  pieces
Rum
⅜ cup scalded milk
1 package active dry yeast
2 tablespoons warm water
  (105°–115° F.)
½ cup all-purpose sifted
  flour
½ cup butter or
  oleomargarine
⅔ cup sugar
3 eggs separated
1½ cups all-purpose sifted
  flour
¼ teaspoon mace

⅜ teaspoon salt
1½ teaspoons grated lemon
  rind
1⅓ cups sugar
⅔ cup water
Additional Rum if needed to
  add to marinade to make
  ⅓ cup
1 quart washed and hulled
  strawberries patted dry and
  sweetened to taste with
  confectioners' sugar or
  2 10-ounce packages
  thawed frozen sweetened
  strawberries
Cointreau

Place citron or mixed fruit in a container and cover with
Rum. Cover container and store in refrigerator overnight. Scald
milk and cool until lukewarm. Stir yeast into warm water and
add lukewarm milk as soon as yeast is dissolved. Beat in ½
cup flour. Cover bowl. Place in warm spot until nearly double
in bulk (approximately 40 minutes).

Cream butter or oleomargarine. Add sugar gradually and beat
until light and fluffy. Add yolks of eggs and beat for 2 minutes.
If using mixer, the foregoing should be done on "creaming
speed." Drain citron or mixed fruit, reserving Rum marinade.
Sift 1½ cups flour, mace, and salt together. Mix drained citron
or fruit with flour. Stir yeast mixture, flour mixture, and lemon
rind into batter with a wooden spoon, beating until smooth.
Beat egg whites until they stand in straight peaks but are not
dry, and fold into batter with a spoon until mixture is smooth.

Grease 10-inch ring mold and spoon dough into mold, spreading it evenly around the center tube. Cover the mold with a slightly damp cloth and let dough stand in warm place until it reaches almost to top of mold (time for this varies from 30–60 minutes, but do not let dough stand longer that 1 hour, for even if it has not reached almost to top of mold, results should be satisfactory).

Bake 15 minutes in 375° F. oven, reduce heat to 350° F., and bake for another 15 minutes. Remove from oven and turn Rum Ring out of mold onto rack at once.

Combine 1⅓ cups sugar and ⅔ cup water. Bring to a boil. Reduce heat to medium and cook 3 minutes. Measure marinade and add additional Rum, if needed, to make ⅓ cup. Mix with syrup.

Turn the ring right side up on another rack. Pour ¾ cup of syrup mixture into bottom of ring mold in which cake was baked. Slide the cake into the mold. Spoon the remaining syrup over top of cake. Let stand until syrup is absorbed (6–8 minutes). Place a rack on a large cooky sheet with ½-inch rim. Turn cake ring out on rack and spoon any of the syrup that runs into cooky tray over top of cake. Cool slightly. Place on serving platter. If using fresh berries, sprinkle with confectioners' sugar and Cointreau. Fill center of ring with berries, reserving some to decorate the platter. If using frozen berries, add Cointreau to taste and, just before serving, pour the berries over the Rum Ring. May be served either warm or cold.

Rum Sponge

½ teaspoon vanilla	1 teaspoon baking powder
½ teaspoon lemon juice	¼ teaspoon salt
4 tablespoons Rum	5 egg yolks
4 tablespoons water (approximate)	1 egg
1½ cups sifted cake flour	1 cup sugar

Pour vanilla, lemon juice, and Rum into measuring cup. Add just enough cold water to make ½ cup. Place in refrigerator.

Sift flour, measure, and add baking powder and salt. Sift. Beat egg yolks and egg until thick and lemon colored (about 5 minutes with rotary egg beater or on maximum mixer speed. Add sugar gradually and beat until light and fluffy. If using mixer add sugar on "creaming speed." Stir in Rum mixture quickly. Sift flour mixture into batter—about 2 tablespoons at a time—and fold in with a wooden or silver spoon, after each addition, until blended. Grease bottom of 10-inch spring form and spoon batter into form. Bake in 325° F. oven about 45 minutes until, when top is lightly pressed with finger, cake will spring back. Remove from oven. Let stand 10 minutes. Loosen cake from sides of form by running knife around the cake. Remove sides of form. Cool. Turn cake over on a rack and remove bottom of form.

Rum Sponge Roll

2 eggs	½ teaspoon salt
2 egg yolks	Confectioners' sugar
1 cup sugar	Desired filling—jelly,
¼ cup dark Rum	preserves, custard, crushed
1 tablespoon lemon juice	fruit or berries, and/or
½ teaspoon vanilla	whipped cream
1 cup sifted cake flour	2 tablespoons dark Rum
1 teaspoon baking powder	

Let eggs stand until room temperature. Mix ¼ cup Rum, lemon juice, and vanilla. Sift flour, baking powder, and salt together. Liberally coat 1 10½×15-inch cooky tray, with ½-inch rim, with salad oil. Line with wax paper, which hangs about 2 inches over each end, and liberally coat paper with salad oil. The paper may smoke when sponge is in the oven, but this may be safely ignored.

Beat eggs and yolks until thick and lemon colored with rotary egg beater or on "creaming speed." Add sugar by spoon-fuls, beating after each addition until all of sugar has been added. Beat for 1 minute. If using food mixer, turn to lowest possible speed. Stir in Rum mixture and then fold in flour mixture quickly and all at one time with a spoon. Spoon batter evenly onto cooky sheet. Bake at 375° F. approximately 15 minutes until top of sponge is golden brown and springs back if lightly touched with finger tip. Run knife around edge of cake to loosen from pan. Sprinkle towel heavily with confectioners' sugar and turn cake out on sugar-sprinkled towel. With a knife loosen wax paper from edges of cake. Make hole in center of paper and pull off gently toward outside edges. Fold ends of towel over cake and roll cake, beginning at 10½-inch side. Let stand until cool. Unroll and spread with jelly, preserves, custard, crushed fruit or berries, and/or whipped cream. Reroll and brush outside of roll with the 2 tablespoons of Rum.

Sherry Apple Cake

¾ cup seedless raisins
Sherry for soaking raisins
1 cup sifted all-purpose
  flour
1 teaspoon cinnamon
¼ teaspoon cloves
¼ teaspoon allspice
1 cup pecans broken into
  small pieces
⅓ cup butter or
  oleomargarine
⅓ cup dark brown sugar
⅓ cup granulated sugar

½ cup unsweetened
  drained and well mashed
  stewed apple
2 eggs
¼ teaspoon soda
1 teaspoon hot water
1 tablespoon Sherry
⅔ cup sifted flour
Additional Sherry, if needed,
  to be combined with
  marinade to make ⅔ cup
  for pouring over cakes
  when they are removed
  from oven

PREPARATION: About 3 or 4 hours before baking, cover raisins with Sherry and store in covered container in refrigerator. Let butter or oleomargarine and eggs stand until room temperature. In very hot weather, use cold eggs. Grease small muffin tins to make 22 cakes. Dissolve soda in hot water. Lift raisins from Sherry with slotted spoon and place them in dish. Sift 1 cup flour, cinnamon, cloves, and allspice. Lift raisins from dish, again using slotted spoon (in this way letting as much Wine as possible drain from dried fruit), and mix with flour and spices. Reserve marinade. Add pecans to flour mixture and set aside. MIXING AND BAKING: Cream butter or oleomargarine just until fluffy. Add sugar slowly and beat for 1 minute after all the sugar is added. Stir in mashed apple and beat for 1 minute. Add eggs and beat 2 minutes. If cake is being made on a mixer all of the foregoing should be done on "creaming speed" and the following should be done on lowest possible speed. Stir in soda, dissolved in water, and then add 1 tablespoon Sherry. Stir only long enough to blend with the batter. Quickly stir in fruit-nut-flour mixture with a spoon and then add ⅔ cup sifted flour, stirring into batter with spoon. Place biscuit pan containing hot water in bottom of 250° F. oven. Spoon cake batter into muffin cups until the cups are ⅔ filled. Place muffin tins on center rack of oven and bake until cake tester inserted in cake comes out clean (60–70 minutes). Additional water may be added to pan in bottom of oven if needed. Remove cakes from oven. Let stand 10 minutes. Turn out on racks. Add enough Sherry to marinade, if necessary, to make ⅔ cup. Immediately spoon Sherry over tops of cakes, being careful to spill as little Wine as possible. (It is advisable to place the rack in a cooky tray with 1-inch sides, so that any Wine that spills can be saved and poured over the cakes.) Let cakes stand until cool and store in covered container. At any time that cakes start to dry out (if they last that long), original freshness can be restored by pouring 1–2 teaspoons of Sherry over each of the cakes.

Tipsy Angel (Angel-Food Cake)

1 cup plus 1 tablespoon sifted cake flour	*1 tablespoon butter or oleomargarine*
¾ cup sugar	*1 cup sifted confectioners' sugar*
1½ cups egg whites	
⅜ teaspoon salt	*1 tablespoon (approximate) Maraschino Liqueur or Almond Cream Marsala*
1½ teaspoons cream of tartar	
1 cup sugar	*1–2 drops red vegetable coloring*
1¼ teaspoons vanilla	
¾ teaspoon almond extract	DOUBLE-BOILER FROSTING *flavored with Rum*

Sift flour, measure, and combine with ¾ cup sugar. Sift 5 times and spoon sugar-flour mixture back into sifter. Let eggs stand until room temperature. Separate whites from yolks (in very hot weather separate whites from yolks while eggs are cold and then let the whites stand until they are room temperature).

Place egg whites in large bowl and add salt. Beat with wire whip or "creaming speed" of mixer until whites are foamy.

Add cream of tartar and beat[1] until whites are stiff enough to stand in peaks that bend. Do not overbeat, as egg whites should not be dry. Add 1 cup sugar gradually and beat only long enough after each addition to blend sugar with egg whites. If using mixer, after all sugar has been added, mixer should be turned to lowest possible speed. Fold in vanilla and almond extract. Sift flour-sugar mixture for the sixth time. Fold into egg white mixture by spoonfuls. Spoon batter into ungreased 10-inch tube pan. Cut through batter with knife or spatula 3 times in circular motion to release the air bubbles. Place in

[1] If using food mixer, after cream of tartar is added, lift the beaters up and down through the whites during 5 or 6 revolutions of the beaters around the bowl.

250°F. oven. Bake 15 minutes. Increase heat to 300°F. and bake 15 minutes. Increase heat to 325°F. and bake 30 minutes. Remove from oven. Invert pan at once and let the cake hang until cool—at least 1 hour. Loosen cake from sides and tube of pan with spatula. Brush crumbs from side of cake. Cream butter or oleomargarine. Beat in confectioners' sugar and Spirit, using just enough of the Spirit to make an icing that can be easily and thinly spread. Add coloring. Spread the icing thinly over the cake. It is not necessary that the entire surface be covered. Prepare Rum-flavored Double-Boiler Frosting and frost cake. Swirl frosting with back of spoon.

Date-Kirsch Torte

½ cup all-purpose flour
½ teaspoon baking powder
3 eggs separated
1 cup sugar
⅞ cup pecans or walnuts
    broken into small pieces
1 pound pitted dates cut
    into small pieces
3 tablespoons Kirsch

1 cup stiffly whipped cream
    sweetened to taste
BAKED PECAN or ALMOND
TOPPING
12 maraschino cherries
    soaked overnight in equal
    parts of their own juice and
    Maraschino Liqueur

Sift flour and baking powder together. Beat egg yolks with rotary egg beater or on maximum food mixer speed for 5 minutes. Add sugar gradually and beat with wooden or silver spoon or on "creaming speed" of mixer until light and fluffy. Stir in flour mixture, nuts, and dates with hands. Beat egg whites until stiff and fold into dough with hands. Cut wax paper to fit the bottom of a 13×9×2-inch pan. Grease bottom and sides of pan well with vegetable shortening. Fit paper into pan and grease paper. Spread dough evenly in pan—about ½ inch thick. Bake in 350°F. oven. Remove from oven when cake tester inserted in center of torte comes out clean (40–45 minutes). Let stand 10 minutes. Loosen torte from sides of pan and turn it out on large board. Remove paper. Brush with Kirsch. Let stand until cool. Cut in 12 3-inch squares. Place each square on an individual serving plate. Place a spoonful of the sweetened whipped cream in center of each square. Sprinkle each serving with Baked Pecan or Almond Topping and top with maraschino cherry.

NOTE: The cut squares may be wrapped in wax paper and stored in a covered container for a week or longer. They may also be kept indefinitely in freezer and they may be served without the cream and/or nut topping and/or cherries.

Pecan Almond Rum Torte

PART 1:

> 5 egg yolks
> 1⅓ cups sifted confectioners' sugar[2]
> 3 tablespoons unsifted all-purpose flour
> ¼ teaspoon baking powder
> 1½ tablespoons dark Rum
> ⅓ cup finely ground almonds, plus enough finely ground pecans to make 2½ cups ground nuts (tightly packed)
> 5 egg whites
> ¼ cup dark Rum

Beat egg yolks until thick and lemon colored. Gradually beat in sugar and beat 1 minute after all sugar is added. Sift

[2] Confectioners' sugar should be sifted and then measured.

flour and baking powder together. Fold flour and 1½ table-spoons Rum into yolks. Stir in ground nuts and when well blended, fold in stiffly beaten egg whites. Continue folding gently until mixture is smooth. Spread evenly in a well-greased 12×8×1-inch pan. Bake in 300° F. oven 45–55 minutes until cake tester inserted in cake comes out clean. Let stand 10 minutes. Turn out on rack and brush with ¼ cup Rum. When cold cut in 3 equal parts—4×8 inches.

PART 2 (BAKED PECAN OR ALMOND TOPPING):

¾ cup pecans broken in very small pieces or blanched and thoroughly dried almond slivers
1 egg white
¼ cup sifted confectioners' sugar

Combine nuts, egg white, and sugar. Spread in a layer about ⅓ inch thick on a cooky tray. Place in 400° F. oven. Bake 2 minutes and reduce temperature to 350° F. Cook 23 minutes more. Loosen from sheet and break into small pieces at once. Let stand until cold before putting into container or using.

PART 3:

1½ cups stiffly whipped cream
Confectioners' sugar to taste

Combine whipped cream with confectioners' sugar. Put the 3 layers of torte together with the sweetened whipped cream. Cover torte with the cream mixture and then sprinkle heavily with the Baked Pecan or Almond topping. Store in refrigerator until ready to serve.
Serves 10.

Almond Brandy Sticks

1 cup butter or
oleomargarine
⅔ cup sugar
½ teaspoon salt
1⅞ cups sifted all-purpose
flour

2¼ cups ground
unblanched almonds
(ground several days
before "sticks" are baked)
¼ cup very cold Brandy
1¼ cups sifted powdered
sugar
3½ tablespoons Cognac
(approximate)

Cream butter or oleomargarine with a wooden spoon, beating 60 strokes. Add sugar and salt gradually and beat until light and fluffy. Add flour and stir in quickly. Blend in ground almonds. Roll a small amount of dough in palms of hands to make a "stick" ¾ ×2¼ inches long. Place "sticks" 2 inches apart on greased cooky trays. Continue rolling "sticks" until all of dough is used. Brush "sticks" with Brandy. Put in 400° F. oven and bake 2 minutes. Reduce heat to 300° F. Bake 20–22 minutes until cookies are a light gold in color. Remove from oven and loosen from cooky sheets. Let stand for 15 minutes and roll in powdered sugar. Remove cookies from sugar and let stand until cold. Sprinkle lightly with the Cognac, using approximately ¼ teaspoon of the Brandy for each cooky. If desired, cookies may be wrapped individually in plastic wrap and then stored in covered containers.

Makes 40 cookies.

Applesauce Cookies with Liqueur Icings

1 teaspoon soda
⅞ cup applesauce
2 tablespoons seedless
  blackberry jam or
  preserves
½ cup butter or
  oleomargarine
¾ cup granulated sugar
¼ cup brown sugar
1 egg
2 cups sifted all-purpose
  flour
½ teaspoon salt
¾ teaspoon cinnamon
½ teaspoon cloves
½ teaspoon allspice
¾ cup raisins
1 cup pecans broken in
  small pieces
¼ cup maraschino cherries
  that have been soaked at
  least 12 hours in equal
  parts of their own juice and
  Maraschino Liqueur and
  then cut in ⅓-inch slices
  and drained

¼ cup small pieces
  crystallized orange peel, if
  desired, made according to
  recipe for CRYSTALLIZED
  CITRUS FRUIT PEEL
8 tablespoons butter or
  oleomargarine
8 cups sifted confectioners'
  sugar
1 tablespoon of each of any
  8 of the following Spirits
  (approximate): Rum,
  Napoleon Brandy,
  Maraschino Liqueur,
  Crème de Menthe, Grand
  Marnier, Sherry, Curaçao,
  Cointreau, Apricot Brandy,
  Anisette, Blackberry
  Brandy, Peach Brandy
  mixed with equal quantity
  Bourbon, Benedictine,
  Kirsch, Kümmel,
  Champagne Cognac,
  Cherry Heering, Applejack,
  Crème de Cassis

Mix soda, applesauce, and jam or preserves. Cream butter or oleomargarine until light. Add sugar gradually and beat until fluffy. Add applesauce mixture and beat 1 minute. Add egg and beat 1 minute more. If using mixer, all of foregoing should be done on ⁹/₁₀ maximum food mixer speed or "creaming speed." Sift flour, measure, and add salt and spices. Combine raisins, nuts, cherries, and, if desired, crystallized orange peel with flour mixture and stir quickly into batter. Drop about 2 inches apart by heaping teaspoonfuls on greased cooky sheets. Bake in 400° F. oven 12–13 minutes. Loosen from pan at once. Cool and ice as follows:

Cream 1 tablespoon butter or oleomargarine. Beat in 1 cup sifted confectioners' sugar and 1 tablespoon desired Spirit. If necessary an additional amount of Spirit may be added to get icing that will spread easily. Ice cooky tops and then make up another batch of icing in a different flavor, but using 1 tablespoon butter or oleomargarine and 1 cup sifted confectioners' sugar. Continue making up icings in various Spirit flavors until all cookies are covered.

Makes 67 cookies.

NOTE: For icing variations:

Add 1 tablespoon of orange marmalade when making up Curaçao or Grand Marnier Icing.

Add 2 tablespoons canned black Bing cherry juice and ⅓ cup chopped canned Bing cherries to 8 tablespoons butter or oleomargarine, 8 cups sifted confectioners' sugar, and enough Napoleon Brandy or Champagne Cognac to make icing that will spread easily and ice all cookies in same flavor.

Add 1 tablespoon strawberry or raspberry preserves to butter-sugar mixture and stir in just enough Cointreau and if necessary additional powdered sugar to make icing that will spread easily.

Sprinkle iced cookies with chopped nuts, chocolate trims, and/or colored sugar crystals. Also, if desired, color the various icings with different vegetable colors.

Kirsch, Cointreau, Rum, or Bourbon Balls

*40 small vanilla wafers
  crushed*
*2 tablespoons white corn
  syrup*
2 tablespoons sifted cocoa
*2 tablespoons drained
  chopped maraschino
  cherries soaked for 12
  hours in equal parts of
  own juice and Maraschino
  Liqueur*

*¼ cup citron cut into small
  pieces*
*⅓ cup pecans broken into
  small pieces*
*¼ cup Kirsch, Cointreau,
  Rum, or Bourbon*
Granulated sugar

Mix all ingredients, except granulated sugar, thoroughly, and roll into 1¼-inch balls between the palms of the hands. Roll balls in sugar.

Makes 20 balls.

Lebkuchen with Rum Icing

⅜ cup raisins
⅜ cup citron
*Rum to cover raisins and
  citron*
*2 ounces unsweetened
  baking chocolate*
4 eggs
2 cups granulated sugar
⅓ cup dark brown sugar
*1¼ cups finely ground
  pecans*
*¼ cup blanched and dried
  finely ground almonds*
*2 teaspoons powdered
  potassium carbonate[8]*
¼ cup Rum
8 ounces honey

*6¼ cups sifted all-purpose
  flour*
½ teaspoon salt
1 teaspoon cinnamon
¼ teaspoon cardamon
½ teaspoon cloves
*¾ cup pecans broken into
  small pieces*
*4 cups sifted confectioners'
  sugar*
1 teaspoon salt
2 teaspoons vanilla
*½ cup Rum (approximate).
  Marinade may be used to
  make up at least part of
  this ½ cup*

[8] White deliquescent granular translucent powder, used in brewing, in mineral waters, and in chocolate preparations.

The day before making Lebkuchen, cover raisins and citron with Rum and store in covered container in refrigerator. Drain raisins and citron, and, if desired, reserve marinade for icing. Melt chocolate over hot, not boiling, water and cool slightly.

Beat eggs until thick and lemon colored with rotary egg beater or on maximum food mixer speed. Add white and brown sugar gradually, beating well after each addition (if using mixer, beat on "creaming speed"). Beat 1 minute after all sugar has been added. Add melted chocolate and beat until blended. Stir ground nuts into egg and sugar mixture. Mix potassium carbonate with ¼ cup Rum and then blend into honey. Sift flour, salt, and spices together. Add drained citron, raisins, and nuts to flour mixture. With a wooden spoon add flour mixture alternately with honey mixture—a small amount of each at a time—starting and ending with flour. Cover bowl in which dough was mixed and place in refrigerator 4½–12 hours. Whenever convenient during this period roll small quantities of dough, letting remainder stay in refrigerator, on floured board or pastry cloth to ¼–⅓-inch thickness (the thicker cookies are softer, but this is a matter of personal taste). Cut into 1¾×2½-inch bars and place on well-greased baking sheets about 2 inches apart. Continue rolling and cutting until all dough is used. Bake in 325° F. oven approximately 20 minutes. Loosen from pan. Combine confectioners' sugar, salt, vanilla, and just enough Rum to make an icing that can be spread easily. Spread icing thinly over cookies and let dry. Store in covered containers.

Makes 42 ⅓-inch-thick cookies.

Pecan Almond Crisps

¾ cup butter or
  oleomargarine
1½ cups sugar
2 eggs
2 tablespoons Rum

1½ cups unsifted all-purpose
  flour
1 cup ground pecans
½ cup ground almonds
¼ cup very cold Rum

Put pecans and almonds (separately) through fine blade of grinder at least 1 day before baking cookies. This may be done several days or weeks ahead of time. Two hours before baking, place ¼ cup Rum in freezer section of refrigerator.

Cream butter or oleomargarine. Add sugar gradually and cream until light and fluffy. Add eggs and beat 1½ minutes. Add 2 tablespoons Rum. Measure flour and sift. Stir in flour and then add ground nuts, stirring only long enough to blend. Drop by half teaspoonfuls on greased cooky sheets, about 2 inches apart. Smooth down and flatten by pressing each cooky with the back of a spoon that has been dipped in the ¼ cup of ice cold Rum. After the cookies have been flattened, using the remainder of the cold Rum, spread the Spirit over the surface of the cookies with a brush (using 2–3 drops for each cooky). Bake in 400° F. oven until a rich brown (8–10 minutes). Remove from oven and loosen with spatula at once. Store in covered containers.

Makes 142 cookies.

Pecan Crisps

Follow recipe for PECAN ALMOND CRISPS, substituting 1½ cups ground pecans for the 1 cup ground pecans and the ½ cup ground almonds.

Frostings
and Dessert Sauces

Many great chefs in years gone by flavored their frostings with Brandy. The first Spirit-flavored icing that I tried was a butter cream, and I used Brandy for the flavor. It was a success, and thus emboldened I tried Rum, different kinds of Brandies, and then the various Liqueurs, and always the flavor of these frostings was something to dream about.

Then I decided that I needed a Brandy- or Rum-flavored DOUBLE-BOILER FROSTING that wouldn't sink into the cake after a day or so, as so often happens even to the best of cooks. Substituting the Spirit for the water doesn't work, as it makes the icing far too sugary. At last I had a happy thought! I dissolved a small amount of gelatine in a little Brandy and added it, with a cup of powdered sugar, to the icing as soon as it was removed from the hot water. The result was a Brandy-flavored marshmallowy frosting that doesn't sink into the cake, is good with coconut or chopped nuts, and just about perfect as an ALLEGRETTI with the melted chocolate dribbled over it.

Equally good are the Spirit-flavored liqueur sauces, and usually they are quite easy to make. Sometimes nothing more than mixing the proper Spirit with a marmalade or preserve is required, but despite their being simple to make, their flavors are tantalizing. Prepare 5 or 6 of these sauces, placing each in an attractive serving bowl, and as an extra added attraction prepare bowls of chopped nuts, BAKED PECAN OR ALMOND TOPPING (which is Part 2 of the recipe for PECAN ALMOND RUM TORTE) and maraschino cherries that have been soaked overnight in equal parts of their own juice and Maraschino Liqueur. Fill a very large soup tureen or a punch bowl with ice cream. Place the ice cream on a table and surround it with the bowls containing the various sauces, cherries, nuts, and topping, and let your guests make their own sundaes. They will love it.

Butter-Cream Frosting

6 cups sifted confectioners' sugar (approximate)
⅔ cup butter or oleomargarine or vegetable shortening
6 tablespoons (approximate) of any of the following:
  Rum, Napoleon Brandy, Cointreau, Curaçao, Grand Marnier,
  Maraschino, Benedictine, Kümmel, Crème de Cassis, Anisette,
  Kirsch, Crème de Menthe, Cherry Heering, Champagne Cognac

Combine 4 cups of sugar with softened butter or oleomargarine or vegetable shortening and mix thoroughly. Add liquid and stir in remainder of sugar. Beat until smooth. More sugar or more liquid may be added to achieve an icing that can be easily spread.
Will ice 1 large cake.

Maraschino Butter-Cream Frosting

For at least 12 hours before making frosting, soak ⅓ cup drained and quartered maraschino cherries in a mixture of 3 tablespoons of Maraschino Liqueur and 3 tablespoons of cherry juice.

Prepare BUTTER-CREAM FROSTING, using the 6 tablespoons of Maraschino Liqueur and cherry juice as the liquid. Stir in the cherries.

Butterscotch Double-Boiler Frosting

2 egg whites	1 teaspoon unflavored
1½ cups firmly packed	gelatine
brown sugar	1 tablespoon Rum
5 tablespoons water	1 cup sifted confectioners'
¼ teaspoon cream of tartar	sugar

Combine egg whites, brown sugar, water, and cream of tartar in top of double boiler. Soak gelatine (in 3-inch-high heatproof cup) in Rum. Place double-boiler top over boiling water and beat egg-white mixture with rotary egg beater (7 minutes) or on "creaming speed" of mixer (about 5 minutes) until frosting stands in peaks. Place cup holding gelatine in pan holding boiling water to a depth of 1½ inches. Add melted gelatine and confectioners' sugar to frosting and beat until smooth. Spread on cake.

Enough icing for 1 large layer cake or cake baked in 10-inch tube pan.

Chocolate Brandy Frosting

6 ounces chocolate	7 tablespoons milk
4½ tablespoons butter	3½ tablespoons Brandy
6 cups sifted confectioners'	1½ teaspoons vanilla
sugar	
¼ teaspoon salt	

Melt chocolate and butter over hot, not boiling, water. Thoroughly mix sugar, salt, milk, Brandy, and vanilla. Stir in butter-chocolate mixture. Let stand, stirring occasionally, with a spoon for just a few minutes until frosting is right consistency to spread.

Will ice 55 Chocolate Sips of Spirits or large layer cake or cake baked in 10-inch tube pan.

Chocolate-Cream Filling

3 tablespoons cornstarch
1 cup sugar
3/8 teaspoon salt
2 slightly beaten egg yolks

2½ ounces melted
    unsweetened chocolate
1⅞ cup scalded milk
2 tablespoons hot Brandy
1 tablespoon Brandy

Sift cornstarch and sugar. Add salt, slightly beaten yolks, and melted chocolate, and stir until blended. Stir in scalded milk and hot Brandy. Cook over medium heat (direct) until boiling point is reached. Lower heat and cook, stirring constantly until mixture is thick. Remove from heat. Cool and add 1 tablespoon Brandy. Blend Spirit with custard.
Makes 2 cups.

Custard Filling

⅔ cup sugar
2 tablespoons cornstarch
2 slightly beaten egg yolks
⅞ cup scalded milk

2 tablespoons Rum, Brandy,
    Cointreau, or Triple Sec
2 teaspoons Rum, Brandy,
    Cointreau, or Triple Sec

Sift sugar and cornstarch. Combine with slightly beaten yolks. Stir in scalded milk, and when completely blended heat 2 tablespoons of desired Spirit and add to milk mixture. Heat to boiling point over direct heat and then lower heat and cook until desired consistency is reached, stirring constantly. Cool and add 2 teaspoons of same Spirit as was used to make custard.
Makes about 1 cup.

Double-Boiler Frosting

2 egg whites
⅛ teaspoon salt
⅓ cup water
1½ cups granulated sugar
¼ teaspoon cream of tartar

1 tablespoon Rum, Brandy,
or Cointreau
1 teaspoon unflavored
gelatine
1 cup sifted confectioners'
sugar

Combine egg whites, salt, water, granulated sugar, and cream of tartar in top of double boiler. Place Rum, Brandy, or Cointreau in 3-inch-high heatproof cup. Sprinkle gelatine over Spirit. Place top of double boiler over rapidly boiling water. Beat egg white mixture with rotary egg beater (7 minutes) or on "creaming speed" of mixer (about 5 minutes) until frosting will hold a peak. Place cup holding gelatine in pan of boiling water to a depth of 1½ inches. Pour melted gelatine and sifted confectioners' sugar into frosting and beat only until smooth. Spread on cake at once.

Will ice 1 large layer cake or cake baked in 10-inch tube pan.

Allegretti Icing

DOUBLE-BOILER FROSTING *flavored with Rum, Brandy, or Cointreau*
2 squares unsweetened chocolate
¼ teaspoon butter or oleomargarine

Prepare frosting. Melt chocolate over hot, not boiling, water with the butter or oleomargarine. Dribble melted chocolate mixture from tip of a teaspoon on frosted cake.

Nesselrode Frosting

DOUBLE-BOILER FROSTING *flavored with Rum, Brandy, or Cointreau*
¼ cup chopped well-drained maraschino cherries
¼ cup drained chopped marrons

Prepare frosting and stir in cherries and marrons.

Brandy Chocolate Sauce

1 cup boiling water
1 ounce unsweetened chocolate melted and cooled slightly

½ cup plus 1 tablespoon sugar
2 tablespoons Napoleon Brandy or Champagne Cognac

Combine water, melted chocolate, and sugar. When blended, cook over medium heat until sauce reaches desired consistency. Cool and stir in Brandy.
Makes ⅞ cup.

Brandy Cocoa Sauce

¼ cup cocoa
1¼ cups sugar
⅛ teaspoon salt

⅓ cup very hot Napoleon Brandy or Champagne Cognac
⅓ cup hot water

Mix cocoa, sugar, and salt. Add hot Brandy and stir until mixture is completely blended. Stir in hot water. Bring to a boil, stirring steadily. Lower heat slightly so that sauce will not boil over pot, but continue boiling for 2½–3½ minutes until desired consistency is reached. Pour into container. Cool and store in refrigerator.
Makes 1 cup.

Butterscotch Sauce with Rum or Brandy

⅞ cup brown sugar
1½ teaspoons cornstarch
  measured then sifted
2 tablespoons white corn
  syrup

⅓ cup Brandy or Rum
2 tablespoons breakfast
  cream

Combine ingredients and stir until blended. Bring to boiling point; lower heat to medium and cook without stirring 3 minutes. Remove from heat. Cool if desired or serve hot.
Makes ¾ cup.

Caramel Sauce with Brandy

½ pound (approximately 1⅓ cups) vanilla caramels
2 tablespoons water
4 tablespoons Cognac or Napoleon Brandy

Melt caramels over hot, not boiling, water, and when they are completely melted, slowly add water, stirring until blended. Gradually add Brandy, stirring constantly as it is added. Serve hot or cold.
Makes 1 cup.

Cherry Anisette Sauce

2½ cups red water-pack
  cherries with juice
2 tablespoons Anisette
1 cup sugar

¼ cup flour
4–5 drops red vegetable
  coloring

Combine cherries and juice with Anisette. Sift sugar and flour into a saucepan. Stir in about ⅓ cup of cherry juice and Anisette mixture gradually and stir until smooth. Add cherries and remainder of juice mixture. Color desired shade. Cook over medium heat until mixture thickens, stirring constantly. Remove from heat and cool. Store in refrigerator.

Serves 12.

Black Cherry-Cointreau-Rum Sauce

¾ cup canned black-cherry   *2 teaspoons cornstarch*
juice   *sifted and then measured*
¼ cup Cointreau   *Drained black cherries from*
⅓ cup sugar   *1-pound can*
⅛ teaspoon salt   *2 tablespoons Rum*

Cook juice, Cointreau, sugar, salt, and cornstarch over medium heat until thickened. Stir in drained cherries and Rum. Cool and store in refrigerator.

Serves 12 but unused portion may be kept in refrigerator for several weeks.

NOTE: ¼ cup Rum may be substituted for ¼ cup of Cointreau and 2 tablespoons of Cointreau may be substituted for 2 tablespoons Rum, thus using only one Spirit (Cointreau or Rum, as desired) in the sauce.

Cointreau and Candied Fruit Sauce

1 cup chopped mixed candied fruit
½ cup Cointreau

Combine fruit and Cointreau. Chill.
Serves 8.

Orange Marmalade-Curaçao Sauce

¾ cup orange marmalade
¼ cup Curaçao

Combine marmalade and Curaçao. Chill.
Serves 6–8.

Orange Marmalade-Grand Marnier Sauce

¾ cup orange marmalade
¼ cup Grand Marnier

Combine orange marmalade and Grand Marnier. Chill.
Serves 6–8.

White Framboise-Raspberry Sauce

1 cup sugar
⅔ cup water

*2 cups chilled slightly
    crushed raspberries*
White Framboise

Boil sugar and water until syrup will spin a thread (230°
F.). Sprinkle berries lightly (White Framboise is very potent,
so use carefully) with Spirit. Stir syrup into berries and chill.
Serves 8.

White Framboise-Frozen Raspberry Sauce

10 ounces thawed frozen sweetened raspberries
White Framboise

Flavor berries to taste with White Framboise (pouring slowly and carefully as Spirit is strong). Chill at least several hours. *Serves 6.*

Cointreau-Strawberry Preserves Sauce

12 ounces strawberry preserves
⅓ cup Cointreau

Combine preserves and Cointreau and chill thoroughly. *Serves 12.*

Kirsch-Strawberry or Raspberry Preserves Sauce

12 ounces strawberry or raspberry preserves
Kirsch

Flavor preserves with Kirsch to taste, adding the Spirit slowly, as it has a strong flavor. *Serves 12.*

Strawberry Sauce

1 cup sugar
⅔ cup water

2 cups chilled crushed
   strawberries
Kirsch

Boil sugar and water until syrup will spin a thread (230° F.). Sprinkle the berries lightly with Kirsch. Stir syrup into berries and chill.
Serves 8.

Frozen Strawberry Sauce

10 ounces thawed frozen sweetened strawberries
Kirsch

Sprinkle berries with Kirsch and chill before serving.
Serves 6.

Whipped-Cream Ice-Cream Sauce

¾ cup chocolate, coffee,
   vanilla, or strawberry ice
   cream
1½ cups stiffly whipped
   cream

2½ tablespoons Rum or
   Cointreau (thoroughly
   chilled)

Beat ice cream just until fluffy but not melted. Fold into whipped cream. Fold Rum into chocolate or coffee ice cream mixture or fold Cointreau into the vanilla or strawberry sauce. Serve at once.
Serves 10.

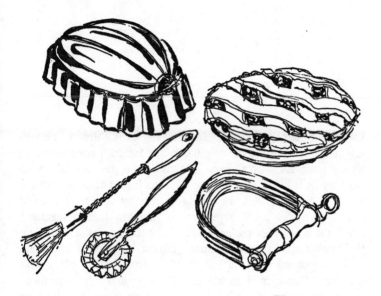

Desserts

Lu Magee, our family cook, inspired my early interest in cooking and also gave me the original recipe for fruit cake. Another legacy from Lu was a marvelous chocolate pie. She left it to me only as a list of ingredients, with no information as to how to put it together. Starting with this sketchy outline, I worked it up, with the usual experimental changes and refinements along the way. This recipe was already unique for a chocolate pie in that the custard mixture (almost as thin as chocolate milk) is poured into the unbaked pie crust before going into the oven. However, I found that I could make it even more special by adding Brandy to the chocolate filling and topping it off with vanilla ice cream or CORDIAL MOUSSE.

A more recent experiment bore fruit just as this book was being completed. I have always thought that PECAN PIE was sickeningly sweet—and that it could be just wonderful if something could be done to rectify this flaw. I decided to try adding Rum to the recipe, and it did indeed do all that I had hoped for.

Another discovery that can prove most valuable to a busy housewife or career woman is the successful storing of prepared CREPES SUZETTES and other elegant desserts, like BAKED ALASKA (minus the meringue of course). I found that I could fry the crepes, spread them with the "butter," roll them, and put them in the freezer wrapped in foil. When I need them, I let them stand at room temperature for several hours, and then put them in the oven (still wrapped in foil) for 10 minutes at 400° F. They come out perfectly—ready to be cooked in Spirits at the table.

CUSTARD DESSERTS

Baked Custard with Grand Marnier-Butterscotch Topping

2 tablespoons butter or
    oleomargarine
½ cup light brown sugar
1 tablespoon grated orange
    rind
¼ teaspoon cinnamon
¼ teaspoon cardamon, if
    desired

⅓ cup hot Grand Marnier
3 eggs
3 rounded tablespoons
    sugar
⅛ teaspoon salt
1 teaspoon vanilla
3 cups milk

Melt butter or oleomargarine. Add brown sugar, orange rind, and spices. Cook over medium heat in small frying pan until sugar is melted. Slowly add Grand Marnier. Cook until just slightly thickened over medium heat. Divide equally between 7 custard cups. Beat eggs slightly with a fork, just enough to combine yolks and whites, but not enough to make the eggs foamy. Add granulated sugar, salt, and vanilla. Scald milk over boiling water and add to egg mixture slowly. Stir until completely blended. Pour over Grand Marnier butterscotch slowly and gently. Place cups in pan into which hot water has been poured to a depth of 1 inch. Bake in 350° F. oven 40–45 minutes until silver knife inserted in custard comes out clean. Remove from oven and place molds in pan into which cold water to a depth of 1 inch has been poured. When custards are cool, refrigerate until ready to serve. Turn them out on individual serving plates or serve in baking cup, as desired.

Benedictine-Crème Brûlée with Macédoine Flambé

4 egg yolks
3 tablespoons Benedictine
1 pint whipping cream
⅓ cup granulated sugar
⅓ cup brown sugar

2 cups drained pitted dark
  sweet cherries (canned)
10 ounces thawed sliced
  frozen peaches
¼ cup Champagne Cognac
  or Napoleon Brandy

Beat yolks on maximum food-mixer speed or with rotary egg beater until very thick. Add Benedictine and beat until blended. Scald cream over hot, not boiling, water. As soon as cream is placed over the hot water, add sugar to yolks and continue beating until cream is scalded. Pour cream into yolks slowly and blend completely. Pour mixture into top of double boiler. Into bottom of double boiler, pour approximately 1½ inches of hot water. Place top of boiler containing yolk mixture over water—the section containing the custard should not touch the water. Cook over hot, not boiling, water, stirring constantly with a wooden spoon until custard thickens (10–12 minutes). During this period, should the custard start to curdle, beat rapidly with rotary egg beater until smooth. When the custard will coat a silver spoon heavily, pour it into an oval baking serving dish (10 inches long×1–1½ inches deep) or into a 9-inch glass pie pan. Cool and place in refrigerator overnight. Just before serving time sprinkle surface evenly with brown sugar. Place dish holding custard in a large shallow pan of ice water (the ice water should not be higher than one half of the baking-dish sides). Gently place pan in broiler about 4 inches under unit, being careful that water does not get into custard. Cook with broiler door slightly open so that brûlée can be carefully watched. When sugar forms a crust, remove custard from broiler and place in refrigerator.

Combine cherries and peaches. Heat and spoon into heated serving bowl. Heat Brandy. Pour about 2½ tablespoons of hot Spirit over fruit. Ignite remainder of Brandy and pour over cherries and peaches. Serve at once with Crème Brûlée which should be spooned over individual portions of the fruit.

Serves 6.

NOTE: Heated bowl of fruit may be brought to table and Brandy ignited there or bowl may be brought in after Brandy is ignited.

Café Brûlot Custard

4 eggs separated	¾ cup black coffee
1 cup sugar	¼ teaspoon cinnamon
3 tablespoons flour measured and then sifted	1½ teaspoons grated orange peel
1 tablespoon melted butter	1½ teaspoons grated lemon peel
¼ cup Cognac	

Beat egg yolks slightly. Add sugar and flour. Stir in butter. Bring Cognac and coffee to a boil. Combine with egg-yolk mixture thoroughly. Stir in cinnamon. Cook in top of double boiler over boiling water, stirring constantly, until custard is thick. Remove from stove. Stir in grated orange and lemon peel. Chill in refrigerator. Beat egg whites until stiff and fold custard over and over them until thoroughly blended.

Serves 5.

Custard

(To be used where a boiled custard is specified in recipes in this book.)

4 eggs separated	*1 cup scalded milk*
1 cup sugar	*1½ tablespoons Rum,*
3 tablespoons flour	*Brandy, Cointreau, or*
measured and then sifted	*Bourbon Whisky*

Beat yolks slightly. Measure sugar and flour and sift. Add dry ingredients to yolks and stir only long enough to blend. Stir in scalded milk and pour mixture into top of double boiler. Cook over boiling water, stirring constantly with a wooden spoon, until thick. Remove from heat and stir in Rum, Brandy, Cointreau, or Bourbon Whisky. Cool. Fold in stiffly beaten egg whites, until custard is smooth. Refrigerate until ready to use. *Serves 5.*

NOTE: If making custards for children, omit Spirit and substitute 1 teaspoon vanilla for the 1½ tablespoons Spirit.

Custard Sponge Roll

RUM SPONGE ROLL	*⅔ cup pecans broken into*
MOCHA RUM CUSTARD or	*small pieces*
CAFE BRULOT CUSTARD or	*or blanched toasted*
LEMON SHERRY CUSTARD	*almond slivers*
	Chocolate trims, if desired

Prepare Rum Sponge Roll and desired 1 of 3 custards listed. In line with instructions for making Rum Sponge Roll, when cool, unroll. Spread with half of custard and sprinkle with half of nuts. Reroll. Place roll on serving platter. As directed in Rum Sponge Roll recipe, brush roll with 2 tablespoons Rum. Cover roll with remaining custard and sprinkle with the remaining nuts. If desired, also sprinkle with chocolate trims. Place in refrigerator for at least 5–6 hours before serving. *Serves 8, but can be stretched.*

Floating Island with Strawberries and Kirsch

3¾ cups milk	2 tablespoons cornstarch
¼ teaspoon salt	measured then sifted
8 egg whites	¼ cup hot Rum
¼ teaspoon cream of tartar	4 cups washed drained and
1 cup sugar	hulled small strawberries
1 cup whipping cream	or thawed drained frozen
8 egg yolks	strawberries
⅔ cup sugar	Kirsch

Scald milk in large skillet (240° F.). Add salt to egg whites and beat until foamy. Add cream of tartar and beat until soft-peak stage is reached. Add 1 cup sugar gradually and beat until whites are stiff. Drop heaping teaspoons of the meringue—about 1 inch apart—on the scalding milk. Cook 3 minutes; turn and cook 3 minutes more. Gently lift the meringues with a slotted spoon and drain on absorbent paper towels (*makes approximately 64 small meringues*). When meringues are cool they may be stored in refrigerator 4–5 hours. When all the meringues have been cooked, combine 2 cups of the scalded milk and 1 cup whipping cream. Scald over hot water.

Beat yolks until thick and lemon colored. Stir in ⅔ cup sugar, cornstarch, and Rum. Gradually add the scalded milk and cream mixture and stir until completely mixed. Cook over boiling water, stirring constantly, until custard is thick enough to heavily coat a silver spoon. Cool and then refrigerate. When ready to serve, place berries in very large glass bowl and sprinkle lib-

erally with Kirsch. Pile meringues on top of berries and spoon custard over meringues.
Serves 16.

Grand Marnier Cream

⅞ cup sugar
⅞ cup of water
2 tablespoons Grand
  Marnier
4 egg yolks
3 tablespoons Grand
  Marnier
1 cup whipping cream

2 tablespoons crystallized
  orange peel made
  according to recipe for
  CRYSTALLIZED CITRUS
  FRUIT PEEL
⅓ cup BAKED PECAN OR
  ALMOND TOPPING

Stir sugar into water and add 2 tablespoons Grand Marnier. Cook over medium heat without stirring until syrup spins a thread (230° F.). Beat yolks until light and fluffy. Pour syrup over yolks in very thin stream, beating constantly—if using electric mixer, use maximum speed. Continue beating until yolk mixture is cool. Stir in 3 tablespoons Grand Marnier. Whip cream until very stiff. Fold cream into yolk mixture and then fold in orange peel. Spoon into dessert cups. Chill for at least 4 hours. Before serving, sprinkle tops with Baked Pecan or Almond Topping.
Serves 6.

Lemon Sherry Custard

2 lemons
4 eggs separated
1 cup sugar
3 tablespoons flour
  measured and then sifted

⅓ cup Sherry
⅔ cup water
1 tablespoon melted butter

Cut lemons in halves and remove seeds. Grate lemons (skin and pulp, but discard membranes). Beat egg yolks slightly. Stir in sugar and flour; bring Sherry and water to a boil. Stir the Wine, water, and melted butter into the egg-yolk mixture. Cook in top of double boiler over boiling water, stirring constantly, until custard is thick. Remove from heat. Stir in grated lemon. Chill thoroughly. Beat egg whites until stiff. Fold custard over and over stiffly beaten egg whites. Spoon into serving bowl or sherbet cups. Refrigerate.

Serves 5.

Marron Champagne Cognac Pudding

4 egg yolks	6 maraschino cherries soaked
1 cup sugar	for at least 12 hours in
3 tablespoons flour	equal parts their own
⅞ cup scalded breakfast	juice and Maraschino
cream	Liqueur
¼ cup Champagne Cognac	Chocolate trims or shaved
½ cup brandied marrons	unsweetened baking
4 stiffly beaten egg whites	chocolate

Beat yolks slightly. Measure sugar and flour and sift. Stir in, until completely blended, cream and 2 tablespoons Champagne Cognac. Cook over simmering water for 10 minutes, stirring constantly with a wooden spoon. Increase heat so that water in bottom of double boiler will boil gently. Continue stirring until custard is thick. Put custard through a fine sieve and stir in 2 tablespoons Champagne Cognac. Chill. Break marrons into pieces. Stir into chilled custard. Fold custard gently over and over stiffly beaten egg whites. Spoon into serving bowl or 6 individual dishes or sherbet cups. Refrigerate. Decorate with cherries and chocolate trims or shaved unsweetened baking chocolate.

Serves 6.

Mocha Rum Custard

4 *eggs separated*
1 *cup sugar*
3 *tablespoons flour*
  measured then sifted
1 *tablespoon butter melted*

2 *tablespoons chocolate*
  syrup
3 *tablespoons Rum*
¾ *cup black coffee*
½ *cup broken pecans*

Beat egg yolks slightly. Add sugar and flour, and, when blended, add butter. Bring chocolate syrup, 2 tablespoons of Rum, and black coffee to a boil. Blend into egg mixture gradually and cook over boiling water, stirring constantly, until custard is thick. Remove from stove. Add remaining Rum. Chill custard. Stir in pecans. Beat egg whites until very stiff. Fold custard over and over the egg whites until thoroughly blended. Refrigerate.
Serves 6.

New Orleans Cream Pie

RUM SPONGE
⅔ *cup sugar*
2 *tablespoons cornstarch*
2 *slightly beaten egg yolks*
⅞ *cup scalded milk*

2 *tablespoons Grand*
  Marnier
Cointreau
Confectioners' sugar

Prepare Rum Sponge. Sift sugar and cornstarch. Combine with slightly beaten yolks. Stir in scalded milk, and when completely blended heat Grand Marnier and add to milk mixture. Heat to boiling point over direct heat and then lower heat and cook until desired consistency is reached, stirring constantly. Cool and then chill in refrigerator. Split cake into 2 layers. Brush cut sides with Cointreau. Put the layers together with the chilled custard filling. Sift confectioners' sugar over top. Refrigerate until ready to serve.
Serves 8.

Tipsy Fellow

CUSTARD *flavored with Rum*
or Bourbon Whisky
(double recipe)

4½ dozen vanilla wafers
(approximate)
Bourbon Whisky or Rum
⅔ cup chopped pecans

Prepare Custard and, when it is chilled, line a bowl about 9 inches in diameter and 1½ inches deep with vanilla wafers, breaking some in order to fit them together in a "solid" shell. Sprinkle with Bourbon Whisky or Rum (using the Spirit with which Custard is flavored). Cover with layer of Custard and top Custard with a layer of vanilla wafers. Sprinkle wafers with Whisky or Rum and pecans. Cover with Custard and sprinkle with pecans. Place in refrigerator overnight.
Serves 8.

Queens' Custard

18 double ladyfingers
separated
2 cups small macaroon
pieces
Cognac
CUSTARD, *Cognac flavored*
(double quantities of all
ingredients specified)
1 cup blanched toasted
slivered almonds

½ cup drained quartered
maraschino cherries that
have been soaked in equal
parts their own juice and
Maraschino Liqueur for at
least 12 hours
1½ cups stiffly whipped and
sweetened cream

Sprinkle ladyfingers and macaroon pieces lightly with **Cognac**. Line large bowl (glass preferred) with ladyfingers. Alternate layers of Custard and macaroons, sprinkling each of the Custard

layers with almonds and cherries. Chill in refrigerator. Just before serving, top with sweetened whipped cream.
Serves 12.

Tropical Custard

4 ounces grated moist
   sweetened canned
   coconut
1 cup breakfast cream
½ cup milk
4 eggs separated
1 cup sugar
3 tablespoons flour
   measured then sifted

1 teaspoon vanilla
12 medium-size double
   ladyfingers
Rum
Maraschino cherries soaked
   for at least 12 hours in
   equal parts their own
   juice and Maraschino
   Liqueur

Soak coconut in cream 2 hours in covered container in refrigerator. Add milk. Beat yolks until thick and lemon colored. Measure sugar and flour and sift. Stir dry ingredients into egg yolks. Scald coconut-cream in top of double boiler over boiling water. Stir into yolk mixture and cook in top of double boiler over boiling water, stirring constantly, until thick. Remove from heat. Stir in vanilla. Cool. Beat egg whites until stiff. Fold into custard. Separate ladyfingers and brush with Rum. *Line 6 sherbet cups* with ladyfingers and fill with custard. Top each serving with cherry and refrigerate until ready to serve.

FROZEN DESSERTS

Apricot Sherbet

6 ounces dried apricots
Sweet Sauterne
½ cup sugar
2 tablespoons lemon juice
¾ cup sugar

2 teaspoons gelatine
2 tablespoons water
¼ cup Apricot Brandy
1 cup milk
1 stiffly beaten egg white

Rinse apricots. Put in saucepan and cover with Sauterne. Bring to a boil and then reduce heat. Allow to simmer 20 minutes. If needed, because of evaporation, additional Wine may be added. Stir in ½ cup sugar and cook over low heat 5 minutes. Pour ¼ cup syrup in which apricots were cooked into blender (if syrup has cooked to less than ¼ cup, add Sauterne enough to make this measurement). Add apricots. Run blender for 30 seconds, turn off motor, and then run an additional 30 seconds. (Fruit may be put through meat grinder and syrup added after fruit is ground, if blender is not available.) Add lemon juice and ¾ cup sugar to puréed fruit. Soak gelatine in water. Bring Apricot Brandy to a boil and pour over gelatine. Stir until dissolved. Blend in apricot pulp. Add milk gradually and stir until completely blended. Spoon into freezer tray and place tray on bottom of freezer unit of refrigerator. After 1 hour place mixture in chilled bowl and beat until fluffy, but not melted, with cold rotary egg beater. Fold in stiffly beaten egg white and spoon back into tray. Return tray to bottom of freezing section of refrigerator and freeze until firm, stirring with a cold wooden spoon from time to time. *Serves 6.*

Apricot Sherbet Cake

APRICOT SHERBET	*Canned drained apricot*
JAM CAKE	*halves chilled*
1 cup apricot preserves	*Apricot Brandy*
2 tablespoons Apricot	*Sprigs of mint*
Brandy, or Cointreau, or	
Kirsch	

Prepare sherbet and after folding egg whites in, spoon into a 9-inch round layer-cake pan that has been lined with aluminum foil so that sherbet may be easily lifted from pan when frozen. Freeze, according to recipe for Apricot Sherbet.

Prepare Jam Cake and cool on racks. About 25 minutes be-

fore serving, place layer of sherbet between the cake layers. Wrap in aluminum foil and quickly place in freezer until ready to serve. Remove wrapping from cake and place it on chilled platter. Cover top with glaze made by heating preserves and Apricot Brandy, Cointreau, or Kirsch, straining it and keeping warm over hot water until ready to use. Garnish platter with apricot halves lightly brushed with Apricot Brandy and sprigs of mint. Serve at once.
Serves 12–16.

Baked Alaska

RUM SPONGE	*Kirsch*
1 pint very firm ice cream or mousse (pink or green tinted if possible)	*¼ teaspoon salt*
	8 egg whites
	½ teaspoon cream of tartar
½ cup thawed frozen strawberries	*1 cup sugar*

After bottom of form has been removed from cake, turn cake right side up. Remove a circle of cake about 2½–3 inches in diameter and about 1 inch thick from the center of the sponge, leaving a shell with walls about 1½ inches thick. Fill sponge shell with very firm ice cream or mousse, piling ice cream or mousse so that it is about an inch higher than the top of cake. Wrap cake and ice cream or mousse in heavy aluminum foil and place in freezer section of refrigerator or in deep freeze for at least 30 minutes (or for weeks or months, if desired). Place several thicknesses of wrapping paper on a wet board or wrap a dry board with several thicknesses of heavy aluminum foil. Defrost and drain strawberries. Sprinkle lightly with Kirsch and let stand several hours. Add salt to egg whites. Beat until foamy. Add cream of tartar and beat to the soft-peak stage. Add sugar gradually and beat until meringue is stiff and glossy. Again drain berries and fold the well-drained berries into the meringue.

Place cake on prepared board and quickly and completely cover with meringue. Bake 3–5 minutes in 500° F. oven. Slide Alaska gently from board to platter or if board was covered with aluminum foil place it on a large heatproof serving tray. Serve at once.

Serves 10–12, according to thickness of slices.

Baked Alaska Flambé

CORDIAL MOUSSE *flavored* *with Curaçao*	*1 cup sugar*
PECAN ALMOND RUM TORTE *(Part 1 only)*	*½ cup crystallized orange* *peel (see recipe for*
¼ *teaspoon salt*	CRYSTALLIZED CITRUS
8 *egg whites*	FRUIT PEEL) *cut into narrow*
½ *teaspoon cream of tartar*	*½-inch-long strips*
	¼ *cup Rum*

Prepare mousse. Cut a sheet of aluminum foil into a rectangle 8×16 inches. Fit the sheet into an 8×2×8-inch aluminum pan so that the two ends of the sheet will hang over the sides of the pan in order that the mousse may be easily lifted when frozen. Spoon mousse into pan and follow instructions given in recipe for Cordial Mousse for freezing.

Prepare torte in accordance with Part 1 of instructions given in recipe for Pecan Almond Rum Torte. When torte is cold, remove mousse from wrapping of aluminum foil and cut into 2 equal parts. (The torte in accordance with the recipe should be cut into 3 4×8-inch parts.) Alternate layers of torte and mousse, starting and ending with torte. Wrap in aluminum foil and place in freezing unit of refrigerator or in deep freeze for at least 30 minutes or for as long as desired. Add salt to egg whites. Beat until foamy. Add cream of tartar and beat to the soft-peak stage. Add sugar gradually and beat until stiff and glossy. Fold in orange peel.

Remove aluminum foil from torte and place on heatproof serving platter or on heavy board covered with several layers of aluminum foil. Cover completely with meringue. Bake in 500° F. oven 3–5 minutes (until meringue is delicate brown). If using board covered with aluminum foil, place on tray with rim. Heat Rum. Pour all but about 1 tablespoon around the Alaska. Ignite remaining hot Spirit and pour lighted Rum over Rum that has already been poured around torte. Serve at once. *Serves 10–12, according to thickness of slices.*

Bananas Flambé with Chocolate Ice Cream

2 tablespoons butter	¼ teaspoon cardamon
½ cup light brown sugar	¼ teaspoon cinnamon
3 small bananas sliced lengthwise (thin slices)	¼ cup Cognac
1 tablespoon grated orange peel	1½ tablespoons Crème de Cacao
	1 quart chocolate ice cream

Melt butter and add sugar in top pan of chafing dish over direct heat. When sugar is dissolved, add banana slices, orange peel, and spices. Cook until bananas are soft and almost transparent, stirring gently from time to time. Heat Cognac and Crème de Cacao. Pour approximately ¼ cup of hot mixture on top of fruit and ignite remaining hot Spirits. Pour lighted mixture over fruit and when flame dies, spoon over *6 individual servings* of ice cream.

Bananas Flambé with Vanilla Ice Cream

3 bananas	¼ cup Rum
3 tablespoons butter	1½ tablespoons Crème de Banana
½ cup brown sugar	1 quart vanilla ice cream
¼ teaspoon cinnamon	
⅛ teaspoon cardamon or nutmeg	

Cut each banana into 4 lengthwise strips. Melt butter in top pan of chafing dish over direct heat. When butter bubbles, place bananas in pan and add sugar and spices. Cook until sugar melts and bananas are soft, stirring occasionally. Combine Rum and Crème de Banana. Heat and pour about ¼ cup of hot mixture of Spirits over bananas. Ignite remaining hot Spirits and pour burning mixture into chafing dish. As soon as flame dies, serve bananas over *6 individual portions* of ice cream.

Biscuit Tortoni

6 egg yolks
⅞ cups sifted confectioners'
   sugar
⅛ teaspoon salt
¼ cup Cointreau
¾ cup very small macaroon
   pieces

½ cup drained sliced
   Maraschino cherries
   that have been soaked
   in equal parts of their own
   juice and Maraschino
   Liqueur
6 egg whites beaten stiff
1 pint heavy cream whipped
   stiff
6 finely crushed macaroons

Beat egg yolks until light and thick. Add sugar and salt gradually, continuing to beat until light and fluffy. Add Cointreau and beat until completely blended. Add macaroon pieces and cherries. Fold in stiffly beaten whites and then fold in stiffly beaten whipped cream. Spoon into freezer tray and place in freezing section of refrigerator, placing tray so that its bottom touches bottom of freezer unit. When frozen, if desired, pack into freezer carton and store in freezer. When ready to serve, garnish with crushed macaroons.
Makes ½ gallon.

Brandy Egg-Custard Ice Cream

3¾ cups milk
¼ teaspoon salt
8 egg whites
¼ teaspoon cream of tartar
1 cup sugar
1 cup whipping cream
8 egg yolks
⅔ cup sugar
2 tablespoons cornstarch
  measured then sifted

¼ cup hot Cognac or
  Napoleon Brandy
1 tablespoon unflavored
  gelatine
¼ cup Cognac or Napoleon
  Brandy
1 cup whipping cream
¼ cup sugar

Scald milk in large skillet (240° F.). Add salt to egg whites and beat until foamy. Add cream of tartar and beat until soft-peak stage is reached. Add 1 cup sugar gradually and beat until whites are stiff. Drop heaping teaspoons of the meringue—about 1 inch apart—on the scalding milk. Cook 3 minutes, turn and cook 3 minutes more. Gently lift the meringues with a slotted spoon and drain on absorbent paper towels. When all the meringues have been cooked, combine 2 cups of the scalded milk and 1 cup whipping cream. Scald over hot water. Beat yolks until thick and lemon colored. Stir in ⅔ cup sugar, cornstarch, and Brandy. Gradually add the scalded milk and cream mixture and stir until completely mixed. Cook over boiling water, stirring constantly, until custard is thick enough to heavily coat a silver spoon.

Sprinkle gelatine over ¼ cup Brandy in a small ramekin about 2½ inches high. Place ramekin in a pan of boiling water to a depth of 1½ inches and remove pan from heat. When gelatine is melted, stir into custard. Cool slightly and fold in meringues, folding until they are almost completely blended with custard and there are only a few tiny pieces of the meringue floating in the gelatine mixture. Pour into an 8×8×3-inch aluminum pan. Place the pan in the freezer so that the entire bottom will be in contact with the bottom of the freezing compartment of the refrigerator. Let stand for 1 hour. Whip 1 cup of cream until stiff and stir in sugar. Remove the custard mixture from freezer. Place custard in chilled bowl and beat for 2 minutes with a cold rotary egg beater. Fold in the whipped cream. In the meantime, keep pan in which ice cream is being frozen in freezer section. Spoon custard mixture back into cold pan and return to freezer; 2 or 3 times during the next 2 or 3 hours stir mixture with a cold wooden spoon. When custard is completely frozen, pack ice cream into a freezer carton and store in refrigerator. Carton should be kept covered. Use as needed.

Makes 1⅔ quarts.

NOTES:

Rum or Cointreau may be substituted for Brandy.

The meringues are cooked because of the particular richness and flavor that is lent to the milk used for this custard ice cream.

Brandy- or Rum-Lemon Ice Cream

1 quart vanilla ice cream   *1½ cups stiffly whipped*
Grated rind 2 lemons   *cream*
5 tablespoons Rum or
Brandy

Soften ice cream slightly. Stir in rind, Rum or Brandy, and fold in stiffly whipped cream. Spoon into freezer tray and place in freezing section of refrigerator, placing tray so that its bottom touches bottom of freezer unit.

Serves 8.

Brandy-Lemon Mousse

Follow recipe for RUM-LEMON MOUSSE, substituting Brandy for Rum.

Makes 1 quart.

Cherries Jubilee

1 cup sweet black pitted
   canned cherries
½ cup cherry juice
1½ tablespoons Kirsch

5 tablespoons heated
   Cognac
1 quart vanilla or custard
   ice cream

Drain cherries. Pour ½ cup juice and the Kirsch over the fruit. Place cherries and liquid in the top pan of a chafing dish over direct heat. When thoroughly heated gently pour 3½ tablespoons (approximate) of the hot Brandy on top of the cherries. Ignite the remaining hot Brandy and pour into chafing dish. Stir and dip the liquid until the flame dies. Pour while hot over *6 individual servings* of ice cream.

Cherry Macaroon Mousse

CORDIAL MOUSSE *flavored with Maraschino Liqueur and colored a pale pink with vegetable coloring*
½ *cup macaroons broken into very small pieces*
½ *cup drained sliced maraschino cherries*

Prepare mousse and after cream is folded in, fold in macaroon pieces and cherries. Freeze as directed for Cordial Mousse.

Chocolate Brandy Biscuit

1½ ounces unsweetened
   chocolate melted and
   cooled
6 egg yolks
¾ cup sugar

⅛ teaspoon salt
¼ cup Brandy
1 pint heavy cream stiffly
   whipped

Melt chocolate over hot, not boiling, water and allow to cool slightly. Beat yolks until light and lemon colored. Add sugar, salt, chocolate, and Brandy. Place bowl in a large pan of cracked ice and beat chocolate mixture until it is chilled. Fold in stiffly whipped cream. Spoon into freezer tray and place in freezing section of refrigerator with the bottom of the tray touching the bottom of the freezer unit. When frozen, if desired, pack in freezer carton, cover, and store in freezer.

Makes 1¾ quarts.

NOTE: If there is no hurry and Biscuit is not needed the same day it is made, it may be packed into the carton after the cream is folded in. If it is packed in a carton, from time to time during the next 24 hours, turn the carton on its side and from one side to the other. The carton of course should touch the bottom of the freezer section of the refrigerator.

Cordial Mousse

2 *tablespoons water*
6 *tablespoons of any of the following Cordials: Maraschino, Crème de Menthe, Kümmel, Curaçao, Cointreau, Chartreuse (Green or Yellow), Benedictine, Cherry Heering, Anisette, Crème de Cassis*

⅔ *cup sugar*
⅛ *teaspoon salt*
1 *egg*
2 *tablespoons Cordial (same Cordial as used for making syrup)*
2 *tablespoons sifted confectioners' sugar*
1 *pint heavy cream stiffly whipped*

Cook water, Cordial, sugar, and salt until syrup will spin a thread (230° F.). Beat egg until light and lemon colored. Add syrup and 2 tablespoons Cordial slowly to the egg, beating constantly, as they are added. Cook in top of double boiler over boiling water, stirring constantly, until thickened (about 5 minutes). Cool, and then chill in refrigerator. When mixture is cold stir until completely blended, as ingredients may separate. Fold the chilled cordial mixture and confectioners' sugar into stiffly whipped cream. Spoon into freezer tray and place in freezing section of refrigerator, placing tray so that its bottom touches bottom of freezer unit. When frozen, if desired, pack in freezer carton, cover, and store in freezer.

Makes 1 quart.

NOTE: If there is no hurry and mousse is not needed for same day it is made, it may be packed into the carton after the Cordial mixture and sugar are folded into the cream. If it is packed into a carton, from time to time during the next 24 hours, turn the carton on its side and from one side to another. The carton of course should touch the bottom of the freezer section of the refrigerator until mousse is firmly frozen.

Cordial Mousse Parfait

> CORDIAL MOUSSE *flavored with Green Crème de Menthe to which green vegetable coloring to obtain desired shade has been added*
> CORDIAL MOUSSE *flavored with Cointreau*
> CORDIAL MOUSSE *flavored with Curaçao and colored to desired shade with yellow vegetable coloring*
> CORDIAL MOUSSE *flavored with Maraschino Liqueur, to which red vegetable coloring has been added to obtain desired shade of pink*
> *Toasted almond silvers or* BAKED PECAN OR ALMOND TOPPING

Prepare and freeze mousses. In the bottom of each parfait glass, place scoop of Crème de Menthe Mousse. Cover with scoop of Cointreau Mousse; then add scoop Curaçao Mousse, and top with scoop of Maraschino Mousse. Sprinkle with almonds or topping and serve at once.

If all of mousse is used at one time, this will serve 25 people generously.

Crème de Cacao Sundae

1 quart rich vanilla ice cream
⅓ cup Crème de Cacao
Toasted almond slivers or BAKED PECAN OR ALMOND TOPPING

Divide ice cream among *6 serving glasses or dishes.* Pour approximately 3 teaspoons Crème de Cacao over each serving and sprinkle with toasted almonds or Baked Pecan or Almond Topping.

Crème de Menthe Sherbet

⅔ cup sugar
1½ cups warm milk
½ cup lemon juice
⅛ teaspoon salt
2 teaspoons gelatine

1 tablespoon cold water
½ cup green Crème de Menthe
1 stiffly beaten egg white

Add sugar to warm milk and stir until dissolved. Add lemon juice and salt.[1] Sprinkle gelatine on cold water. Dissolve over boiling water and stir into milk mixture. Add Crème de Menthe. Spoon into freezer tray and place tray on bottom of freezer unit of refrigerator. After 1 hour place mixture in chilled bowl and beat with chilled rotary egg beater until fluffy but not melted. Fold in stiffly beaten egg white and spoon back into tray. Return tray to bottom of freezing section of refrigerator and freeze until firm, stirring with a cold wooden spoon from time to time.
Makes 1½ pints.

[1] Milk will appear to be curdled when lemon juice is added.

Frozen Egg Nog

3 egg yolks
⅔ cup powdered sugar
¼ cup Bourbon Whisky
2 teaspoons Jamaica Rum

3 egg whites
2 cups stiffly whipped
cream

Beat yolks until thick and lemon colored. Gradually add sugar and beat until light. Beat in Whisky and Rum. Beat egg whites until stiff and fold stiffly beaten whites and whipped cream into yolk mixture. Spoon into refrigerator tray. Set freezing controls of refrigerator at highest point. Place tray where entire bottom is in contact with bottom of freezing unit. When mixture is partially frozen and is firm around the sides of the tray, place in cold bowl and beat with rotary egg beater until smooth but not melted. In the meantime, keep freezing tray in freezer until ready to use. Spoon mixture back into tray and return to freezer compartment, being sure that entire bottom of tray is in contact with bottom of freezer section. From time to time during the freezing process, stir the mixture with a cold wooden spoon. When frozen, if desired, pack into freezer carton, cover, and store in freezer.
Serves 6.

Fruit Brandy Mousse

Follow recipe for CORDIAL MOUSSE, using Fruit Brandy. If desired, 1 cup of drained canned chopped peaches or apricots may be added to Peach or Apricot Brandy Mousses, respectively, when cream is folded in.

Grand Marnier Melon

Follow recipe for WHITE FRAMBOISE MELON, making the following substitutions:

> Grand Marnier-flavored CORDIAL MOUSSE *for* White Framboise
>   Mousse
> *Orange sherbet for raspberry or strawberry sherbet*
> ORANGE MARMALADE-GRAND MARNIER SAUCE *for* WHITE
>   FRAMBOISE-RASPBERRY SAUCE

Pineapple and Cherries with Apricot Sherbet

2 medium-size pineapples	⅓ cup Kirsch
2 cups pitted fresh or	Sugar
drained canned black	APRICOT SHERBET
cherries	

Cut both pineapples into 2 parts lengthwise. Scoop out pulp and cut pulp into bite-size chunks. Combine with cherries and Kirsch and sprinkle with sugar. Place pineapple shells and fruit mixture in the refrigerator until thoroughly chilled. At serving time arrange fruit in shells and sprinkle lightly with liquid from bowl in which it was chilled. Dot fruit with small scoops of Apricot Sherbet and serve at once.
Serves 10–12, depending on size of pineapple.

Pistachio Ice Cream with Raspberries and White Framboise

> 1 quart pistachio ice cream
> 10 ounces thawed frozen raspberries
> White Framboise

Divide ice cream between *6 glasses or dishes*. Flavor raspberries to taste with White Framboise. Spoon the raspberries over the ice cream and serve at once.

Rum-Lemon Mousse

2 tablespoons lemon juice
2 teaspoons grated lemon
    rind
3 tablespoons water
3 tablespoons dark Rum
⅔ cup sugar
⅛ teaspoon salt

1 egg
2 tablespoons dark Rum
2 tablespoons sifted
    powdered sugar
1 pint heavy cream stiffly
    whipped

Cook lemon juice, rind, water, 3 tablespoons Rum, sugar, and salt until syrup will spin a thread (230° F.). Beat egg until light and lemon colored. Add syrup and 2 tablespoons Rum slowly, beating constantly as they are added. Cook in top of double boiler over boiling water, stirring constantly until thickened (about 5 minutes). Cool and then chill in refrigerator. When mixture is cold, stir, as ingredients may separate, until completely blended. Fold the chilled lemon-Rum mixture and powdered sugar into stiffly whipped cream. Spoon into freezer tray and place in freezing section of refrigerator, placing tray so that its bottom touches bottom of freezer unit. When frozen, if desired, pack in freezer carton, cover, and store in freezer.
    Makes 1 quart.
NOTE: If there is no hurry and mousse is not needed for same day it is made, it may be packed into the carton after the Rum mixture and sugar are folded into the cream. If it is packed into a carton, from time to time during the next 24 hours turn the carton on its side and from one side to another. The carton of course should touch the bottom of the freezer section of the refrigerator until mousse is firmly frozen.

Spirit Fantasy

CORDIAL MOUSSE *flavored with Maraschino Liqueur and tinted delicate pink*
RUM-LEMON MOUSSE
6 egg whites
⅛ teaspoon salt
1 cup firmly packed brown sugar
1 cup granulated sugar
1½ teaspoons vinegar
1¾ cups chopped hazelnuts (filberts)
BRANDY CHOCOLATE SAUCE
Crème de Menthe

Prepare mousses and freeze. Beat egg whites and salt until they will hold a soft peak. Add brown sugar gradually. Alternately add granulated sugar and vinegar, continuing to beat. Fold in nuts. Drop by small spoonfuls in 9 circles or mounds on brown paper placed on large cooky sheet. The circles should be at least 2 inches apart. Hollow out mounds with back of spoon. Bake in 275° F. oven for 40 minutes. Cool and remove paper from pan and meringues from paper. Cool. When ready to serve, place meringues on individual serving plates. Fill each meringue with a scoop of Cordial (Maraschino) Mousse and a scoop of Rum-Lemon Mousse. Dribble the Brandy Chocolate Sauce over the mousses and then dribble the Crème de Menthe so that it crisscrosses the chocolate. Use both the sauce and the Crème de Menthe sparingly.
Serves 9.
NOTE: The meringues may be prepared well in advance and stored in freezer, wrapped in aluminum foil separately.

Tutti-Frutti Ice Cream

ONE:

½ pound candied sliced
cherries soaked overnight
in Maraschino Liqueur
⅓ pound candied diced
pineapple soaked overnight
in Rum
¼ pound candied orange
peel diced and soaked
overnight in Curaçao

4 ounces candied citron
diced and soaked
overnight in Cointreau
1½ quarts vanilla ice cream
⅛ teaspoon cardamon, if
desired
⅛ teaspoon nutmeg
⅛ teaspoon cinnamon
1¼ cups stiffly whipped
cream

Drain fruit. Put ice cream in large chilled bowl. Allow to soften slightly. Fold spices into stiffly whipped cream. Whip ice cream with chilled wooden spoon until it is fluffy but not melted. Fold in cream and drained fruit. Spoon into freezer tray and place in freezing section of refrigerator, placing tray so that its bottom touches bottom of freezer unit. When frozen, if desired, pack in freezer carton, cover, and store in freezer. *Serves 8–10.*

TWO:

Follow TUTTI-FRUTTI ICE CREAM recipe given above, making the following substitutions:

Use ⅓ pound candied diced apricots soaked overnight in Apricot
Brandy instead of pineapple soaked in Rum
Use ¼ pound candied diced plums soaked overnight in
Cointreau instead of citron

White Framboise Melon

FRUIT BRANDY MOUSSE (*double recipe*) *made with White
   Framboise without fruit* (*2 quarts*)
2 quarts raspberry sherbet or strawberry sherbet (*approximate*)
WHITE FRAMBOISE-RASPBERRY SAUCE (*double recipe*)

Rinse a gallon melon mold with ice water. Dry quickly and
place mold in refrigerator until it is chilled. Line mold with
mousse, which has been stirred with cold wooden spoon until
just slightly softened but not melted. Place in freezer section of
refrigerator or in deep freeze until very firm. Fill center of mold
with sherbet. Seal mold and return to freezer section of refrigerator or to deep freeze and let stand until firm. Unmold on
chilled serving platter and either dribble sauce over the "melon"
or serve sauce with it.
Serves 24.
NOTE: For smaller groups, use ½-gallon mold and cut recipe
accordingly.

Wine Sherbet

See recipe for CREME DE MENTHE SHERBET and substitute
½ cup sweet White or Red Wine for ½ cup Crème de
Menthe.

GELATINE DESSERTS

Egg Nog Pudding

2 tablespoons unflavored
  gelatine
¼ cup cold water
¾ cup boiling water
8 egg whites
¾ cup sugar
8 egg yolks
½ cup sugar
⅓ cup Bourbon Whisky
2 teaspoons Jamaica Rum
18 medium-size double
  ladyfingers
¼ cup Rum (approximate)

½ cup small macaroon
  pieces
⅓ cup pecans broken into
  small pieces
12 drained maraschino
  cherries that have been
  soaked in equal parts of
  their own juice and
  Maraschino Liqueur for at
  least 12 hours and then
  cut in slices
½ pint heavy cream stiffly
  whipped

Soak gelatine in cold water. Pour boiling water over it and stir until dissolved. Beat egg whites until soft-peak stage is reached and add ¾ cup sugar gradually, continuing to beat until whites are stiff. Beat in gelatine and continue beating for 5 minutes. Beat yolks until thick and lemon colored. Add ½ cup sugar gradually and beat 1 minute after all sugar is added. Add Whisky and 2 teaspoons Jamaica Rum. Fold yolk mixture into whites of eggs. Separate ladyfingers and sprinkle lightly with ¼ cup Rum. Line spring mold with the cake. Spoon gelatine mixture into mold, and, when mold is filled, refrigerate for at least 12 hours. Just before serving remove sides of mold. Fold macaroon pieces, pecans, and cherries into stiffly whipped cream. Top pudding with cream mixture and refrigerate until ready to use.

Serves 12 generously but can be stretched.

Fruit with Cointreau-Curaçao Gelatine

2 tablespoons gelatine
1 cup cold water
1¾ cups boiling water
⅔ cup sugar
¼ teaspoon salt
6 tablespoons lemon juice
3 tablespoons Cointreau
3 tablespoons Curaçao
4–5 drops green food coloring

Seeded black grapes, pitted
cherries, green seedless
grapes, sliced fresh or
canned peaches, peeled
diced pears, cooked or
canned pineapple, peeled
diced apple, or peeled
sliced oranges

Soak gelatine in cold water. Add boiling water and stir until gelatine is dissolved. Add sugar, salt, lemon juice, Cointreau, and Curaçao. Tint to desired shade of green with food coloring. Place in refrigerator to congeal. Half fill sherbet cups with desired fruit from those listed above. Break gelatine into small bits and fill sherbet glasses with the bits of gelatine.
Serves 12.
NOTE: This gelatine may be stored in refrigerator in covered container for weeks without deteriorating in any way.

Macaroon Bavarian Cream

⅞ cup sugar
¼ cup water
¼ cup Brandy
1 tablespoon gelatine
2 tablespoons cold water
2 egg whites stiffly beaten
1½ cups stiffly whipped
    cream

⅓ cup drained maraschino
    cherries that have been
    soaked in equal parts of
    their own juice and
    Maraschino Liqueur
1 cup very small pieces of
    macaroons

Boil sugar with water and Brandy for 3 minutes. Soak gelatine in 2 tablespoons cold water. Dissolve gelatine with boiling syrup. Pour gelatine mixture slowly over the stiffly beaten egg whites, beating constantly until cool. Fold in whipped cream, cherries, and macaroons. Spoon into oiled mold and refrigerate until firm. Unmold and serve.

Serves 8.

Prune Whip

1 tablespoon unflavored
  gelatine
½ cup cold water
¼ cup Brandy
¼ cup boiling water
½ cup stewed prune pulp
  put through fine blade of
  food grinder or through
  food mill
⅔ cup sugar

½ cup half-and-half (half
  milk and half cream)
1½ cups stiffly whipped
  cream
2 stiffly beaten egg whites
¼ cup BAKED PECAN OR
  ALMOND TOPPING
⅔ cup sweetened whipped
  cream

Soak gelatine in cold water 5 minutes. Add Brandy to boiling water and bring to boiling point. Stir into gelatine and continue stirring until gelatine is completely dissolved. Add prune pulp and sugar and stir until blended. Cool and place in refrigerator to congeal. Remove from refrigerator and place prune mixture container in bowl of chopped ice. Beat until light and fluffy. Add half-and-half and fold in whipped cream and egg whites. Pour into oiled mold and chill until firm. Fold Baked Pecan or Almond Topping into ⅔ cup sweetened whipped cream and top Prune Whip with the whipped cream mixture (after it has been turned out on serving platter).

Serves 8.

Wine Gelatine

2 tablespoons gelatine
3½ cups Red or White Wine
⅔ cup sugar
¼ teaspoon salt

¾ cup sweetened whipped
cream
Canned or fresh fruits, if
desired

Dissolve gelatine in ½ cup Wine. Bring 3 cups of Wine to a boil and stir boiling Wine into gelatine. Stir until dissolved. Add sugar and salt, and stir until these ingredients are also dissolved. Cool. Pour into oiled mold or into glass (cut glass, if available, is very effective) bowl. Store in refrigerator until firm. Gelatine may be unmolded or served in glass bowl with sweetened whipped cream and, if desired, with fruit.
Serves 6 without fruit; serves 12 with fruit.

MISCELLANEOUS DESSERTS

Chocolate Ice-Box Cake

2½ ounces unsweetened
baking chocolate
2 tablespoons Cognac
2 tablespoons water
⅔ cup granulated sugar
4 egg yolks
⅞ cup butter (unsalted, if
obtainable)
1¼ cups sifted confectioners'
sugar
1 teaspoon vanilla
4 egg whites

30 medium-size double
ladyfingers
Cognac, Rum, or Apricot
Brandy
½ cup BAKED PECAN OR
ALMOND TOPPING
12 maraschino cherries
soaked overnight in equal
parts their own juice and
Maraschino Liqueur
drained and sliced
½ pint stiffly whipped cream

Melt chocolate over hot, not boiling, water in top of double boiler. Mix Cognac and water. Add granulated sugar and then

Brandy mixture to melted chocolate. Stir until smooth. Beat egg yolks until thick and lemon colored and combine with chocolate mixture. Place over boiling water and cook, stirring constantly, for 5 minutes. Remove from heat and allow to cool. Cream butter and gradually add sugar, beating until mixture is light and fluffy. Stir in vanilla and chocolate mixture and blend completely. Beat egg whites until stiff and fold them into the chocolate mixture, continuing to fold until smooth. Separate ladyfingers and line bottom and sides of large spring mold with them. Sprinkle with Cognac, Rum, or Apricot Brandy. Spoon layer of chocolate mixture into mold and cover with layer of ladyfingers. Sprinkle cake with Spirit. Alternate layers of chocolate mixture with ladyfingers, sprinkled with Cognac, Rum, or Apricot Brandy, until mold is nearly filled, ending with layer of chocolate. Store in refrigerator overnight. Remove sides of mold. Just before serving fold Baked Pecan or Almond Topping and drained, sliced cherries into whipped cream. Pile on top of "cake" and serve shortly thereafter, storing in refrigerator in the meantime.
Serves 12.

Cake Syllabub

RUM SPONGE
Dessert Sherry
Peel of 1 lemon
8 large lumps sugar
1 pint heavy cream stiffly
　whipped

Juice of 1 lemon
Sifted confectioners' sugar to
　taste
Fresh or thawed frozen
　(chilled) strawberries

Cool sponge and cut into 2 layers. Place on large serving platter with cut surfaces up. Brush cake layers liberally with Sherry. Rub off peel of lemon with lump sugar and pound sugar until it is completely pulverized. Fold sugar into whipped cream. Fold in lemon juice and sweeten to taste with confectioners' sugar. Pile cream on cake and garnish with berries.
Serves 12.

Cheese, Kirsch, and Guava Jelly

8 ounces processed cream
cheese
3 tablespoons Kirsch²

2½ tablespoons guava jelly
Toasted crackers or
Euphrates wafers

Combine cheese, Kirsch, and jelly. Beat until smooth. Serve
with toasted crackers or wafers.
Allowing 1½–2 tablespoons per person, will serve 6–8.

Crepes Suzettes

¼ cup butter
⅓ cup confectioners' sugar
Grated rind of 1 orange
1 tablespoon orange juice
¼ teaspoon lemon juice
1 tablespoon Cognac or Rum
1 tablespoon Grand Marnier
or Curaçao
1½ teaspoons Benedictine

Dessert pancakes, prepared
according to Part 1 of
recipe for DESSERT
PANCAKES
2½ tablespoons Cognac
1 tablespoon Grand Marnier
or Curaçao
1½ tablespoons Cognac

Cream butter and sugar. Stir in rind and juice of orange,
lemon juice, 1 tablespoon Cognac or Rum, 1 tablespoon Grand
Marnier or Curaçao, and Benedictine. Beat until completely
blended. Chill (Suzette butter may be prepared ahead of time
and stored in refrigerator or freezer). Prepare batter for Dessert Pancakes and, in accordance with instructions, store for
several hours before cooking. Remove Suzette butter from refrigerator or freezer and let stand until room temperature. Cook
crepes in accordance with directions given in recipe. As soon
as the "cakes" are a light brown on both sides, spread 1 side
with "butter" and roll. Immediately place in top pan of chaf-

² While Kirsch is preferred, Cognac may be substituted.

ing dish over boiling water or on hot heatproof platter in warm oven. Cook the crepes, spread with the Suzette butter, and roll until all batter is used. Combine 2½ tablespoons Cognac and 1 tablespoon Grand Marnier or Curaçao. Heat and sprinkle crepes with hot Spirit mixture. Heat 1½ tablespoons Cognac and ignite. Pour burning Spirit over the crepes at table, if this is at all possible; otherwise, carry burning crepes to table without delay.

Makes 12 crepes.

Dessert Pancakes

PART 1

¾ cup unsifted flour
4 teaspoons sugar
¼ teaspoon salt
3 eggs
⅞ cup milk
¾ cup breakfast cream
1 tablespoon melted butter or oleomargarine

1⅔ tablespoons (1 tablespoon plus 2 teaspoons) Cognac, Napoleon Brandy, or Grand Marnier

Sift flour, sugar, and salt. Beat eggs until light and fluffy. Stir in milk, cream, melted butter or oleomargarine, Cognac, Napoleon Brandy, or Grand Marnier, and flour mixture. Stir only until batter is smooth—a minute or less. Store batter in refrigerator for at least several hours.[3] Grease 5-inch griddle lightly. Heat to 380° F. (a drop of water will dance on griddle). Pour in just enough batter to cover bottom (approximately ¼ cup). Cook 2 minutes, loosen with spatula, and turn. Cook 2 minutes more.

Makes 12 crepes.

[3] When batter is removed from refrigerator stir quickly until smooth.

PART 2

DESSERT PANCAKES, *prepared*   *Cointreau or Kirsch*
    according to recipe above   *Powdered sugar*
1 cup preserves or jam

As soon as the "cakes" are taken from the griddle, spread with preserves or jam, flavored to taste with Cointreau or Kirsch. Roll the pancakes and place on slightly heated platter in warm oven. Sprinkle with powdered sugar. Serve as soon as all the pancakes have been cooked and rolled.

NOTE: Leftovers may be wrapped in aluminum foil and placed in freezer. When ready to use, put in 400° F. oven for 10 minutes.

Strawberries Romanoff

6 cups thoroughly chilled   *1 cup stiffly whipped cream*
    strawberries   *5 tablespoons Cointreau*
Kirsch (chilled)[4]   *(chilled)*
Sugar to taste
1½ pints (3 cups)
    vanilla ice cream

Wash berries in ice water, drain, and pat dry. Place 4 cups of the berries in a chilled serving bowl and return to refrigerator. Slightly mash the remaining berries and flavor to taste with Kirsch and sugar. Sprinkle Kirsch over whole berries. Whip the ice cream just until it is creamy, and fold into whipped cream. Fold in Cointreau. Pour mashed berry mixture over whole berries and quickly spoon ice cream-whipped cream mixture over them. Serve at once.

Serves 12.

[4] If Kirsch is not available, Champagne Cognac or Napoleon Brandy may be substituted.

Syllabub

1½ pints chilled whipping cream
¼ pound sifted confectioners' sugar
5 tablespoons Dessert Sherry or Madeira

Whip cream until very stiff. Fold in sugar and then fold in
Wine. Serve in parfait glasses.
Serves 8.

PASTRY DESSERTS

Almond Shell Flan

½ cup ground blanched
almonds (do not use until
24 hours after nuts are
ground)
¾ teaspoon almond extract
⅓ cup butter or
oleomargarine
¼ cup sugar
1 scant teaspoon grated
lemon rind
⅛ teaspoon nutmeg
1 egg white
¾ cup sifted all-purpose
flour
1½ tablespoons cold Rum
4 eggs separated
1 cup sugar

3 tablespoons flour
measured then sifted
1 cup scalded milk
1 tablespoon melted butter
or oleomargarine
1 teaspoon vanilla
6 double medium-size
ladyfingers
2 tablespoons Cointreau
14 large canned drained
apricot halves
(approximate)
24 large canned pitted
sweet black cherries
(approximate)
⅔ cup apricot preserves
2 tablespoons Cointreau

Mix almonds and extract. Cream butter or oleomargarine.
Add sugar slowly and beat until fluffy on "creaming speed" in

small mixer bowl or with wooden spoon. Beat in almond-extract mixture, lemon rind, and nutmeg. Add egg white and beat for 1 minute (if using mixer, beat on maximum speed). Stir flour in slowly with a fork. Grease and flour 8 inch round × 1½ inch deep layer-cake pan. With fingers, pat the dough evenly on bottom and sides of pan to make a shell. Place in refrigerator for 1–3 hours (as convenient). Brush shell with cold Rum. Put in 400° F. oven and bake 2 minutes. Reduce oven temperature to 300° F. and cook until a light golden brown (about 30 minutes). Cool 15 minutes. Turn the shell[5] out on rack and let stand until cool.

Beat egg yolks slightly. Stir in sugar and flour, and mix only until blended. Add scalded milk and melted butter or oleomargarine. Mix well. Cook in top of double boiler, over boiling water, stirring constantly, until thick. Remove from over water and cool. Stir in vanilla. Chill in refrigerator and when cold, fold in stiffly beaten egg whites, continuing to fold until custard is smooth. Spoon half of custard evenly into the bottom of the shell. Separate double ladyfingers and place a layer of the cake on top of the custard, breaking some of the "fingers" into smaller pieces if it is necessary to fit the pieces to make a "solid" layer. Sprinkle ladyfingers with 2 tablespoons of Cointreau. Cover with remainder of custard. Around the edges of the custard filling, arrange a circle of the apricot halves. Completely fill the circle with the cherries. Heat the apricot preserves and 2 tablespoons of Cointreau until the preserves are melted. Strain and keep warm over hot water until ready to serve the flan. Brush surfaces of cherries and apricot halves with apricot glaze and serve at once.

Serves 6 generously, but can be stretched to 8.

[5] This almond shell may be made and stored in refrigerator for several days or in freezer, wrapped in aluminum foil, for an indefinite period before the flan is made.

Chocolate Brandy Pie

5 egg yolks
1⅔ cups sugar
2½ tablespoons flour
3⅓ tablespoons cocoa
3⅓ tablespoons boiling
 Cognac or Napoleon
 Brandy
⅓ cup butter or
 oleomargarine
1½ teaspoons vanilla

1⅔ cups milk
Unbaked 9-inch pie shell
Vanilla ice cream topping
 OR CORDIAL MOUSSE top-
 ping (Cointreau-flavored)
 OR sweetened whipped
 cream topping
Chocolate trims or shaved
 chocolate

MEASUREMENT EXPLANATION:

For flour measure, use 2 tablespoons, plus 1½ teaspoons (2½ tablespoons);

For cocoa measure, use 3 tablespoons, plus 1 teaspoon (3⅓ tablespoons);

For Brandy measure, use 3 tablespoons, plus 1 teaspoon (3⅓ tablespoons).

Beat egg yolks slightly. Sift sugar and flour and add to eggs. Stir only until ingredients are blended. Measure cocoa and sift. Dissolve cocoa in boiling Brandy. Stir into egg mixture. Melt butter or oleomargarine and stir into the egg mixture. Add vanilla and milk and blend thoroughly. Pour into unbaked pie shell. Place in 425° F. oven. Cover pie, including shell, with sheet of aluminum foil. Cook 35 minutes. Reduce heat to 350° F. and bake 20 minutes more. Cool. Place pie in refrigerator for at least several hours.

VANILLA ICE CREAM OR CORDIAL MOUSSE TOPPING: Line 8-inch round layer pan with aluminum foil. Fill with slightly softened ice cream or mousse. Place in freezer and, when firm, remove ice cream from pan and wrap in aluminum foil. Store in freezer until ready to use and, immediately before serving, place topping on pie.

OR Whip ½ pint heavy cream until stiff. Fold in sifted confectioners' sugar to taste and pile sweetened whipped cream on custard.

Sprinkle ice cream or mousse topping with chocolate trims or shaved chocolate. (To shave chocolate, hold square of baking chocolate with wrapping in palm of hand until chocolate is slightly softed from heat of hand. With vegetable parer, shave side of square.)

Serves 8.

Custard Tarts

6 medium-size baked tart shells
MOCHA RUM CUSTARD or
   CAFE BRULOT CUSTARD or
   LEMON SHERRY CUSTARD

Fill tarts with desired chilled custard and serve at once. *Serves 6.*

Fruit Tarts Glacé

2¾ cups berries or seeded
grapes or halved or sliced
canned or fresh peaches or
apricots or canned or fresh
pitted cherries

Kirsch
1 cup apricot preserves
1½ tablespoons Kirsch
6 large baked tart shells

Sprinkle fruit very, very lightly with Kirsch. Combine apricot preserves with Kirsch. Cook over medium heat until preserves are melted, and put through strainer. Place fruit in tart shells and brush with glaze. Serve at once. *Serves 6.*

Pecan Pie

2 tablespoons dark Rum	3 tablespoons butter melted
½ cup sugar	2 tablespoons dark Rum
1 cup dark corn syrup	1½ cups chopped pecans
3 eggs	Unbaked pie shell

Cook 2 tablespoons dark Rum, sugar, and corn syrup until syrup will spin a thread (230° F.). Beat eggs with rotary egg beater or on maximum food mixer speed until thick and lemon colored (about 5 minutes). Add hot syrup gradually to eggs, beating constantly. Add butter, remaining Rum, and nuts. Pour into unbaked pie shell. Bake at 450° F. for 10 minutes. Reduce heat to 350° F. and bake 35–40 minutes more until pie filling is set.
Serves 8.

SWEET OMELETS AND SOUFFLÉS

Chocolate Soufflé

2½ ounces unsweetened cooking chocolate broken into small pieces	⅔ cup sugar
	5 egg yolks
	⅛ teaspoon salt
3 tablespoons butter	7 egg whites
3 tablespoons flour measured and then sifted	¼ teaspoon cream of tartar
	Cognac
¾ cup scalded milk	1 cup sweetened stiffly whipped cream
¼ cup hot Cognac or Champagne Cognac	

Melt chocolate over hot, not boiling, water and, when melted, cool. Melt butter in top of double boiler. Remove from heat and stir in flour with a wooden spoon. Return to heat and cook until thick (about 15 seconds), stirring constantly with the wooden spoon. Again remove from over hot water; stir in scalded milk and hot Brandy. Stir until smooth and again place over the hot water. Cook for 1 minute, stirring constantly. Remove from heat, and beat in first the chocolate and then the sugar. Beat until smooth and completely blended. Beat egg yolks until thick and lemon colored. When sauce is lukewarm, fold into the yolks until thoroughly mixed. Add salt to egg whites. Beat until foamy. Add cream of tartar and beat until stiff. Fold 2 kitchen spoons of the whites into the chocolate mixture and then slowly pour the chocolate sauce over the remaining egg whites, folding while pouring. Spoon into 2½-quart buttered and sugared soufflé dish or casserole. Bake in 350° F. oven. Test at end of 22 minutes by gently pushing dish in oven. If soufflé shakes just slightly, it is done; if it is not done, cook 3 minutes more and test again. Stir Cognac to taste into sweetened whipped cream. Serve soufflé as soon as it is removed from oven with Cognac-Whipped-Cream Sauce.

Serves 6 generously.

NOTE: This soufflé will be soft and runny in center.

Coffee Soufflé

3 tablespoons butter	4 egg yolks
3 tablespoons flour measured then sifted	⅛ teaspoon salt
½ cup scalded milk	5 egg whites
¾ cup hot strong black coffee	¼ teaspoon cream of tartar
¼ cup hot Brandy	1 cup sweetened whipped cream
¼ teaspoon cinnamon	1 tablespoon Brandy
¼ teaspoon cloves	¼ cup BAKED PECAN OR ALMOND TOPPING
⅔ cup sugar	

Melt butter in top of double boiler. Remove from over hot water and stir in flour. Cook, stirring constantly, over hot water

1 minute. Remove from heat and add milk. Stir until smooth. Combine hot coffee and Brandy with cinnamon and cloves, and stir into milk mixture. Stir in sugar. Cook over boiling water until thick, continuing to stir. Remove from heat and beat until very smooth. Cool until lukewarm. Beat egg yolks until light and lemon colored. Stir coffee mixture into yolks and continue stirring until completely blended. Add salt to egg whites and beat until foamy. Add cream of tartar and continue beating until stiff. When egg-yolk mixture is cool, fold 2 kitchen spoons of egg whites into it and continue folding until blended. Very slowly pour the egg-yolk mixture over remainder of whites, folding while pouring. Spoon into buttered and sugared 2½-quart soufflé dish or casserole. Bake in 350° F. oven 22 minutes and test by gently pushing dish in oven. If soufflé shakes slightly, it is done. If it is not done, cook 3 minutes more and test again. While soufflé is in oven, combine the whipped cream and Brandy and stir in the Pecan or Almond Topping. Serve soufflé as soon as it is removed from oven with sauce.

Serves 6 generously.

NOTE: Center of this soufflé will be runny.

Lemon Soufflé

3 tablespoons butter
3 tablespoons flour
   measured then sifted
½ cup breakfast cream
3 tablespoons Cointreau
Milk to make 1 cup with
   cream and Cointreau
4 egg yolks
⅔ cup sugar

1 tablespoon grated lemon
   rind
3 tablespoons lemon juice
5 egg whites
⅛ teaspoon salt
¼ teaspoon cream of tartar
COINTREAU-STRAWBERRY
   PRESERVE SAUCE or WHITE
   FRAMBOISE-RASPBERRY
   SAUCE

Melt butter in top of double boiler. Remove from heat and stir in flour with a wooden spoon. Stir over boiling water until thickened. Combine cream, Cointreau, and enough milk to make 1 cup. Remove roux from heat and stir in milk mixture. Cook over boiling water, continuing to stir, until thick and smooth. Cool until lukewarm. In the meantime beat yolks until thick and add sugar gradually, beating until light and fluffy. Stir a small amount of sauce into yolk mixture and then stir the mixture into the remainder of the lukewarm sauce. Add lemon rind and juice; stir until blended. Beat egg whites and salt until foamy. Add cream of tartar and beat until stiff. Add 2 kitchen spoons of whites to yolk mixture and fold until blended. Slowly pour the yolk mixture over remaining whites, folding the yolk sauce, as it is poured, into the stiffly beaten whites. Spoon into buttered and sugared 2½-quart soufflé dish or casserole and bake in 350° F. oven. After 22 minutes test by gently pushing dish in oven. If soufflé shakes just slightly, it is done. If not done, cook 3 minutes more and test again. Serve at once with Cointreau-Strawberry Preserve Sauce or White Framboise-Raspberry Sauce.

Serves 6 generously.

NOTE: This soufflé will be soft and runny in center.

Orange Soufflé

Follow recipe for LEMON SOUFFLE, substituting 1 tablespoon grated orange rind for lemon rind and 1½ tablespoons orange juice mixed with 1½ tablespoons Curaçao or Grand Marnier for lemon juice.

Rum Omelet Flambé

10 ounces thawed frozen
  strawberries
2 tablespoons Cointreau
6 eggs
2 tablespoons cream

Salt
2 tablespoons butter
2 cups heated brandied
  peaches or pears
⅓ cup Rum

Combine strawberries and Cointreau. Heat and keep warm over hot water until ready to use. Beat eggs until fluffy. Add cream and season to taste with salt, continuing to beat while these ingredients are added. Melt butter in skillet over medium heat and, when it sizzles, add eggs. Lower heat and cook slowly over low heat until the undersurface of the omelet is set. Lift edge of omelet with spatula and tilt pan slightly and gently to allow the uncooked egg to run underneath. Complete cooking over low heat. Place omelet on ovenproof heated platter. Working quickly, cover half of omelet with berries and fold other half over them. Arrange Brandied fruit around omelet. Heat Rum and pour all but 1½ tablespoons (approximate) over the hot brandied fruit. Ignite remaining Rum and pour lighted Spirit over fruit. Serve at once.

Serves 4.

BAKED PUDDINGS

Bread Pudding

3 eggs slightly beaten
⅞ cup sugar
3 tablespoons melted butter
  or oleomargarine
3¾ cups scalded milk
⅜ teaspoon salt
¾ teaspoon vanilla

1 tablespoon Rum
3¾ cups bread cut into very
  small cubes
⅔ cup raisins
½ cup peeled apples cut into
  small pieces
⅓ cup Rum

Beat eggs with fork until mixed. Combine sugar, slightly beaten eggs, melted butter or oleomargarine, scalded milk, salt, vanilla, and 1 tablespoon Rum. Mix bread cubes, raisins, and apple pieces in a large deep baking dish. Sprinkle with ⅓ cup Rum, mixing the bread and fruit while sprinkling so that all the cubes and pieces will be sprinkled with the Spirit. Pour milk mixture over bread mixture and let stand 10 minutes. Place baking dish in a pan filled to depth of 1½ inches with hot water in a 350° F. oven. Bake 60 minutes. Remove from oven. If pudding is not brown on top, brown slightly under broiler unit.

Serves 8.

Macaroon Pudding

1⅓ cups macaroon crumbs
1¾ cups scalded breakfast cream
¼ cup Dessert Sherry
⅔ cup sugar
½ teaspoon cinnamon
¼ teaspoon nutmeg
2 tablespoons Dessert Sherry

⅔ cup chopped pecans
¼ cup sliced drained maraschino cherries that have been soaked for 12 hours in equal parts of their own juice and Maraschino Liqueur
2 eggs separated

Mix crumbs and scalded cream. Stir in ¼ cup Sherry. Cook over boiling water, stirring from time to time until thick (about 10 minutes). Cool. Stir in sugar, cinnamon, nutmeg, remaining Sherry, pecans, sliced cherries, and slightly beaten egg yolks. Beat egg whites until stiff and fold into mixture. Spoon into individual baking serving dishes (small). Place ramekins in pan filled to a depth of ½ inch with boiling water. Bake 25 minutes in 350° F. oven. Place molds in pan filled to depth of ½ inch with ice water and, when they are cold, place in refrigerator.

Serves 12.

Rum Sponge Cake Pudding

3 tablespoons butter
¾ cup sugar
3 eggs slightly beaten
3¾ cups milk scalded
¼ teaspoon salt
1 teaspoon vanilla
1 tablespoon Rum
½ cup chopped pecans
3⅔ cups RUM SPONGE
　broken into small pieces

¼ pound candied chopped
　cherries soaked in
　Maraschino Liqueur
　overnight
2 slices chopped candied
　pineapple soaked in
　Cointreau overnight
Rum

Melt butter and combine with sugar, eggs, milk, salt, and vanilla. Stir in 1 tablespoon Rum. Mix pecans and cake pieces. Drain fruit. Place a layer of cake and nuts in bottom of a greased large baking dish and sprinkle with Rum. Cover with chopped cherries and pineapple. Alternate layers of cake and nuts, sprinkled with Rum, with layers of fruit until baking dish is ⅔ filled. Pour egg mixture over cake and fruit. Let stand for 10 minutes. Place in pan filled to a depth of 1½ inches with boiling water. Bake in 350° F. oven 45–50 minutes. Remove from oven and place in pan filled to a depth of 1½ inches with ice water. When cold, place in refrigerator.
Serves 8.

Spirits Used in

The Art of Cooking with Spirits

LIQUEURS

Anisette

Benedictine

Chartreuse
  (green and yellow)

Cherry Heering

Cointreau

Crème de Banana

Crème de Cacao

Crème de Cassis

Crème de Menthe
  (green and white)

Curaçao

Grand Marnier

Kümmel

Maraschino

Triple Sec

BRANDIES

Applejack

Apricot Brandy

Blackberry Brandy

Champagne Cognac

Cognac

Kirsch

Napoleon Brandy

Peach Brandy

White Framboise

LIQUORS

Bourbon   Rum (light and dark)
Gin

WINES

Champagne   Port (Ruby)
Madeira   Rosé
Marsala (Almond)   Sherry
                                  Vermouth

RED   ### WHITE

Claret   Burgundy
Burgundy   Chablis
                                  Moselle
                                  Rhine
                                  Sauterne

INDEX

Allegretti icing, 256
Almond:
  Brandy sticks, 244
  shell flan, 300–1
  topping (baked), 243
Angel-food cake. *See* Tipsy angel
Appetizers:
  apple and grape cocktail, 20
  avocado pear and Rum cocktail, 21
  crabmeat Lorenzo (cold), 26–27
  fruit, 20–26
  grapefruit and orange cocktail, 22
  grapefruit halves with peach or apricot preserves, 21
  honeydew melon and Rum cocktail, 22
  melon and Cointreau or Triple Sec cocktail, 23
  melon and Wine cocktail, 23
  peach and Wine cocktail, 24
  pear and Wine cocktail, 24
  raspberries and White Framboise Liqueur, 24
  seafood, 26–27
  seafood cocktail, 27
  strawberries:
    and grapefruit cocktail, 25
    and orange cocktail, 25
    and pineapple cocktail, 26
  See also Aspics; Hors d'oeuvres
Apples:
  baked, 189
  and grape cocktail, 20
  rings, spiced, 190
  stewed, 190–91
  stuffing, 216
Applesauce, 189
  cookies with Liqueur icings, 245–46
Apricot sherbet, 274–75
Apricot sherbet cake, 275–76
Artichokes:
  hearts:
    with chicken and ham, 172
    with tomato juice-Moselle aspic, 9
    with tomato juice-Moselle aspic and crabmeat, 9–10
  stuffed, 173
  with truffle stuffing, 173–74
Asparagus:
  in bouillon aspic, 27–28
  sauce, 205
  with Sherry-flavored cream or cheese sauce, 174

Aspics:
  asparagus in bouillon aspic, 27–28
  avocado and grapefruit in lime gelatine, 29
  carrot and pineapple, 29–30
  chicken, 34–35
  crabmeat timbales, 30–31
  crawfish, 34–35
  eggs and caviar, 16
  fruit-flavored gelatine with grapefruit and orange, 31
  lime-avocado-asparagus, 31–32
  lobster, 34–35
  pear and pineapple in lime gelatine, 32
  relish, 32
  ring with eggs au pâté, 28–29
  seafood sauce gelée, 33
  shrimp, 34–35
    in clear aspic, 33–34
  Thousand Island, 35–36
  tomato juice-Moselle, 36
  turkey, 34–35
  See also Appetizers; Hors d'oeuvres
Avocado:
  and grapefruit in lime gelatine, 29
  pear and Rum cocktail, 21

Baked:
  Alaska, 276–77
  Alaska flambé, 277–78
  apples, 189
  bananas, 191
  beefsteak with vegetables, 133
  boned broilers, 98–99
  custard with Grand Marnier-butterscotch topping, 265
  fish:
    diablo, 65
    flambé, 66
    with marinière sauce, 66–67
    with oyster stuffing, 67–68
  ham steak:
    with pineapple juice and Cointreau, 153
    with raisin sauce, 153
  peaches, 194
  pears, 196
  pecan or almond topping, 243
  puddings, 308–10
  stuffed oysters, 87
  stuffed tomato, 184–85

Bananas:
  baked, 191
  flambé, 191–92
  flambé with chocolate ice cream, 278
  flambé with vanilla ice cream, 278–79
Barbecued spareribs, 149
Barbecue sauce for chicken or meat, 205
Bavarian cream, macaroon, 293–94
Beans:
  Boston baked, 174–75
  butter or lima, with hot Sauterne mayonnaise, 175
  dried red or lima, 176
  soup, dried, 46
    blender-made, 46–47
Béarnaise sauce, 206
Beef:
  baked with vegetables, 133
  chart (roasting time/temperature), 142–43
  chili, 135
  corned, 135–36
  daube, 136
    jellied, 137–38
    with spaghetti, 136–37
  ground, with tomatoes and corn, 138
  hamburger with Wine, 139
  hash, 160–61
  Irish stew, 163–64
  meat sauce, quick, 140
  pot roast, 139–40
  ragout of, 141
  roast, 142–43
  sauerbraten, 143–44
  Stroganoff, 134
Benedictine-crème brûlée with macédoine flambé, 266–67
Biscuits, cheese, with deviled ham, 12
Biscuit tortoni, 279
Bisque, Creole crawfish, 44–45
Black cherry-Cointreau-Rum sauce, 259
Bluefish, baked, with oyster stuffing, 67–68
Boiled:
  chicken, 99
  crabs, 80–81
  shrimp, 80–81
Bordelaise sauce, 206–7
Borsch, 39
Boston baked beans, 174–75
Bouillabaisse, 40
Bouillon (chicken, veal, beef), 41
Bourbon balls, 247
Brandied:
  cherries, 192
  peaches, 195
  pears, 196
  plums, 197
Brandies, list, 311

Brandy:
  chocolate sauce, 257
  cocoa sauce, 257
  egg-custard ice cream, 280–81
  -lemon mousse, 281
  or Rum-lemon ice cream, 281
Bread, cheese garlic, 61
Bread pudding, 308–9
Bread stuffing, 216–17
Broiled chicken, 99–100
Broiled fillet of sole Marguery, 68
Broiled quail, 125–26
Broilers, baked boned, 98–99
Brown sauce, 207
Burgundy sauce for steak, 208
Butter beans with hot Sauterne mayonnaise, 175
Butter-cream frosting, 253
Butterscotch double-boiler frosting, 254
Butterscotch sauce with Rum or Brandy, 258

Café brûlot custard, 267
Cake fillings and frostings:
  allegretti icing, 256
  butterscotch double-boiler frosting, 254
  butter-cream frosting, 253
  chocolate Brandy frosting, 254
  chocolate-cream filling, 255
  custard filling, 255
  double-boiler frosting, 256
  icing for lettering, 229
  icing variations, 246
  maraschino butter-cream frosting, 253
  nesselrode frosting, 257
  pecan or almond topping, 243
Cakes:
  angel-food (see Tipsy angel)
  apricot sherbet, 275–76
  chocolate ice-box cake, 295–96
  chocolate sips of Spirits, 227–29
  fruit cake of the twelve Spirits, 230–33
  icings (see Cake fillings and frostings)
  jam cake, 233–34
  jam cakes (individual), 234
  Rum ring, 235–36
  Rum sponge, 236–37
  Rum sponge roll, 237–38
  Sherry apple cake, 238–39
  syllabub, 296
  tipsy angel, 240–41
  See also Cookies; Tortes
Camembert butter, 10
Candied sweet potatoes, 181
Caper sauce, 208
Capon:
  roast, 114
  smothered, with mushrooms, 115–16

Caramel sauce with Brandy, 258
Carrot and pineapple aspic, 29–30
Celery, stuffed, #1, #2, #3, #4, 10–12
Champagne-onion soup, 41–42
Charts (time/temperature):
  beef, roasting, 142–43
  lamb, roasting, 148
  pork, roasting, 151
  steak, broiling, 145
  veal, roasting, 158
Cheese:
  biscuits with deviled ham, 12
  camembert butter, 10
  cucumbers stuffed with Roquefort or
    bleu cheese, 15–16
  eggs au gratin, 55
  fondue with shrimp or crawfish, 13
  garlic bread, 61
  Kirsch, and guava jelly, 297
  sauce, 209
Cherries:
  Anisette sauce, 258–59
  brandied, 192
  jubilee, 282
  macaroon mousse, 282
Cherry Anisette sauce, 258–59
Cherry macaroon mousse, 282
Chestnut stuffing, 217
Chicken:
  à la king, 101
  à la Maryland, 102
  -artichoke-tomato casserole, 103–4
  aspic, 34–35
  barbecue sauce for, 205
  boiled, 99
  breasts:
    with mushrooms and hearts of arti-
      chokes, 102–3
    pan-broiled, 100
  broiled, 99–100
  cacciatore, 104–5
  with Chablis, Madeira, and Cointreau,
    105–6
  with pâté Brandy stuffing, 106
  creamed, with mushroom omelet, 56–
    57
  Florentine, 106–7
  fricassee, 107–8
    spring, 108
  krispy, 112–13
  livers:
    and eggplant, 177
    eggs à la turke, 56
  mousse, 109
  paprika, 109
  pie, 110
  potted, 113
  poulet sous cloche, 113–14
  and rice casserole, 110–11

salad with sour cream, 111
smothered, 115
  with mushrooms, 115–16
soup, cream of, 42–43
stewed, 116
  with dumplings, 117
Virginia breast of, 118
with Wine and herbs, 112
Chili, 135
Chocolate:
  Brandy biscuit, 282–83
  Brandy frosting, 254
  Brandy pie, 302–3
  -cream filling, 255
  ice-box cake, 295–96
  shaving, 303
  sips of Spirits, 227–29
  soufflé, 304–5
Cocktail patties #1, #2, 13–14
Coffee soufflé, 305–6
Cointreau:
  balls, 247
  and candied fruit sauce, 259
  -strawberry preserves sauce, 261
Cold fish platter, 69
Consommé, jellied, 42
Cookies:
  almond Brandy sticks, 244
  applesauce, with Liqueur icings, 245–
    46
  Bourbon balls, 247
  Cointreau balls, 247
  icing variations, 246
  Kirsch balls, 247
  lebkuchen with Rum icing, 247–48
  pecan almond crisps, 249
  pecan crisps, 249
  Rum balls, 247
  See also Cakes; Tortes
Cordial mousse, 283–84
  parfait, 284
Corned beef, 135–36
Crabmeat:
  au gratin, 83
  balls, 14–15
  bordelaise, 82
  croquettes, 80
  gumbo, quick, 48
  Lorenzo (cold), 26–27
  mousse, 83–84
  Newburg, 84
  omelet, 57
  poached, 85
  and shrimp Remick, 91
  timbales, 30–31
  See Crabs
Crabs:
  boiled, 80–81
  stuffed, 81–82

Cranberry sauce, 192–93
Crawfish:
    aspic, 34–35
    bisque, Creole, 44–45
    cheese fondue with, 13
Creamed chicken with mushroom omelet,
    56–57
Creamed sweetbreads, 164
Cream of chicken soup, 42–43
Cream of shrimp-Sherry dressing, 214
Cream of vegetable soup, 43
Cream sauce, 203
Crème brûlée, Benedictine, with macé-
    doine flambé, 266–67
Crème de Cacao sundae, 285
Crème de Menthe sherbet, 285
Creole crawfish bisque, 44–45
Crêpes suzettes, 297–98
Croquettes:
    crabmeat, 80
    meat, 160
    sweetbread, 165–66
Crown roast of lamb, 146
Crystallized citrus fruit peel, 193
Cucumbers stuffed with Roquefort or
    bleu cheese, 15–16
Curried hard-cooked eggs, 54–55
Curry dressing with Wine, 215
Custard, 268
    filling, 255
    sponge roll, 268–69
    tarts, 303
Custard desserts, 265–74
    almond shell flan, 300–1
    baked custard with Grand Marnier-
        butterscotch topping, 265
    Benedictine-crème brûlée with macé-
        doine flambé, 266–67
    café brûlot custard, 267
    chocolate-cream filling, 255
    custard, 268
    custard sponge roll, 268–69
    filling, 255
    floating island with strawberries and
        Kirsch, 269–70
    Grand Marnier cream, 270
    lemon Sherry custard, 270–71
    marron Champagne Cognac pudding,
        271
    mocha Rum custard, 272
    New Orleans cream pie, 272
    queen's custard, 273–74
    sponge roll, 268–69
    tarts, 303
    tipsy fellow, 273
    tropical custard, 274

Date-Kirsch torte, 241–42
Daube, 136

jellied, 137–38
with spaghetti, 136–37
Desserts:
    almond shell flan, 300–1
    apricot sherbet, 274–75
    apricot sherbet cake, 275–76
    baked Alaska, 276–77
        flambé, 277–78
    baked custard with Grand Marnier-
        butterscotch topping, 265
    baked puddings, 308–10
    bananas flambé:
        with chocolate ice cream, 278
        with vanilla ice cream, 278–79
    Benedictine-crème brûlée with macé-
        doine flambé, 266–67
    biscuit tortoni, 279
    Brandy egg-custard ice cream, 280–81
    Brandy-lemon mousse, 281
    Brandy- or Rum-lemon ice cream, 281
    bread pudding, 308–9
    café brûlot custard, 267
    cake syllabub, 296
    cheese, Kirsch, and guava jelly, 297
    cherries jubilee, 282
    cherry macaroon mousse, 282
    chocolate:
        Brandy biscuit, 282–83
        Brandy pie, 302–3
        ice-box cake, 295–96
        soufflé, 304–5
    coffee soufflé, 305–6
    Cordial mousse, 283–84
        parfait, 284
    Crème de Cacao sundae, 285
    Crème de Menthe sherbet, 285
    crêpes suzettes, 297–98
    custard, 268, 265–74
        sponge roll, 268–69
        tarts, 303
    egg nog pudding, 292
    floating island with strawberries and
        Kirsch, 269–70
    frozen, 274–91
    frozen egg nog, 286
    fruit Brandy mousse, 286
    fruit with Cointreau-Curaçao gelatine,
        293
    fruit tarts glacé, 303
    gelatine, 292–95
    Grand Marnier cream, 270
    Grand Marnier melon, 287
    lemon Sherry custard, 270–71
    lemon soufflé, 306–7
    macaroon Bavarian cream, 293–94
    macaroon pudding, 309
    marron Champagne Cognac pudding,
        271
    mocha Rum custard, 272

New Orleans cream pie, 272
orange soufflé, 307
pancakes, 298–99
pastry, 300–4
pecan pie, 304
pineapple and cherries with apricot
    sherbet, 287
pistachio ice cream with raspberries
    and White Framboise, 287
prune whip, 294
queen's custard, 273–74
Rum-lemon mousse, 288
Rum omelet flambé, 308
Rum sponge cake pudding, 310
Spirit fantasy, 289
strawberries Romanoff, 299
sweet omelets and soufflés, 304–8
syllabub, 300
tipsy fellow, 273
tropical custard, 274
tutti-frutti ice cream, 290
White Framboise melon, 291
Wine gelatine, 295
Wine sherbet, 291
See also Cakes; Cookies; Ice creams;
    Mousse; Pies; Puddings; Sherbets;
    Soufflés; Tortes
Double-boiler frosting, 256
Dried bean soup (lima or red bean), 46
blender-made, 46–47
Dried red beans, 176
soup, 46
    blender-made, 46–47
Duck:
    ducklings, flambé, 121–22
    glazed roast, 118–19
    hash, 119–20
    wild, roasted, 121
Ducklings, flambé, 121–22

Egg nog:
    frozen, 286
    pudding, 292
Eggplant:
    and chicken livers, 177
    stuffed (with shrimp, crabmeat, and
        ham), 178
Eggs:
    à la turke, 56
    aspic ring au pâté, 28–29
    au gratin, 55
    and caviar in aspic, 16
    curried hard-cooked, 54–55
    omelets:
        crabmeat, 57
        mushroom, creamed chicken with,
            56–57
        Rum, flambé, 308
        shrimp and mushroom, 58

    Spanish, 58
    strawberry, 58–59
    sweet (dessert) and soufflés, 304–8
    savory, 59
    Spanish, 60
    See also Soufflés
Egg sauce, 209

Fillet of sole:
    broiled, Marguery, 68
    ravigote, 71–72
    thermidor, 70–71
Fillings. See Cake fillings and frostings
Fish and seafood:
    baked:
        diablo, 65
        flambé, 66
        with marinière sauce, 66–67
        with oyster stuffing, 67–68
    on bed of onions, mushrooms, and
        potatoes, 73
    bluefish, baked, with oyster stuffing,
        67–68
    cocktail patties #1, 13
    cold platter, 69
    crabmeat:
        au gratin, 83
        balls, 14–15
        bordelaise, 82
        croquettes, 80
        gumbo, quick, 48
        Lorenzo (cold), 26–27
        mousse, 83–84
        Newburg, 84
        omelet, 57
        poached, 85
        and shrimp Remick, 91
        timbales, 30–31
    crabs:
        boiled, 80–81
        stuffed, 81–82
    crawfish:
        aspic, 34–35
        bisque, Creole, 44–45
        cheese fondue with, 13
    fillet of sole:
        broiled, Marguery, 68
        ravigote, 71–72
        thermidor, 70–71
    fillets:
        amandine, 72–73
        on bed of onions, mushrooms, and
            potatoes, 73
        poached, 75
        skillet-broiled, 78–79
    flounder:
        with caviar, 74
        fillet of (thermidor), 70–71
        with herbs, 74–75

herring, pickled, 16–17
lobster:
  aspic, 34–35
  au gratin, 83
  bordelaise, 82
  mousse, 83–84
  Newburg, 84
  poached, 85
  royal, 85–86
  thermidor, 86
oyster(s):
  baked stuffed, 87
  Bienville, 88
  in brown sauce with spaghetti ring, 89–90
  cocktail patties #2, 14
  crab, and shrimp gumbo, 47
  sauce, 212
  in Sherry sauce, 90
  and shrimp jambalaya, 93
  stuffing, 220–21
pompano in White Wine, 75–76
red fish:
  baked diablo, 65
  baked, with oyster stuffing, 67–68
  Chambord, 76–77
  cold platter, 69
  court bouillon of, 70
red snapper:
  baked diablo, 65
  baked, with oyster stuffing, 67–68
  Chambord, 76–77
  cold platter, 69
  Sharfe, 78
Sharfe (stewed fish), 78
shrimp:
  aspic, 34–35
  au gratin, 83
  boiled, 80–81
  cheese fondue with, 13
  in clear aspic, 33–34
  and crabmeat Remick, 91
  diablo, 92
  and mushroom omelet, 58
  and mushroom sauce, 213
  and olive casserole, 92
  and oyster jambalaya, 93
  poached, 85
skillet-broiled, 78–79
sole (see Fillet of sole)
stewed (see Sharfe)
stuffing, ham-rice-tomato, 218
trout:
  baked, with oyster stuffing, 67–68
  Marguery, 79–80
tuna balls, 14–15
turtle soup, 51–52
Flaming stuffed pork chops, 150
Floating island with strawberries and Kirsch, 269–70

Flounder:
  with caviar, 74
  fillet of (thermidor), 70–71
  with herbs, 74–75
Fondue, cheese, with shrimp or crawfish, 13
French dressing with Wine, 215
French mushrooms, 179
Frostings. See Cake fillings and frostings
Frozen desserts:
  apricot sherbet, 274–75
  apricot sherbet cake, 275–76
  baked Alaska, 276–77
  baked Alaska flambé, 277–78
  bananas flambé with chocolate ice cream, 278
  bananas flambé with vanilla ice cream, 278–79
  biscuit tortoni, 279
  Brandy egg-custard ice cream, 280–81
  Brandy-lemon ice cream, 281
  Brandy-lemon mousse, 281
  cherries jubilee, 282
  cherry macaroon mousse, 282
  chocolate Brandy biscuit, 282–83
  Cordial mousse, 283–84
  Cordial mousse parfait, 284
  Crème de Cacao sundae, 285
  Crème de Menthe sherbet, 285
  frozen egg nog, 286
  fruit Brandy mousse, 286
  Grand Marnier melon, 287
  pineapple and cherries with apricot sherbet, 287
  pistachio ice cream with raspberries and White Framboise, 287
  Rum-lemon ice cream, 281
  Rum-lemon mousse, 288
  Spirit fantasy, 289
  tutti-frutti ice cream, 290
  White Framboise melon, 291
  Wine sherbet, 291
Frozen egg nog, 286
Frozen strawberry sauce, 262
Fruit:
  appetizers, 20–26
  apples:
    baked, 189
    and grape cocktail, 20
    rings, spiced, 190
    stewed, 190–91
    stuffing, 216
  applesauce, 189
  avocado pear:
    and grapefruit in lime gelatine, 29
    and Rum cocktail, 21
  bananas:
    baked, 191
    flambé, 191–92

with chocolate ice cream, 278
with vanilla ice cream, 278–79
Brandy mousse, 286
cake of the twelve Spirits, 230–33
cherries:
    Anisette sauce, 258–59
    brandied, 192
    jubilee, 282
    macaroon mousse, 282
    with Cointreau-Curaçao gelatine, 293
    cooked, 188–99
    cranberry sauce, 192–93
    crystallized citrus peel, 193
    -flavored gelatine with grapefruit and
        orange, 31
    grapes, poached, 194
    peaches:
        baked, 194
        brandied, 195
        stewed, 195
        and Wine cocktail, 24
    pears:
        baked, 196
        brandied, 196
        and pineapple in lime gelatine, 32
        stewed, 196–97
        and Wine cocktail, 24
    peel, crystallized citrus, 193
    pineapple:
        and cherries with apricot sherbet,
            287
        pickled, 198
    plums:
        brandied, 197
        greengage, stuffed, 197
    sautéed canned, 192
    Spirit-flavored preserves or jam, 194
    tarts glacé, 303
    watermelon rind, pickled, 198–99

Gelatine:
    desserts, 292–95
    fruit with Cointreau-Curaçao, 293
    fruit-flavored, with grapefruit and
        orange, 31
    wine, 295
Giblet stuffing, 217
Gin 'n' sauce, 209
Glazed roast duck, 118–19
Goose, roast, 122–23
Grand Marnier cream, 270
Grand Marnier melon, 287
Grapefruit:
    halves with peach or apricot preserves,
        21
    and orange cocktail, 22
Grapes, poached, 194
Gravy, pan-brown, 210
Greengage plums, stuffed, 197

Grillades (veal steaks), 156–57
Guinea hens baked in cream and to-
    matoes, 123
Gumbo:
    crab, quick, 48
    oyster, crab, and shrimp, 47

Ham:
    Olympus (with cherry-Madeira-Coin-
        treau glaze), 154–55
    picnic, with Wine, 155–56
    -rice-tomato stuffing for fish, 218
    steak:
        baked with pineapple juice and Coin-
            treau, 153
        baked with raisin sauce, 153
Hamburger:
    soufflé, 60–61
    with Wine, 139
Hash:
    beef, 160–61
    duck, 119–20
    lamb, 160–61
    veal, 160–61
Hen, roast, 114
    See Chicken
Herring, pickled, 16–17
Honeydew melon and Rum cocktail, 22
Hors d'oeuvres:
    artichoke hearts:
        filled with tomato juice-Moselle as-
            pic, 9
        filled with tomato juice-Moselle as-
            pic and crabmeat, 9–10
    Camembert butter, 10
    cheese biscuits with deviled ham, 12
    cheese fondue with shrimp or crawfish,
        13
    cocktail patties, #1, #2, 13–14
    crabmeat balls, 14–15
    cucumbers stuffed with Roquefort or
        bleu cheese, 15–16
    eggs and caviar in aspic, 16
    lime-avocado-asparagus dip, 17
    pickled herring, 16–17
    radishes with chive cheese or bleu
        cheese, 18
    steak bits, 18–19
    stuffed celery #1, #2, #3, #4, 10–12
    tomatoes:
        plum, filled with olive aspic, 19
        plum or cherry, stuffed, 19–20
    tuna balls, 14–15
    See also Appetizers; Aspics

Ice creams. See Frozen desserts
Icing for lettering, 229. See Cake fillings
    and frostings
Irish stew, 163–64

Jam, spirit-flavored, 194
Jam cake, 233–34
Jam cakes (individual), 234
Jellied daube, 137–38
Jellied tongue, 166

Kirsch balls, 247
Kirsch-raspberry preserves sauce, 261
Kirsch-strawberry preserves sauce, 261

Lamb:
  chart (roasting time/temperature), 148
  chops flambé, 147
  crown roast of, 146
  hash, 160–61
  roast, 148–49
  stew, 147–48
Lebkuchen with Rum icing, 247–48
Lemon Sherry custard, 270–71
Lemon soufflé, 306–7
Lima beans, 176
  with hot Sauterne mayonnaise, 175
  dried, soup, 46
    blender-made, 46–47
Lime-avocado-asparagus aspic, 31–32
Lime-avocado-asparagus dip, 17
Liqueurs, list, 311
Liquors, list, 312
Liver, bacon, and onions, 162–63
  See also Chicken livers
Lobster:
  aspic, 34–35
  au gratin, 83
  bordelaise, 82
  mousse, 83–84
  Newburg, 84
  poached, 85
  royal, 85–86
  thermidor, 86

Macaroon Bavarian cream, 293–94
Macaroon pudding, 309
Madeira mushrooms, 179–80
Madrilène, 48–49
Maître d'hôtel sauce, 210–11
Maraschino butter-cream frosting, 253
Marchand de Vin, 211
Marron Champagne Cognac pudding, 271
Mayonnaise, Sauterne, 215
Meat:
  balls, Swedish, with sour cream, 161–62
  barbecue sauce for, 205
  bouillon (chicken, veal, beef), 41
  beef:
    baked, with vegetables, 133
    chart (roasting time/temperature), 142–43

chili, 135
corned, 135–36
daube, 136
  jellied, 137–38
  with spaghetti, 136–37
ground, with tomatoes and corn, 138
hamburger with Wine, 139
hash, 160–61
Irish stew, 163–64
meat sauce, quick, 140
pot roast, 139–40
ragout of, 141
roast, 142–43
sauerbraten, 143–44
Stroganoff, 134
chili, 135
corned beef, 135–36
croquettes, 160
daube, 136
  jellied, 137–38
  with spaghetti, 136–37
grillades (veal steaks), 156–57
ham:
  olympus (with cherry-Madeira-Cointreau glaze), 154–55
  picnic, with Wine, 155–56
  -rice-tomato stuffing for fish, 218
  steak, baked with pineapple juice and Cointreau, 153
  steak, baked with raisin sauce, 153
hamburger:
  soufflé, 60–61
  with Wine, 139
hash:
  beef, 160–61
  duck, 119–20
  lamb, 160–61
  veal, 160–61
Irish stew, 163–64
lamb:
  chart (roasting time/temperature), 148
  chops flambé, 147
  crown roast of, 146
  hash, 160–61
  roast, 148–49
  stew, 147–48
liver, bacon, and onions, 162–63
mutton: Irish stew, 163–64
pork:
  chart (roasting time/temperature), 151
  chops:
    flambé, 152
    flaming stuffed, 150
    with Wine, 152
  roast, fresh, 151–52
pot roast, 139–40
sauce, quick, 140

sauerbraten, 143–44
spareribs, barbecued, 149
steak:
  bits, 18–19
  Burgundy sauce for, 208
  chart (broiling time), 145
  with Roquefort, 144–45
  with Sherry, 145–46
stock, 50
sweetbreads:
  and artichokes, 165
  creamed, 164
  croquettes, 165–66
tongue, 135–36
  corned, 135–36
  jellied, 166
tripe, stewed, 167
veal:
  chops with Wine, 159
  grillades, 156–57
  hash, 160–61
  Irish stew, 163–64
  ragout of, 157–58
  roast, 158
  roasted in barbecue sauce, 159–60
Melon:
  and Cointreau or Triple Sec cocktail,
    23
  honeydew, and Rum cocktail, 22
  and Wine cocktail, 23
Menus, festive dinner, 97–98
Mocha Rum custard, 272
Mousse:
  chicken, 109
  crabmeat, 83–84
  See also Frozen desserts
Mushrooms:
  French, 179
  Madeira, 179–80
  omelet, creamed chicken with, 56–57
Mustard sauce, 211
Mutton: Irish stew, 163–64

Nesselrode frosting, 257
New Orleans cream pie, 272
Nut stuffing, 218

Omelets:
  crabmeat, 57
  mushroom, creamed chicken with, 56–
    57
  Rum, flambé, 308
  shrimp and mushroom, 58
  Spanish, 58
  strawberry, 58–59
  sweet (dessert) and soufflés, 304–8
Onion-Champagne soup, 41–42
Orange marmalade-Curaçao sauce, 260

Orange marmalade-Grand Marnier sauce,
    260
Orange soufflé, 307
Oysters:
  baked stuffed, 87
  Bienville, 88
  in brown sauce with spaghetti ring, 89–
    90
  cocktail patties #2, 14
  crab, and shrimp gumbo, 47
  sauce, 212
  in Sherry sauce, 90
  and shrimp jambalaya, 93
  stuffing, 220–21

Pan-broiled chicken breasts, 100
Pan-brown gravy, 210
Pancakes, dessert, 298–99
  See also Crêpes suzettes
Partridge, roast, 124
Pastry desserts, 300–4
Pâté:
  Brandy-oyster stuffing, 220
  Brandy stuffing, 106, 218–20
Peaches:
  baked, 194
  brandied, 195
  stewed, 195
  and Wine cocktail, 24
Pears:
  baked, 196
  brandied, 196
  and pineapple in lime gelatine, 32
  stewed, 196–97
  and Wine cocktail, 24
Peas, black-eyed, 176
Pecan:
  almond crisps, 249
  almond Rum torte, 242–43
  or almond topping, 243
  crisps, 249
  pie, 304
Pheasant, roast, with Chablis and Bour-
    bon, 124–25
Pickled:
  herring, 16–17
  pineapple, 198
  watermelon rind, 198–99
Picnic ham with Wine, 155–56
Pies:
  almond shell flan, 300–1
  chicken, 110
  chocolate Brandy, 302–3
  New Orleans cream, 272
  pecan, 304
Pineapple:
  and cherries with apricot sherbet, 287
  pickled, 198

Pistachio ice cream with raspberries and White Framboise, 287
Plums:
  brandied, 197
  greengage, stuffed, 197
Plum tomatoes filled with olive aspic, 19
Poached fish fillets, 75
Poached grapes, 194
Pompano, in White Wine, 75–76
Pork:
  chart (roasting time/temperature), 151
  chops:
    flambé, 152
    flaming stuffed, 150
    with Wine, 152
  roast fresh, 151–52
Potato:
  soup with Swiss or Gruyère cheese, 49
  stuffed baked, with Vermouth, 180
    and cheese, 181
  sweet (see Sweet potatoes)
Pot roast, 139–40
Potted chicken, 113
Poulet sous cloche, 113–14
Poultry and fowl:
  bouillon (chicken, veal, beef), 41
  broilers, baked boned, 98–99
  capon:
    roast, 114
    smothered, with mushrooms, 115–16
  chicken:
    à la king, 101
    à la Maryland, 102
    -artichoke-tomato casserole, 103–4
    aspic, 34–35
    barbecue sauce for, 205
    boiled, 99
    breasts:
      with mushrooms and hearts of artichokes, 102–3
      pan-broiled, 100
    broiled, 99–100
    cacciatore, 104–5
    with Chablis, Madeira, and Cointreau, 105–6
    with pâté Brandy stuffing, 106
    creamed, with mushroom omelet, 56–57
    Florentine, 106–7
    fricassee, 107–8
    spring, 108
    krispy, 112–13
    livers:
      and eggplant, 177
      eggs à la turke, 56
    mousse, 109
    paprika, 109
    pie, 110
    potted, 113

poulet sous cloche, 113–14
  and rice casserole, 110–11
  salad with sour cream, 111
  smothered, 115
    with mushrooms, 115–16
  soup, cream of, 42–43
  stewed, 116
    with dumplings, 117
  Virginia breast of, 118
  with Wine and herbs, 112
  cocktail patties #1, 13
  duck:
    glazed roast, 118–19
    hash, 119–20
  ducklings, flambé, 121–22
  goose, roast, 122–23
  Guinea hens, baked in cream and tomatoes, 123
  hen, roast, 114
  partridge, roast, 124
  pheasant, roast, with Chablis and Bourbon, 124–25
  quail, broiled, 125–26
  Rock Cornish game hens:
    baked in Brandy, 126
    with kumquats and wild rice, 127
  squab, roast, 127–28
  stock, 50
  stuffing, pâté Brandy, 106
  turkey:
    à la king, 101
    aspic, 34–35
    chart (roasting time/temperature), 128–29
    flambé, 129
    Florentine, 106–7
    roast, 128–29
    salad with sour cream, 111
    with truffles and ham, 130
  wild ducks, roasted, 121
Preserves, Spirit-flavored, 194
Prune whip, 294
Puddings:
  baked, 308–10
  bread, 308–9
  egg nog, 292
  macaroon, 309
  marron Champagne Cognac, 271
  Rum sponge cake, 310
  squash, 184
  sweet potato, 183

Quail, broiled, 125–26
Queen's custard, 273–74

Radishes with chive cheese or bleu cheese, 18

Ragout:
  of beef, 141
  of veal, 157–58
Raspberries and White Framboise Liqueur, 24
Red cabbage with raisins and chestnuts, 176–77
Red fish:
  baked:
    diablo, 65
    with oyster stuffing, 67–68
  Chambord, 76–77
  cold platter, 69
  court bouillon of, 70
Red snapper:
  baked diablo, 65
  baked, with oyster stuffing, 67–68
  Chambord, 76–77
  cold platter, 69
  Sharfe, 78
Relish aspic, 32
Roast:
  beef, 142–43
  capon, 114
  goose, 122–23
  hen, 114
  lamb, 148–49
  partridge, 124
  pheasant with Chablis and Bourbon, 124–25
  squab, 127–28
  turkey, 128–29
  veal, 158
  wild ducks, 121
Rock Cornish game hens:
  baked in Brandy, 126
  with kumquats and wild rice, 127
Rum:
  balls, 247
  -lemon ice cream, 281
  -lemon mousse, 288
  omelet flambé, 308
  ring, 235–36
  sponge, 236–37
  sponge cake pudding, 310
  sponge roll, 237–38

Sage stuffing, 221
Salad dressings:
  cream of shrimp-Sherry, 214
  curry, with Wine, 215
  French, with Wine, 215
  Sauterne mayonnaise, 215
  Sherry Roquefort, 216
Salads:
  chicken, with sour cream, 111
  turkey, with sour cream, 111

Sauces:
  asparagus, 205
  barbecue, for chicken or meat, 205
  béarnaise, 206
  black cherry-Cointreau-Rum, 259
  Bordelaise, 206–7
  Brandy chocolate, 257
  Brandy cocoa, 257
  brown, 207
  Burgundy, for steak, 208
  butterscotch, with Rum or Brandy, 258
  caper, 208
  caramel, with Brandy, 258
  cheese, 209
  cherry Anisette, 258–59
  Cointreau and candied fruit, 259
  Cointreau-strawberry preserves, 261
  cranberry, 192–93
  cream, 203
  diablo, 202, 212
  egg, 209
  Gin 'n' sauce, 209
  Kirsch-raspberry preserves, 261
  Kirsch-strawberry preserves, 261
  maître d'hôtel, 210–11
  marchand de Vin, 211
  meat, quick, 140
  mustard, 211
  orange marmalade-Curaçao, 260
  orange marmalade-Grand Marnier, 260
  oyster, 212
  pan-brown gravy, 210
  shrimp and mushroom, 213
  strawberry, 262
    frozen, 262
  tomato, 214
  tomato cream, 213
  tomato-mayonnaise-Gin, 213–14
  whipped cream ice-cream, 262
  white (thick or thin), 204
  White Framboise-raspberry, 260
  White Framboise-frozen raspberry, 261
Sauerbraten, 143–44
Sautéed canned fruits, 192
Sauterne mayonnaise, 215
Savory eggs; 59
Seafood:
  appetizers, 26–27
  cocktail, 27
  sauce gelée, 33
  See Fish and seafood
Sharfe (stewed fish), 78
Sherbet. See Frozen desserts
Sherry apple cake, 238–39
Sherry Roquefort dressing, 216
Shrimp:
  aspic, 34–35
  au gratin, 83
  boiled, 80–81

cheese fondue with, 13
in clear aspic, 33–34
and crabmeat Remick, 91
diablo, 92
and mushroom omelet, 58
and mushroom sauce, 213
and olive casserole, 92
and oyster jambalaya, 93
poached, 85
Skillet-broiled fish or fillets, 78–79
Smothered chicken, 115
with mushrooms, 115–16
Soufflés:
chocolate, 304–5
coffee, 305–6
hamburger, 60–61
lemon, 306–7
orange, 307
Soups:
borsch, 39
bouillabaisse, 40
bouillon (chicken, veal, beef), 41
Champagne-onion, 41–42
consommé, jellied, 42
crab gumbo, quick, 48
cream of chicken, 42–43
cream of vegetable, 43
Creole crawfish bisque, 44–45
diablo, 50
dried bean, 46
blender-made, 46–47
madrilène, 48–49
meat stock, 50
oyster, crab, and shrimp gumbo, 47
potato, with Swiss or Gruyère cheese,
49
poultry stock, 50
stock, 50
turtle, 51–52
vichyssoise (chilled), 52
Spanish eggs, 60
Spanish omelet, 58
Spareribs, barbecued, 149
Spiced apple rings, 190
Spirit fantasy, 289
Spring chicken fricassee, 108
Squab, roast, 127–28
Squash:
pudding, 184
stuffed (with shrimp, crabmeat, and
ham), 178
Steak:
bits, 18–19
Burgundy sauce for, 208
chart (broiling time), 145
with Roquefort, 144–45
with Sherry, 145–46
Stew:
Irish, 163–64

lamb, 147–48
See also Ragout
Stewed:
apples, 190–91
chicken, 116
and dumplings, 117
peaches, 195
pears, 196–97
Stock, poultry or meat, 50
clearing, 50
Strawberries:
and grapefruit cocktail, 25
omelet, 58–59
and orange cocktail, 25
and pineapple cocktail, 26
Romanoff, 299
sauce, 262
Stuffed:
artichokes, 173
baked potato with Vermouth, 180
and cheese, 181
celery #1, #2, #3, #4, 10–12
crabs, 81–82
cucumbers with Roquefort or bleu
cheese, 15–16
greengage plums, 197
plum or cherry tomatoes, 19–20
tomato, baked, 184–85
Stuffings:
apple, 216
bread, 216–17
chestnut, 217
giblet, 217
ham-rice-tomato, for fish, 218
nut, 218
oyster, 220–21
pâté Brandy, 218–20
pâté Brandy-oyster, 220
poultry, pâté Brandy, 106
sage, 221
wild rice, 221–22
Swedish meat balls with sour cream,
161–62
Sweetbreads:
and artichokes, 165
creamed, 164
croquettes, 165–66
Sweet omelets and soufflés, 304–8
Sweet potatoes:
candied, 181
flambé, 182
pudding, 183
Syllabub, 300

Tarts:
custard, 303
fruit, glacé, 303
Thousand Island aspic, 35–36
Tipsy angel (angel-food cake), 240–41

Tipsy fellow, 273
Tomato(es):
    baked stuffed, 184–85
    cream sauce, 213
    grilled with White Wine and cheese, 185
    juice-Moselle aspic, 36
    -mayonnaise-Gin sauce, 213–14
    plum or cherry, stuffed, 19–20
    plum, filled with olive aspic, 19
    sauce, 214
Tongue, corned, 135–36
    jellied, 166
Topping. *See* Cake fillings and frostings
Tortes:
    date-Kirsch, 241–42
    pecan almond Rum, 242–43
Tripe, stewed, 167
Tropical custard, 274
Trout:
    baked, with oyster stuffing, 67–68
    Marguery, 79–80
Tuna balls, 14–15
Turkey:
    à la king, 101
    aspic, 34–35
    chart (roasting time/temperature), 128–29
    flambé, 129
    Florentine, 106–7
    roast, 128–29
    salad with sour cream, 111
    with truffles and ham, 130
Turtle soup, 51–52
Tutti-frutti ice cream, 290

Veal:
    chops with Wine, 159
    grillades, 156–57
    hash, 160–61
    Irish stew, 163–64
    ragout of, 157–58
    roast, 158
    roasted in barbecue sauce, 159–60
Vegetables:
    artichokes:
        hearts:
            with chicken and ham, 172
            with tomato juice-Moselle aspic, 9
            -and crabmeat, 9–10
        stuffed, 173
        with truffle stuffing, 173–74
    aspargus:
        in bouillon aspic, 27–28
        sauce, 205
        with Sherry-flavored cream or cheese sauce, 174
    beans:
        Boston baked, 174–75

    butter or lima, with hot Sauterne mayonnaise, 175
    dried red or lima, 176
    soup, dried, 46
        blender-made, 46–47
    black-eyed peas, 176
    carrot and pineapple aspic, 29–30
    eggplant:
        and chicken livers, 177
        stuffed (with shrimp, crabmeat, and ham), 178
    mushrooms:
        French, 179
        Madeira, 179–80
        omelet, creamed chicken with, 56–57
    potato:
        soup with Swiss or Gruyère cheese, 49
        stuffed baked, with Vermouth, 180
            and cheese, 181
        sweet (*see* Sweet potatoes)
    red cabbage with raisins and chestnuts, 176–77
    soup, cream of, 43
    squash:
        pudding, 184
        stuffed (with shrimp, crabmeat, and ham), 178
    sweet potatoes:
        candied, 181
        flambé, 182
        pudding, 183
    tomatoes:
        baked stuffed, 184–85
        cream sauce, 213
        grilled with White Wine and cheese, 185
        juice-Moselle aspic, 36
        -mayonnaise-Gin sauce, 213–14
        plum or cherry, stuffed, 19–20
        plum, filled with olive aspic, 19
        sauce, 214
    vegetable pears, stuffed (with shrimp, crabmeat, and ham), 178
Vichyssoise (chilled), 52
Virginia breast of chicken, 118

Watermelon rind, pickled, 198–99
Whipped cream ice-cream sauce, 262
White Framboise-frozen raspberry sauce, 261
White Framboise melon, 291
White Framboise-raspberry sauce, 260
White sauce (thick or thin), 204
Wild ducks, roasted, 121
Wild rice stuffing, 221–22
Wine, list, 312
Wine gelatine, 295
Wine sherbet, 291

on duty

LIFE WITH THE
NAVY SEALS

Robert C. Kennedy

HIGH
interest
books

Children's Press
A Division of Grolier Publishing
New York / London / Hong Kong / Sydney
Danbury, Connecticut

Book Design: Nelson Sa
Contributing Editor: Mark Beyer
Photo Credits: Cover © Leif Skoogfors/Corbis; pp. 5, 7 © Corbis; pp. 9 © Jim Sugar/Corbis; pp. 11, 12, 16, © Leif Skoogfors/Corbis; p. 19 © Jim Sugar/Corbis; p. 21 © Leif Skoogfors/Corbis; p. 23 © Jim Sugar/Corbis; p. 24 © Corbis; p. 27 © Jim Sugar/Corbis; p. 29, 31, 33 © Leif Skoogfors/Corbis; p. 34 © Jim Sugar/Corbis; p. 37 © Jim Sugar/Corbis; p. 41 © Jim Sugar/Corbis.

Library of Congress Cataloging-in-Publication Data

Kennedy, Robert C.
Life with the Navy Seals / by Robert C. Kennedy
p. cm.—(On duty)
Includes bibliographical references and index.
ISBN 0-516-23351-3 (lib. bdg.) – 0-516-23551-6 (pbk.)
1. United States. Navy. SEALs–Juvenile literature. [1.United States. Navy. SEALs.] 1.
Title II. Series

VG87.K46 2000
359.9'84–dc21

00-029527

CONTENTS

Introduction 4

1 Let the Journey Begin 6

2 Boot Camp and "A" School 18

3 BUD/S 28

4 Seals in Action: 36

A Seal Warning Order

New Words 42

For Further Reading 44

Resources 45

Index 47

About the Author 48

Introduction

The name "SEAL" comes from the words SEa, Air and Land. SEALs are tough enough to work or fight in all three. To be a SEAL means being smart enough to know your strengths and weaknesses. SEAL teams know what each team member is able to do. They know how to work together to complete a mission successfully.

To join the SEALs, you have to be tough enough to set a goal, then achieve it. If you aren't in top-notch physical condition, you must start a good training program. If you have some academic shortcomings, you have to figure out how to change that. If you are really serious about wanting to be one of the very best, a SEAL recruiter can put you on track!

SEALs carry with them all the gear that they need to complete a mission.

Let the Journey Begin

HOW THE SEALS GOT THEIR NAME

The Navy SEALs started as the naval construction battalions (CBs) of World War II (1939-1945). They were called SeaBees. SeaBees helped to clear obstacles from beaches so that troops could land and attack. These obstacles included steel barriers, floating mines, barbed wire, and buried mines.

In 1943, men in the SeaBees were asked to volunteer for some dangerous missions. Those men formed Navy combat demolition units (NCDUs). They were asked to break through the beach barriers in small groups. Once through the barriers, they secretly attacked enemy positions. These smaller forces were able to attack because they were small. Large attacking forces were difficult to manage and

SEALs move through enemy territory in secret.

could easily be detected. The NCDUs, on the other hand, could sneak through enemy lines. They could hide in a jungle and not be seen. Once they attacked, they could more easily escape enemy territory. The NCDUs saw plenty of combat action in the western part of the Pacific Ocean.

During the Korean War (1950–1952), NCDUs became underwater demolition teams (UDTs). The UDTs also saw a lot of combat. Their missions were much like those of the NCDUs of World War II.

In the early 1960s, President John F. Kennedy told the American military forces to build a special warfare unit. President Kennedy had volunteered for a special boats unit in World War II. He rode in a patrol torpedo (PT) boat. PT boats were fast and sneaky. Their crews patrolled waters near island coasts. PT boats were deadly weapons against Japanese ships in World War II. President Kennedy knew

SEAL members use special rifles for some missions.

that a small, special warfare unit could do a lot that larger forces could not do.

To carry out the president's order, the Navy changed its UDTs into special warfare units. For a long time, they were called UDT/SEALs. In 1983, the UDT was dropped from the name. Now, the teams are simply called SEALs.

WHAT SEALS DO

Most SEAL missions are top secret. Yet, there is some basic information that is known. The Navy SEAL teams:

- Map and pinpoint obstacles that could stop landings on enemy beaches
- Disarm mines on a beach where friendly forces will land
- Destroy steel and concrete obstacles on beaches before a landing
- Destroy big guns that overlook and protect beaches and harbors
- Perform underwater mapping of enemy harbors before a submarine attack
- Blow up enemy ships in harbors that friendly submarines can't attack
- Cut or blow away steel nets blocking the entrance to an enemy harbor
- Destroy enemy guerrilla forces near rivers and canals in friendly territory
- Rescue air crews that are shot down or hostages held by an enemy

Sometimes SEAL missions require the use of armed vehicles.

•Train friendly government troops to do what SEALs do

GETTING INTO THE SEALS

SEALs are combat units. Therefore, only men can join. By law, women cannot be members of combat units. A recruit must enter SEAL training from the Navy, as either an enlisted man or an officer. As an enlisted man, a recruit must have a job skill needed by the SEALs. This skill is a recruit's source rate. A source rate is earned by training in a special field, such as electronics, weaponry, or intelligence.

Navy SEAL recruiters explain to recruits all of the options available. Recruits receive a SEAL warning order and a SEAL challenge contract. These papers tell recruits exactly what they must do to qualify for SEAL training.

ENTERING THE NAVY AS AN OFFICER

Recruits between twenty and twenty-eight years old may go into the Navy as officers following college graduation. After graduation, a recruit enters the Navy as a reserve (temporary) or regular (permanent) commissioned (selected) officer. There are three ways to enter the Navy as an officer.

Naval Reserve Officers' Training Corps (NROTC)

NROTC pays college tuition and other benefits worth up to $70,000 by end of service. Graduates receive the degree they earned and a reserve commission.

SEAL recruits must be physically fit.

13

Officer Candidate School (OCS)

After college graduation, this thirteen-week course earns recruits a reserve commission.

U.S. Naval Academy

Admission to the Naval Academy is by recommendation from a member of Congress from a recruit's home district. The Academy is a four-year college program. Recruits earn a Bachelor of Science degree and a regular Navy commission.

ENTERING THE NAVY AS AN ENLISTEE

About 95 percent of all newbies enter as enlistees. Recruits must be high school graduates between the ages of seventeen and twenty-eight. Seventeen-year-old enlistees must have permission from their parents.

The Navy has high-tech jobs such as working with electronics and computers. Therefore, high school courses in math and science are important. These subjects can get recruits into a source-rate Navy school that is required to get into the SEALs.

The SEAL challenge contract guarantees recruits four opportunities during boot camp to pass the SEAL physical screening test. Recruits must pass that test to enter SEAL training. The physical screening test requires recruits to complete a 4-mile run, swim underwater for 50 meters (170 feet), and master underwater knot tying.

Part of being physically fit means that recruits must pass a physical screening test.

LIFE WITH THE NAVY SEALS

After passing the physical screening test, recruits have a three-phase training schedule:
Phase 1: Finish Navy boot camp
Phase 2: Complete a source-rate training program
Phase 3: Pass the basic underwater demolition/SEAL (BUD/S) course

HOW SEALS ARE ORGANIZED

All special warfare units are under the command of the U.S. Special Operations Command. The Naval Special Warfare Center is at Coronado, California. All naval special warfare units are trained there.

Naval special warfare units are the SEALs, SEAL delivery vehicle (SDV) teams, and special boat units (SBUs).

Seal delivery vehicles are water craft such as rubber boats or high-tech underwater craft. The minisubmarines and other underwater craft are designed to be undetectable by radar (electronic search) equipment. The special boat units and SDV teams are involved in most SEAL operations.

17

Special boat units (SBUs) carry SEAL teams into and out of a mission.

Boot Camp and "A" School

RECRUIT TRAINING COMMAND (RTC)

The Navy's only boot camp for training new recruits is the Recruit Training Command at Great Lakes, Illinois.

During boot camp, recruits have to accept discipline as a way to manage themselves and others. They also must accept the responsibility for their own mental attitude and physical condition. Correcting any shortcomings in these areas becomes the recruit's most important mission.

IN-PROCESSING AT GREAT LAKES

On arrival, recruits enter a beehive of instructions, forms, and physicals. During the first few days, recruits have physical and dental exams,

The first step to becoming a SEAL is boot camp.

disease inoculations (shots), haircuts, and a swim survival test. Recruits are housed in a thousand-man barracks. All meals are served at a recruit galley (dining room). All meals are served at exact times. Recruits must be on time and eat in a certain amount of time.

A recruit's first uniform is a Navy sweat suit. Recruits wear sweat suits until they have been issued uniforms. A recruit's first lessons are how to stand at the position of attention, clean and maintain his barracks, wear and care for his uniforms, and recognize all ranks. A recruit must learn how and when to salute. Saluting is a sign of respect.

All naval personnel must be in excellent physical condition. Therefore, all recruits go through physical training. This includes daily exercises featuring running, push-ups, sit-ups, chin-ups, and swimming. There is a lot of swim training during Navy boot camp. Recruits who are going through boot camp with their eyes on becoming SEALs may think this training is easy. For a SEAL, boot camp training is easy. You'll soon find out why.

BOOT CAMP

Classroom instruction teaches Navy rules, organization, ships, submarines, and airpower. Divisions (large groups of Navy personnel) compete against one another for things such as cleanest barracks and best military drill. Such competition teaches pride in achievement.

Most boot camp training teaches recruits how to work within the Navy. Not all Navy jobs include time at sea on a ship. However, all recruits must learn how to act and work on a ship. Subjects such as ordnance (military supplies), gunnery, seamanship, swimming, water survival, and fire fighting must be thoroughly learned. SEAL recruits won't actually fire a weapon until they get into BUD/S, because Navy recruits train on weapon simulators (video training).

Recruits want to succeed with personal and professional honor. To do this, many get into a "leadership mode" (act like a leader) and stay there. They set the standard in both physical training and military subjects. After a week of in-processing, recruits receive eight weeks of hard training in military subjects and seamanship.

Seamanship covers everything from swabbing (cleaning) decks to fire fighting. A SEAL

Recruits don't fire a weapon until BUD/S training.

must know how to care for a wounded man or tie a rubber dinghy (small boat) to a submarine. During the seventh week of training, a final physical training test determines the fitness of each trainee. This test will show how recruits are able to handle other assignments in the Navy. Recruits hoping to get into SEAL training have now had every opportunity to pass the SEAL physical screen test. Only an outstanding score on this final test will get a recruit into SEAL training.

The final tests for recruits are battle stations. Battle stations test all the strengths of a group on handling simulated battle situations. Such situations include fire drills, war damage drills, attack drills, and medical drills. Each situation requires teamwork. In some cases, recruits will have to help weaker trainees with tasks beyond their physical strengths. In teamwork like this, a leader always appears. He makes split-second decisions and assigns tasks to each team member according to that person's abilities.

GRADUATION

Boot camp graduation is celebrated with a ceremony and parade. As relatives and friends watch, the class of recruits is congratulated by a number of high-ranking naval officers. Some graduates may be singled out for special praise and awards. Each division marches past a review stand and exchanges military honors with the high-ranking officers on the reviewing stand.

Battle stations test a recruit's ability to use his training skills in a simulated battle situation.

Phase one of the three-phase mission has been successfully completed!

"A" SCHOOL

This is the advanced school. It's where recruits learn all of the skills required to work in their source rate. Recruits study hard and work hard to gain the experience they need to work in their specialties.

Physical conditioning is still a part of a recruit's training. However, most training takes place in the classroom or in on-the-job training. This means that all recruits must spend many off-duty hours in the gym to stay in top physical condition.

Most A School training takes ten weeks. The amount of time spent at A school depends on what type of training a recruit is receiving. Study and training are intense, and tests are hard. To pass A School, recruits must be dedicated and willing to take direction.

"A" School training takes ten weeks to complete.

Recruits who are not going on to SEAL training leave A School for duty around the world. They have learned what they need to know as sailors, and are ready for duty.

For recruits who are working toward SEAL duty, the prize for completing A School is entrance into BUD/S. This is the final, and most difficult, SEAL training.

BUD/S

THE BASICS OF BUD/S

The basic underwater demolition/SEAL (BUD/S) course is given at Coronado, California. Those sailors who have gone through BUD/S say it's the toughest physical and mental training in the world.

INDOCTRINATION

This takes two weeks. It lets all students know what is expected of them. Expectations include physical training that is demanding and often dangerous. Then, those who have not yet passed the BUD/S physical screen test (PST) must do so. Recruits who pass the PST are formed into classes and begin training. Recruits who fail the PST are returned to duty elsewhere in the Navy.

Much of BUD/S training takes place in the water.

FIRST PHASE: PHYSICAL CONDITIONING

This is eight weeks long. Training emphasizes building endurance by doing calisthenics, running, and swimming. As the weeks pass, all of these become harder because the recruits are required to do more of each. There are weekly runs, obstacle courses, long ocean swims with fins, and small boat seamanship classes.

The fifth week is Hell Week. It tests the stamina and self-control built up in the first month. This puts a recruit's mental and physical ability to an extreme test. It decides whether a recruit really has what it takes to become a SEAL.

Hell Week lasts five and a half days. Recruits are allowed to sleep a total of four hours during the five and a half days. Throughout the five days, recruits must complete the following:

- 50-meter (170-feet) underwater swim
- underwater knot tying
- basic lifesaving test

Ocean swims are just one part of Hell Week.

- 1,200-meter (3,750-feet) pool swim with fins (in 45 minutes)
- 1-mile swim (in an ocean bay) with fins (in 50 minutes)
- 1-mile ocean swim with fins (in 50 minutes)
- 1-1/2 mile ocean swim with fins (in 70 minutes)
- 2-mile ocean swim with fins (in 95 minutes)
- obstacle course (in 15 minutes)
- 4-mile timed run (in 32 minutes)

The training and the test show which recruits are capable of becoming SEALs. Recruits learn that a SEAL's survival depends on teamwork. Recruits will prove to themselves that the human body can do ten times the amount of work expected of an average man. More than a third of all SEAL recruits do not pass Hell Week.

Usually, those who make it through Hell Week will make it through BUD/S. As a reward for a recruit's endurance, the last three weeks of this phase are spent in studying and making charts of a body of water.

SECOND PHASE: COMBAT DIVING

This is seven weeks long. Physical training is more difficult, to make sure recruits are capable of completing the training. A self-contained underwater breathing apparatus (SCUBA) is used. Scuba training qualifies recruits as Navy combat divers. No other special operations force has this skill, so it sets SEALs apart from all the rest.

Heavily armed sand vehicles are just one way for SEALs to get from one place to the next during a mission.

THIRD PHASE: GROUND WARFARE

Ground warfare training takes ten weeks. It teaches weapons, demolitions (explosives), and small-unit tactics (fighting plans). A recruit's physical stamina is increased by having longer runs. Rappelling (dropping from a cliff by rope), map reading, and land navigation are learned. The last four weeks of BUD/S are spent in a realistic combat exercise that makes a total test of a recruit's ability as a SEAL.

Passing the third phase of BUD/S means that a recruit has become a Navy SEAL.

FURTHER TRAINING

Airborne School

BUD/S training gives SEALs their basic skills and proves their full abilities as naval soldiers. However, training never stops with any soldier. This is even truer of SEALs.

After BUD/S, SEALs are trained in parachuting. Training is given at airborne school. This is a three-week program that is given in three parts.

Week 1: Ground Week

Instructors teach how to care and use parachute equipment. They teach how to control a

parachute during the drop and landing, and parachute landing falls (PLFs). Hitting the ground without getting hurt is important in a SEAL's airborne training. Recruits jump from an aircraft door mock-up and a low tower to practice PLFs.

Week 2: Tower Week

SEALs practice jumping from towers. A wind machine forces SEALs to master slant landing methods. It also gives SEALs practice going into the landing zone at less than a perfect down-wind fall. Teamwork and mass exit methods also are taught.

WEEK 3: JUMP WEEK

There are five jumps that a SEAL is required to take to pass airborne training. These jumps are taken during Jump Week. On Friday morning of Jump Week, SEALs are graduated from airborne training in a graduation ceremony. Just days afterward, SEALs leave for their duty assignments.

SEALs also begin missions by dropping into enemy ground from a helicopter.

Seals In Action:
A Seal Warning Order

Before every mission, each SEAL receives a warning order. This order tells him what he needs for the mission and how long the mission will take to complete. The warning order also will state what additional training a SEAL needs before going on the mission. Such special training may include operation of underwater vehicles, explosives use, or special climate warfare (jungle, mountain, or arctic areas).

A warning order cannot tell everything about a mission. Missions are planned around what needs to be done, and how to do it. For example, a SEAL team may have to get to and destroy a communications tower in enemy territory. They know they must swim from a submarine to a beach. Once on the beach, they will have to travel through a forest to the

Navy SEALs go into every mission prepared to handle anything that comes their way.

communications tower. Finally, they will have to destroy the tower using explosives. Do you think this sounds easy for a SEAL team? Keep in mind that they may not know certain things that could make the mission easier. The missing information may be how many enemy troops are guarding the tower. Or, it may be what the weather conditions are. It could be what the ground is like around the tower. Many of these things can be found out. Others cannot, but still the mission must be completed. This is when SEAL training and equipment become important.

WEAPONS

SEAL teams use a variety of weapons, but not all at the same time. Rifles, pistols, grenades, and explosives are just some of the weapons that SEALs have with them on certain missions.

Rifles that are used include the M-16 assault rifle. This rifle has an M-203 grenade launcher attached beneath the barrel. The M-14 rifle is a weapon used by SEAL snipers. The CAR-15 rifle is a short, powerful semi-automatic rifle that also has an M-203 grenade launcher attached. The Barret .50 caliber sniper rifle is a weapon feared by SEAL enemies. This rifle can shoot with accuracy from two miles away. Finally, the Mk-19 40mm grenade launcher sits on a tripod or can be mounted on the tops of minisub-marines. The common pistol used by SEAL members is the HK USP semi-automatic pistol.

No SEAL wants to use his weapon. However, when his weapon is needed, he knows that it is capable of doing the job.

INSERTIONS

SEALs are brought to the area where their mission begins by boat, helicopter, parachute, or submarine. Which transporting vehicle is used depends on the type of mission. If SEAL teams need to go into an area far from the water, but cannot get in secretly by helicopter, they will jump from a plane and parachute in. If near a coast, rubber boats or submarines will be able to get them to the shore. Once in enemy territory, SEAL teams are on their own until it is time to leave the area.

ON A MISSION

SEAL teams traveling in enemy territory move secretly. They are small teams and can do great damage to the enemy. However, if they are found by the enemy they can be in great danger. Therefore, SEALs know how to move through enemy territory in silence. They move slowly, steadily, and often communicate only through hand signals.

When a SEAL team reaches its target, it moves swiftly and acts decisively. Whatever the goal of the mission, they work quickly and as a team to complete the mission. Once completed, they get out of the area faster than they came in. The damage has been done, and it is time to escape.

EXTRACTION

Leaving enemy territory must be done quickly and quietly. SEAL teams have escape routes planned. Ships, submarines, or helicopters are waiting to pick them up once at sea or out of enemy territory. No mission is considered a success unless all members have gotten out. In fact, SEALs take pride in completing a mission without having let the enemy know they were there.

THE FUTURE OF THE SEALS

Countries today are less likely to become involved in large wars. The world may never

40

The different looks of these SEALs show that the Navy SEALs are prepared for many different types of missions.

see another war like World War II. That war had more than seventy countries fighting on both sides. Today, small wars in hostile countries are more likely. This means small teams such as Navy SEALs will be used. They can easily get into and out of enemy territory. They are also highly trained to complete a variety of missions. Fighting teams such as the SEALs will be what the U.S. military will rely on when action is needed.

New Words

A School advanced school; where recruits are
   taught special skills

barracks where recruits live and sleep

boot camp a period of basic training in
   which recruits learn to live the Navy way

BUD/S basic underwater demolition training
   which includes combat diving

demolition the use of explosives

division a large group of Navy personnel

galley the dining area where recruits eat

guerilla an unconventional means of warfare

New Words

mine a bomb that explodes when something touches it

radar (RAdio Detecting And Ranging) using radio waves to locate objects

rappel to scale a wall by using a rope

scuba (Self-Contained Underwater Breathing Apparatus) used to breathe underwater

SEAL SEa, Air and Land teams

SEAL delivery vehicle teams (SDVs) SEAL teams that operate water craft

source rate job skill

For Further Reading

Halberstadt, Hans. *U.S. Navy SEALs.* New York: Barnes & Noble, Incorporated, 1999.

Halberstadt, Hans. *U.S. Navy SEALs in Action.* Osceola, WI: MBI Publishing Company, 1995.

Streissguth, Thomas. *U.S. Navy SEALs.* Mankato, MN: Capstone Press, 1996.

Stubblefield, Gary. *Inside the U.S. Navy SEALs.* Osceola, WI: MBI Publishing Company, 1995.

Resources

Web Site
NAVYSEALS.COM
www.navyseals.com/main/main.html
Here you can learn more about SEAL history and get details of past operations. This site has an explanation of what SEAL training is like and the equipment that Navy SEALs use. It also includes current SEAL news, articles, and interviews.

UDT Seal Museum
3300 N A1A N. Hutchinson Island
Ft. Pierce, FL 34949
(561) 595-5845
The museum is dedicated to educating the public about the history of the Frogmen. Their exhibits include Navy SEAL gear and pictures of the Frogmen.

Resources

U.S. Navy SEALs Recruiting
www.sealchallenge.navy.mil
This is the official recruiting site of the U.S. Navy SEALs. It gives information on becoming a Navy SEAL, including screen test locations and a list of frequently asked questions. The site also includes contact information for recruiters in many areas.

Index

A

"A" School, 26, 27

airborne school, 34

B

barracks, 20, 21

battle stations, 25

boot camp, 16, 18, 20–22, 25

BUD/S, 16, 22, 27, 28–35

C

CAR-15 rifle, 38

combat diving, 32

D

demolition(s), 6, 8, 16, 28, 33

E

extraction, 40

G

galley, 20

ground week, 34

guerilla, 10

H

Hell Week, 30, 32

HK USP semi-automatic
    pistol, 38

J

Jump Week, 35

K

Kennedy, John F., 8

Korean War, 8

M

mine(s), 6, 10

M-14 rifle, 38

M-16 assault rifle, 38

M-203 grenade launcher, 38

N

Naval Reserve Officers' Training
    Corps, 13

Naval Special Warfare Center, 17

Navy combat demolition units
    (NCDUs), 6, 8

O

Officer Candidate School, 14

ordnance, 22

P

parachute landing falls (PLFs), 35

physical screening test, 15,
    24, 28

Index

R
radar, 17
rappelling, 33
Recruit Training Command, 18

S
scuba, 32
SeaBees, 6
SEAL challenge contract, 13
SEAL delivery vehicle teams
    (SDVs), 17

SEAL warning order, 13, 36
seamanship, 22
snipers, 38
source rate, 12, 15, 16, 26
special boat units (SBUs), 17
special climate warfare, 36

T
tower week, 35

U
underwater demolition teams
    (UDTs), 8, 9
UDT/SEALs, 9
U.S. Naval Academy, 14
U.S. Special Operations
    Command, 17

W
weapon simulators, 22
World War II, 6, 8, 41

About the Author

Robert C. Kennedy entered the U.S. Army at age seventeen and attended various specialized schools. He served with a military intelligence detachment during the Korean War and with a special operations detachment during the Vietnam War, in 1967. He ended his career as an instructor for the Military Intelligence Officer Advanced Course, which he helped to develop, in 1968.